THE TASK OF THE CRITIC

THE TASK OF THE CRITIC

Terry Eagleton in Dialogue

Terry Eagleton and Matthew Beaumont

VERSO
London • New York

First published by Verso 2009
© Terry Eagleton 2009
Commentary and introduction © Matthew Beaumont 2009

1 3 5 7 9 10 8 6 4 2

Verso
UK: 6 Meard Street, London W1F 0EG
US: 20 Jay Street, Suite 1010, Brooklyn, NY 11201
www.versobooks.com

Verso is the imprint of New Left Books

ISBN-13: 978-1-84467-340-7 (hbk)
ISBN-13: 978-1-84467-339-1 (pbk)

British Library Cataloguing in Publication Data
A catalogue record for this book is available from the British Library

Library of Congress Cataloging-in-Publication Data
A catalog record for this book is available from the Library of Congress

Typeset by Hewer Text UK Ltd, Edinburgh
Printed in the US by Maple Vail

To

Alice, wishing her words

(T. E.)

and to

Jordan and Aleem

(M. B.)

Contents

Acknowledgements

Interviews, as Peter Osborne has observed, are 'careful fictions, conjuring the promise of the actual from the signs of the present'; 'Creatures of context and occasion, they are nonetheless ultimately the products of the artful edit.' Almost all of the material collected and edited for *The Task of the Critic* comes from discussions that I conducted with Terry Eagleton in London, Manchester and Oxford over the course of approximately nine months in 2008 and 2009. On the odd occasion, however, I have supplemented it with statements made by Eagleton in interviews that have previously appeared in other, generally specialist publications that I have listed in the bibliography. These statements have then been revised and updated by Eagleton himself. So in this respect, if not others, the book is a careful fiction. I am first and foremost grateful to Terry Eagleton himself for the thoughtfulness, generosity and good humour with which he both discussed his intellectual biography and read and corrected the manuscript. This manuscript evolved from transcripts that had themselves evolved from sometimes inchoate recordings, and I am extremely thankful to Natalie Howe for producing them with such efficiency and skill. I am also grateful, for encouragement or support of one kind and another, to Tariq Ali, Joanna Beaumont, Michael Beaumont, Tony Pinkney, Mark Martin, Stephen Regan, Jane Shallice, Natasha Shallice, Susan Watkins and Tony Wood. Particular thanks go to Sebastian Budgen.

M. B.

Introduction

The section 'The Task of the Critic' will include a critique of the great figures of today, a critique of the sects. Physiognomic criticism. Strategic criticism. Dialectical criticism: judgment and the events within the work itself.

Walter Benjamin, 'The Task of the Critic'

In the opening months of 1930, Walter Benjamin planned a collection of essays on literature intended to 'recreate criticism as a genre'. A publisher's contract, drafted in April, referred to thirteen essays, incorporating both pieces that hadn't so far been composed and articles that had already appeared (like 'Surrealism' and 'The Task of the Translator'). To Benjamin's disappointment, the book never materialized; and, like the project on the Parisian arcades that he was also outlining in 1930, he subsequently regarded it as one of the 'large-scale defeats' of his life. Vital residues of his attempt to recreate criticism at this time have however survived. His 'Programme for Literary Criticism', for example, crystallizes his reflections on the importance of quotations to good criticism; and 'Criticism as the Fundamental Discipline of Literary History' asserts that the 'distinction between literary history and criticism must be rejected'.[1]

---

1 Walter Benjamin, 'Criticism as the Fundamental Discipline of Literary History', in *Selected Writings: Volume 2, 1927–1934*, trans. Rodney Livingstone et al., eds Michael W. Jennings, Howard Eiland and Gary Smith (Cambridge, MA: Belknap Press, 1999), p. 415.

Among these glittering deposits from the beginning of the 1930s are the notes he made for an essay on 'The Task of the Critic', one of the pieces he had scheduled for the unpublished collection on literature. The second paragraph of this tantalizing fragment refers to 'the terrible misconception that the quality indispensable to the true critic is "his own opinion"'. Benjamin emphasizes that 'the more important the critic, the more he will avoid baldly asserting his own opinion', and 'the more his insights will absorb his opinions':

> Instead of giving his own opinion, a great critic enables others to form *their* opinion on the basis of his critical analysis. Moreover, this definition of the figure of the critic should not be a private matter but, as far as possible, an objective, strategic one. What we should know about a critic is what he stands for. He should tell us this.[2]

In contrast to so many of his contemporaries, we still know what Terry Eagleton stands for. Unlike those seduced by the slippery intellectual opportunities that postmodernism presented to a generation of critics disappointed by the political defeats of the epoch that succeeded the late 1960s, his commitments have not faltered. Most fundamentally, amidst the temptations of post-Marxism, and in particular the post-structuralists' enticing promise to transpose the insurrectionary energies of the *soixante-huitards* from the street to the sentence, he has remained a Marxist. He has told us this repeatedly, as Benjamin argues the critic should, in a range of different registers, in response to a series of different historical or ideological situations. On occasion, and in some of his interlocutors, this has created a sense of incomprehension that is almost comic. So, in a frequently obtuse interview with Eagleton for a book about Lukács from 1993, Eva L. Corredor seems positively baffled by his repeated affirmations of commitment to a Marxism that is at once orthodox and heterodox. 'You are a left-wing critic and a sociocritic,' she insists, 'but if you are a Marxist,

---

2   Walter Benjamin, 'The Task of the Critic', in *Selected Writings: Volume 2, 1927–1934*, p. 548.

you are writing your own Marxism.' Eagleton, for his part, appears equally mystified by her crudely monolithic conception of Marxism. He insists both that 'Marxism is a text, open to many different meanings and readings', and that 'there must be feasible limits on what is meant by the word Marxism'. Corredor apparently cannot assimilate this dialectical attitude to her rigidly postmodernist frame of mind. She remains frankly incredulous as he insists on the importance of simultaneously defending and reinventing concepts like the totality. 'I am surprised by your surprise,' Eagleton eventually says in a tone of polite exasperation, 'because I have never had any doubt, nor have the vast majority of my critics ever been in doubt, that I am in some significant sense a Marxist and that I continue to be a Marxist after the recent collapse of Stalinism.'[3]

In the course of more than forty years as a critic, Eagleton has endlessly re-examined what it means to remain a Marxist. He has consistently sifted the claims of competing theories, and competing forms of political practice, especially feminism, to seek opportunities for reaffirming Marxism. Perhaps most provocatively, in the early 1980s, an exceptionally prolific period even by his standards, Eagleton appropriated some of the profoundest insights of post-structuralism itself, but did not for a moment compromise his adherence to historical materialism. In *The Rape of Clarissa* (1982), for example, which seizes on Samuel Richardson's immense novel in the irreverent spirit of Brecht, implausibly reclaiming it for a contemporary readership, perhaps even a non-academic one, Eagleton is adamant that, though his critical method is manifestly indebted to psychoanalytic and feminist models, these do not supplant the Marxist tradition in which his thought is so deeply imbricated. 'Sexuality,' he insists, 'far from being some displacement of class conflict, is the very medium in which it is conducted.'[4] His recourse to Lacanian concepts in this book

---

3 Eva L. Corredor, ed., *Lukács after Communism: Interviews with Contemporary Intellectuals* (Durham: Duke University Press, 1997), pp. 135–6.
4 Terry Eagleton, *The Rape of Clarissa: Writing, Sexuality and Class Struggle in Samuel Richardson* (Oxford: Blackwell, 1982), p. 88.

thus resolutely resists the logic of the supplement, which depletes or empties out that to which it is added. Eagleton has frequently mediated Marxism through other hermeneutics, testing its limits, reformulating it, transforming it, but he has never displaced it.

To think that Eagleton's critical project can even in part be detached from his commitment to Marxism is equivalent to assuming that, because *Literary Theory: An Introduction* (1983), Eagleton's most successful publication, does not contain a section on Marxist criticism, he has therefore failed to identify himself as a Marxist – no doubt because he is either a conspirator or a tergiversator. Of course, the scrupulous liberal critic would insist on including a section on Marxism in such a book, as proof of their supposed neutrality or disinterestedness. The absence of Marxist thought in Eagleton's book, conversely, is a sign of its ubiquitous presence, and of his partisan commitment to it. Like the mass in Baudelaire's poems, according to Benjamin, it is a constant background hum. Infiltrating the theories that are explicated as discrete or semi-discrete methods, in the form of an immanent criticism, it thus remains resistant to reification. 'No doubt we shall soon see Marxist criticism comfortably wedged between Freudian and mythological approaches to literature,' Eagleton prognosticated in 1976, 'as yet one more stimulating academic "approach", one more well-tilled field of enquiry for students to tramp.'[5] In *Literary Theory*, Eagleton refused to package Marxism as a neat methodology. 'Any reader who has been expectantly waiting for a Marxist theory has obviously not been reading this book with due attention,' he sternly remarks in the book's conclusion. The point, finally, is not simply to explain or interpret the field of literary theory so much as to challenge and change it. 'I am countering the theories set out in this book not with a *literary* theory, but with a different kind of discourse,' he adds; a discourse 'which would include the objects ("literature") with which these other theories deal, but which would transform them by setting them in a wider context.'[6] And this discourse, in the end, is Marxism;

---

5   Terry Eagleton, *Marxism and Literary Criticism* (London: Methuen, 1976), p. vii.
6   Terry Eagleton, *Literary Theory: An Introduction* (Oxford: Blackwell, 1983), pp. 204–5.

not an academic Marxism, it should be added, but one indissociable from the socialist and feminist movements.

The title of the final chapter of *Literary Theory*, 'Conclusion: Political Criticism', is deliberately tautological. Eagleton has argued throughout the book that all criticism is in some sense political, both because it is shaped by the ideological conditions in which its various currents emerge and because, however scrupulously it posits itself as apolitical, it performs a tactical role in the dissemination and interpretation of culture that has inescapably political implications. Socialism and feminism, in contrast to the numerous dispositions of liberal humanism, are self-consciously strategic in performing this role. In this respect they radicalize liberal humanism, and in so doing fatally critique it, rather than crudely rejecting it. 'Liberal humanist critics are not merely out for a more complete account of literature: they wish to discuss literature in ways which will deepen, enrich and extend our lives,' Eagleton writes. 'Socialist and feminist critics are quite at one with them on this: it is just that they wish to point out that such deepening and enriching entails the transformation of a society divided by class and gender.'[7] Liberal humanists shore up culture against the collapse of civilization. Socialists and feminists, in contrast, operate on the assumption that there is no document of culture that is not at the same time a document of barbarism, and that to reclaim literature from the conditions of exploitation that make its production and consumption possible consequently entails the abolition of capitalism. To use another Benjaminian distinction, the Marxist critic reads literature through the eyes of our enslaved ancestors, in the name of our liberated grandchildren. Marxism is at the same time a hermeneutic of suspicion and of redemption.

In his recent critical introduction to Eagleton's work, James Smith comments that 'while many critics would speak of the influence that Eagleton's writing has had upon their field, it would be difficult to identify any distinctly "Eagletonian" critical practice

---

7   Eagleton, *Literary Theory*, p. 210.

or theory that can be distilled down to a clear methodology, or point to any schools or disciples who would cite Eagleton as their founder, unlike many of the other names who rose to a similar prominence in the wave of literary and cultural theory which swept the academy in the 1970s and 1980s'.[8] Smith's point, in this sympathetic, insightful monograph, is that Eagleton's thought has never settled into a static method because it has so restlessly, so inventively responded to contemporary intellectual developments. Eagleton, according to him, 'has occupied a more difficult terrain, with his position constantly adapting, reacting, and evolving throughout his career, his publications frequently situating themselves as polemical interventions in existing debates, displaying an uncanny ability for gauging and anticipating intellectual movements and currents, as well as for fastening upon and opening up areas of acute sensitivity and importance.' The thread that binds together the 'seemingly diffuse range of positions' he has adopted, Smith argues, is a commitment to exploring 'how criticism can be pushed into new social and intellectual engagements, and the responsibility of the critic towards fulfilling a political function within society.'[9]

Smith is correct to underline Eagleton's consistent commitment to rearticulating the task of the critic. Throughout the last four decades, he has interrogated the role of the intelligentsia in capitalist society again and again, reconstructing the archaeology of the traditional intellectual and digging out the political possibilities open to the organic intellectual. *The Function of Criticism* (1984), a nuanced but compellingly readable historical critique of the ideology of disinterestedness that has sustained the crypto-political ambitions of modern European criticism, is perhaps his most important publication in this respect. It systematically

---

8   James Smith, *Terry Eagleton: A Critical Introduction* (Cambridge: Polity, 2008), p. 2. Willy Maley has mischievously defined 'an Eagletonism', in purely rhetorical terms, as 'a flexible polemical device which takes the form of a rhetorical flourish designed to debunk an image of high culture, through a gesture in the direction of some banal, bizarre, or brute "reality".' See 'Brother Tel: The Politics of Eagletonism', *Year's Work in Critical and Cultural Theory* 1:1 (1991), p. 273.
9   Smith, *Terry Eagleton*, p. 2.

deconstructs T. S. Eliot's symptomatic claim, in an essay also called 'The Function of Criticism' (1923), that the task of the critic is, in general, 'the disinterested exercise of intelligence' and, in particular, 'the elucidation of works of art and the correction of taste'.[10] In innumerable other publications, too, Eagleton has probed the ethico-political responsibilities of saints, scholars and rebels, assessing their respective contributions to the critique of capitalism and reconceptualizing the exemplary role of the radical critic, it might be speculated, in terms of an unstable composite of these archetypes. Smith is correct too to celebrate Eagleton's polemical skills, his ability to fasten upon and open up 'areas of acute sensitivity and importance' and so to join the practice of radical criticism to its theory. For as Benjamin recommended, Eagleton's polemics 'approach a book as lovingly as a cannibal spices a baby'.[11] A fine recent example of this is *Reason, Faith, and Revolution* (2009), his delicious attack on the writings of those Enlightenment fundamentalists, like Richard Dawkins and Christopher Hitchens, who have summarily dismissed the entire history of religion as so much false consciousness. Like Slavoj Žižek, another great contemporary polemicist, Eagleton believes that Marxism and a certain form of Christianity should 'fight on the same side of the barricade against the onslaught of new spiritualisms', and that 'the authentic Christian legacy is much too precious to be left to the fundamentalist freaks.'[12]

In the spirit of Ernst Bloch – a philosopher with whom, regrettably, he has postponed an appointment, in spite of the commitments they have in common – Eagleton insists in *Reason, Faith, and Revolution* that it is materialists who must assume the important, eminently dialectical task of rescuing the critical-utopian

---

10   T. S. Eliot, 'The Function of Criticism', in *Selected Prose*, ed. Frank Kermode (London: Faber & Faber, 1975), p. 69.

11   Walter Benjamin, 'One-Way Street', in *Selected Writings: Volume I, 1913– 1926*, eds Marcus Bullock and Michael W. Jennings (Cambridge, MA: Belknap Press, 1999), p. 460.

12   Slavoj Žižek, *The Fragile Absolute, Or, Why Is the Christian Legacy Worth Fighting For?*, 2nd edition (London: Verso, 2008), p. xxix.

core of Christianity from its ideological forms.[13] He argues, for example, for a dialectical understanding of the relationship between faith and knowledge, in an everyday context, that is derived from Christian orthodoxy, and he does so, startlingly, in relation to 'Vladimir Lenin's claim that revolutionary theory can come to completion only on the basis of a mass revolutionary movement': 'Knowledge is gleaned through active engagement, and active engagement implies faith.'[14] It is in thus extricating and reclaiming certain fundamental Christian tenets from liberals and conservatives, atheists and theists, in a rhetorical style at once playful and deadly, that he has reached perhaps the broadest audience of his career as a public intellectual. He has made influential polemical interventions in both publications like the *Guardian* and the *London Review of Books* and substantial books like *After Theory* (2003). Most famously, his vituperative criticism of Martin Amis's appalling racist attacks on the Muslim community in the UK caused some controversy in 2007.[15]

In this polemical climate, as if for old times' sake, Eagleton has been attacked for being a Leninist. (Long ago, in his most significant theological statement to emerge from the late 1960s, Eagleton had announced, not a little scandalously, and unconscious of contemporary debates in Latin America about liberation theology, 'that the priest is best understood as a revolutionary leader on the Leninist model'.)[16] Magnificently, Eagleton's successor as the Thomas Warton Professor of English Literature at Oxford, David Womersley, recently castigated *Literary Theory*, which had been reissued in its third edition in 2008, as 'a Leninist attempt to debauch

---

13   See, for example, Ernst Bloch, *Atheism in Christianity*, trans. J. T. Swann (London: Verso, 2009).
14   Terry Eagleton, *Reason, Faith, and Revolution: Reflections on the God Debate* (New Haven: Yale University Press, 2009), p. 121.
15   For a bitter flavour of this episode, see Geoffrey Levey, 'Spicier than a Novel: The Literary Feud Raging between the Amis Dynasty and the Marxist Critic', *MailOnline*, 11 October 2007, www.dailymail.co.uk.
16   Terry Eagleton, *The Body as Language: Outline of a 'New Left' Theology* (London: Sheed & Ward, 1970), p. 76.

the intellectual currency of literary study'.[17] Womersley would no doubt be scandalized, if also gratified, to discover that, like others on the left, Eagleton has recently re-examined Lenin himself, championing him, though not uncritically, as a revolutionary activist and intellectual who has become more rather than less relevant in the epoch of postmodernism.[18] An increasingly strident ideologue of the UK's resurgent right, Womersley cannot stomach the fact that his predecessor is, to use Smith's phrase, 'fulfilling a political function within society' – even though this is of course precisely what he himself is doing.

One effect of Smith's emphasis on the polemical responsiveness of Eagleton's work to contemporary intellectual developments – its pragmatic, reactive quality – is however to understate the systematic character of his work. For if Eagleton is a supremely sprightly, combative intellectual tactician, as the pieces collected in *Figures of Dissent* (2003) most brilliantly illustrate, he is also a strategic thinker. 'The critic,' Benjamin urges, 'is the strategist in the literary struggle.'[19] I am thinking in the first instance of Eagleton's restlessly inventive but single-minded attempt, since at least the beginning of the 1970s, to demonstrate that historical, materialist critics make the finest close readers of literature because and not in spite of the fact that, as he put it in the introduction to *Myths of Power* (1975), they interpret the 'words on the page' as the 'opaque but decipherable signs' of history itself. In an apparently old-fashioned idiom, he there claimed that the aim of 'historical criticism' is 'to posses the work more deeply'.[20] Since then, in both specialist and populist publications, Eagleton has ceaselessly reaffirmed his commitment to promoting a close rhetorical analysis of the words on the page that is at all times premised on a deep,

---

17   David Womersely, 'Overrated: Terry Eagleton', *Standpoint*, April 2009 http://www.standpointmag.co.uk/overrated-april-09-terry-eagleton.
18   See 'Lenin in the Postmodern Age', in *Lenin Reloaded: Towards a Politics of Truth*, eds Sebastian Budgen, Stathis Kouvelakis and Slavoj Žižek (Durham: Duke University Press, 2007), pp. 42–58.
19   Benjamin, 'One-Way Street', p. 460.
20   Terry Eagleton, *Myths of Power: A Marxist Study of the Brontës*, anniversary edition (Basingstoke: Palgrave Macmillan, 2005), pp. 13–14.

probing understanding of the ideology of form in its historical development.[21] From Eagleton's perspective literary criticism is not a negligible discipline, in spite of its marginal status in capitalist society. 'Language is the medium in which both Culture and culture – literary art and human society – come to consciousness,' he has recently argued; 'and literary criticism is thus a sensitivity to the thickness and intricacy of the medium which makes us what we are.' If in consequence literary analysis has an important critical vocation it has a utopian dimension too: 'To attend to the feel and form of words is to refuse to treat them in a purely instrumental way, and thus to refuse a world in which language is worn to paperlike thinness by commerce and bureaucracy.'[22] Its gratuitousness can dramatize or distil a kind of grace.

In the second instance, and in more philosophical terms, I am thinking of his cumulative effort, since the late 1960s, to construct a materialist account of the dialectical relations between ethics and aesthetics, one that proceeds from the oppressed, labouring body under capitalism but at the same time points to its redemptive possibilities under communism. Eagleton initiated this critical-utopian project at least as far back as *The Body as Language* (1970). There he insisted that Marxism commenced, in the *Economic and Philosophical Manuscripts* of 1844, 'with a discussion of alienation at once sociological, centred in the inhuman contradictions of capitalism, and phenomenological, analyzing the nature of human subjectivity, objectivation, objectification etc.'[23] The sociological and phenomenological registers that shaped Eagleton's early theological writings subsequently evolved into a thoroughgoing historical-materialist discourse. His concerns have remained roughly the same, from his earliest celebrations of the utopian promise of communal liberation in terms of the Christian notion of grace, as in *The New Left Church* (1966), to his most recent celebrations of what he has characterized as 'political love', as in

---

21   For a fine recent analysis of the politics of form in general, see Terry Eagleton, 'Capitalism and Form', *New Left Review* 2:14 (2002), pp. 119–31.
22   Terry Eagleton, *How to Read a Poem* (Oxford: Blackwell, 2007), pp. 9–10.
23   Eagleton, *The Body as Language*, p. 107.

Trouble with Strangers (2008). And Christ has continued to function in his thinking, more or less openly, as a sacramental image of the shattered human body that, in an authentic communist society, might finally be healed and made whole. For Eagleton, to put it in metaphorical terms, Christ's crucified hand closes to assume the form of Lenin's fist – as in some luridly colourful lenticular postcard of an icon. The sign of oppression is equally the sign of redemption, just as for the satanic-angelic Roy Batty, at the climax of Ridley Scott's film *Blade Runner*, the nail driven through his palm becomes a stiletto that functions as the lethal instrument of his *ressentiment*. According to Eagleton, the political scapegoat or the *pharmakos* 'bears the seeds of revolutionary agency in its sheer passivity'.[24] The stigmatized or excluded community, like the proletariat for Marx, is the agent of militant change.

The Ideology of the Aesthetic (1990) and *Trouble with Strangers*, to some extent companion volumes, are to date probably the most significant contributions to this ongoing enterprise, this ethics of the alienated and disalienated body. In the conclusion to the former book, Eagleton argues that 'a materialist ethics is "aesthetic" in that it begins with a concrete particularity, taking its starting-point from the actual needs and desires of human beings.'[25] It is these non-identical needs that open the individual up to the collective, in all its contradictions. Radical politics is then the attempt to respect and fulfil them on a universal as well as a particular level, so that (in Marx's formulation) the development of each is the condition of the development of all. Ethics is thus inseparable from politics. It is not automatically a displacement of it, as Fredric Jameson assumes, according to Eagleton, when he contends that its appearance is 'the sign of an intent to mystify', a symptom of merely moral as opposed to properly dialectical thought.[26] Ethics

24 Terry Eagleton, *Sweet Violence: The Idea of the Tragic* (Oxford: Blackwell, 2003), p. 279.
25 Terry Eagleton, *The Ideology of the Aesthetic* (Oxford: Blackwell, 1990), p. 413.
26 Fredric Jameson, *Fables of Aggression: Wyndham Lewis, the Modernist as Fascist* (Berkeley: University of California Press, 1979), p. 56, cited in Terry Eagleton, *After Theory* (London: Allen Lane, 2003), p. 143.

and politics, so Eagleton argues in *Trouble with Strangers*, 'are not separate spheres but different viewpoints on the same object – the former investigating such matters as needs, desires, qualities and values, the latter examining the conventions, forms of power, institutions and social relations within which alone such things are intelligible.'[27] There is perhaps a slightly idealist strain to this sentence, but Eagleton is forcefully committed to the idea that, in their dialectical relationship to one another, these 'viewpoints' have revolutionary social implications. 'To realize one's nature in ways which create the space for others to do so', as he summarizes his ethics at one point, entails in practice the complete political transformation of class society.[28] *The Ideology of the Aesthetic* frames this argument in opposition to the particularistic politics of postmodernism, insisting that 'difference must pass through identity if it is to come into its own'.[29] *Trouble with Strangers*, for its part, frames it in opposition to the Lacanian 'ethics of the Real' that has recently been promoted by Badiou, Žižek and others, and so counterposes an ethics of love, in its political as well as interpersonal sense, to one of desire. But these are different aspects of a unified critical enterprise.

Smith's point that there is no distinctively 'Eagletonian' critical theory or practice, to return to the implications of this claim, concedes too much to Eagleton's opponents. For critics of Eagleton have themselves solemnly argued, as if articulating an indubitable logic, that because there is no school of Eagletonians, as there is a school of Derrideans or Lacanians, he therefore cannot be an original or systematic thinker. To make this oddly sectarian claim is, finally, to misunderstand his commitment to Marxism, in its numerous, sometimes contradictory traditions, as the grammar that informs his thought. If there are no Eagletonians, then this is because his acolytes, like those of Engels, say, in England in the 1880s, generally call themselves Marxists. One suspects,

---

27 Terry Eagleton, *Trouble with Strangers: A Study of Ethics* (Oxford: Blackwell, 2008), p. 316.
28 Eagleton, *Trouble with Strangers*, p. 308.
29 Eagleton, *The Ideology of the Aesthetic*, p. 414.

incidentally, that critics who call themselves 'Jamesonians', to take an adjacent example, are those who more or less secretly hope that Jameson's interpretations of postmodernism can be understood in detachment from his Marxist dialectics. Eagleton's thought, like Jameson's, cannot be abstracted from the tradition of historical materialism to which it is itself such a vital, constantly evolving contribution. 'We Marxists live in tradition,' Trotsky announced in *Literature and Revolution* – a statement that, in the face of the sustained postmodernist attempt to discredit the idea of tradition *tout court*, Eagleton has relished repeating almost as a slogan. Emulating either Eagleton or Jameson in the field of literary and cultural theory implies the necessity of coming to terms with this irreducibly Marxist tradition, its totalizing critique of the history of class society and its living narrative of revolutionary attempts to overthrow capitalism. This rigorously materialist tradition should in any case be properly suspicious of the reifying effects of deriving convenient labels from the names of influential intellectuals. To put too much faith in a theory that is divorced from a historical or political practice is to capitulate to the idealism that Eagleton once identified as 'the spontaneous ideology of intellectual life'.[30] It might even be said, in sum, that if the term Eagletonian had any valence it would testify to the failure of Eagleton's project.

In a predictably penetrating introduction to a recent collection of his previously published interviews, Jameson has looked back on his career as an intellectual and characterized it in terms of his various restive attempts, in innumerable publications, to apprehend new languages with which to reformulate and illuminate the old epistemological problems. It is a question, according to him, of learning and relearning codes. 'Influence,' as Jameson dismissively puts it, 'is one of the stupider ways of talking about it, which should rather be turned inside out and described in terms of need, and indeed, the need for a new language':

---

30 Terry Eagleton, *Scholars and Rebels in Nineteenth-Century Ireland* (Oxford: Blackwell, 1999), p. 8.

xxiv   *Introduction*

A philosophy grips us because it suddenly has answers for our questions and solutions to our problems: but that is the least of it, and the answers and solutions are what become most quickly dated. What electrifies us is not so much those, but rather the new language in which the need – the questions and problems – suddenly become visible in the first place. Now suddenly the syntax of this new language makes it possible to think new thoughts and to perceive the landscape of a whole new situation, as though the mist of old commonplaces had begun to burn away.

Jameson then lists some of the languages he has in mind, from structuralism and 'Frankfurt School dialectics' to Heideggerianism and Deleuzianism, and admits that he finds the interviews from which he constructs this overview of his career interesting 'to the degree that they put [him] on the track of some inner unity between all these interests, whether they are intellectual or aesthetic flirtations or deeper passions and commitments'.[31] The same assessment might profitably be made of Eagleton's intellectual biography, which in its rather different national and cultural context has likewise been adrenalized by a succession of 'language conversions'. Eagleton has over a period of almost half a century adopted a series of theoretical discourses – existentialism, feminism, Lacanian post-structuralism, to name some of them – and adroitly adapted them to his uninterrupted attempt to renew and redefine the explanatory power of Marxism.

The interviews that constitute *The Task of the Critic* are a testament to these adventures in Marxism (to appropriate the title of a book by Marshall Berman).[32] Chronological in its approach, *The Task of the Critic* represents a comprehensive retrospective account of the evolution of Eagleton's thought in relation to the biographical, political and intellectual forces that have shaped him. It details his conceptual encounters with some of the most important

31   Fredric Jameson, 'Introduction: On Not Giving Interviews', in *Jameson on Jameson: Conversations on Cultural Marxism*, ed. Ian Buchanan (Durham: Duke University Press, 2007), pp. 1–3.
32   Marshall Berman, *Adventures in Marxism* (London: Verso, 1999).

theoreticians of the last century, including Williams, Wittgenstein, Lukács, Goldmann, Althusser, Benjamin, Brecht, Adorno, Lacan, Jameson and Žižek; and it explores his personal and political responses to some of the most important historical events for the left in the last fifty years. The book begins, in the first chapter, with a detailed discussion of the working-class Irish Catholic community from which Eagleton emerged, and of the deeply disjunctive experience, at once liberating and oppressive, of going to Cambridge to study English literature as an undergraduate. The second chapter focuses on his formative relationship, in his early twenties, both with Raymond Williams, his most enduring point of reference, and with the heretical culture of the Catholic left in the 1960s. From the second chapter on, the dialogue is structured in relation to Eagleton's most important publications as they appear, from *The New Left Church* to *Trouble with Strangers*, and including his creative writing. In each of the book's chapters a slightly different problematic is explored, generally in terms of the binary opposition signalled by the chapter titles – binary oppositions, it scarcely needs to be underlined, that Eagleton's thought either spontaneously or strategically deconstructs. The conclusion, in which nothing is of course concluded, revisits some of the themes that seem most pressing at the present time, including the role of theology in his current thinking. Throughout, it is I think possible simultaneously to grasp both his probing critical engagements with the various theoretical codes or languages he encounters, and the 'inner unity between all these interests'.

In Benjamin's notes on the task of the critic, as I have indicated, he emphasizes that 'a great critic enables others to form *their* opinion on the basis of his critical analysis.' It is to be hoped that this book exemplifies that dictum in respect to Eagleton, and not least because, as Stuart Hall has observed, 'the interrogative form' of a book of interviews, potentially at least, 'invites the reader to become involved in what is in any case a dialogue.' Hall is commenting on *Politics and Letters* (1979), the monumental, consistently scintillating collection of interviews that some of the representatives of *New Left Review* conducted with Raymond Williams in the late 1970s. Although transparently inspired by this example, *The Task of the Critic* does not imitate it. It is however premised on the conviction that, as Hall puts it in relation to Williams, the self-reflexivity that the extensive interview form demands suits Eagleton. Like his chief mentor, Eagleton has displayed an exemplary capacity 'simply *to go on thinking*, to go on developing and changing in response to new intellectual challenges.'[33] *The Task of the Critic*, a book in which the critic's insights effortlessly absorb his opinions, is an attempt to dramatize both the dialogic quality of Eagleton's thought and its strategic importance.

Matthew Beaumont

---

33   Stuart Hall, 'Politics and Letters', in *Raymond Williams: Critical Perspectives*, ed. Terry Eagleton (Cambridge: Polity, 1989), pp. 54–6.

CHAPTER ONE

Salford/Cambridge

Could I begin by asking you to say something about your family background? You were born in Salford in 1943...

I was born in Salford, in one of the few pleasant areas of the city, in a house on the edge of a moor where the Manchester Chartists used to meet a century before. But the house was rented and run-down, the landlord was a bully who wanted us out, and we were very poor. There was fresh air and a pleasant view but no money, in contrast to our relatives who lived deeper in the city, who had neither. My parents were first-generation English, of Irish descent. That's to say, my grandparents were all Irish, two of them from what's now the Republic and two from Ulster. The Irish family on my mother's side was pretty republican politically. I was aware of rather banal Irish rebel songs at the age of seven, for example, and I was once prevented by my mother from singing one on the top of a bus in my innocent treble – a slight sense that this was not quite done. My father was one of a family of twelve, a typical sort of Irish family in those days. My mother's parents had immigrated first of all to the Lancashire mill towns, where my mother was born; and I imagine that in the thirties, during the Depression, they then gravitated to the city. My grandmother on my mother's side was a barmaid, my grandfather worked in a gasworks. Coincidentally, so did my other grandfather. My father's family was very much lower working-class, though, and was looked down upon by my mother's family, who were a fairly snobbish bunch.

My father and mother were both upward-aspiring working-class people, classically ambitious for their children, so they were desperate for us to get some secondary education – obviously the first generation that might get some. I went to a very rough primary school. It was almost a Charles Dickens situation, the blacking factory situation. I knew that I had to get the eleven-plus to get out of the place, and if I didn't – everything hung on this – I was in that life forever. So being told by my headmaster that I had got the eleven-plus to the local Catholic grammar school was one of the great liberatory moments of my life. Even then I was aware of what was at stake, and of what was socially implied by all that.

My father had left school at fifteen. The family rumour was that he had got to the grammar school but that they couldn't afford to pay for him – as in those days they had to – so he didn't go. He was a very intelligent man indeed. He went into what was then I think the largest engineering factory in Britain: Metropolitan-Vickers in Old Trafford, Manchester. He went in as a manual labourer, although he didn't often talk about that. Then when I was still a child he was promoted to a small-time clerkship, a white-collar job. He'd always wanted to be his own gaffer, as he put it, his own boss. And at great risk he drew a bit of superannuation money, perhaps a few hundred pounds, and bought an off-licence in a slum area of Salford. This area is not only long gone now but was I think on the verge of being demolished even then. Anyway, he sweated away, glad to be his own boss for once. He was an enterprising man, a man of initiative and resourcefulness. In class terms, I suppose he just about gravitated up into the *petite bourgeoisie*. But he only survived a year, because he died of cancer a year after taking on the shop. That was when I was going to Cambridge. My mother then struggled on with the shop for a bit, before managing to sell it. She had a rather serious nervous breakdown. I think this was mainly because she had had to get on with running the shop and hadn't had time to mourn my father's death. She came back from the funeral and opened the shop. There was no time for her to work through her grief and loneliness.

Was your father involved in trades unionism at all?

No, I don't think so. But I think that his family had certain political legacies. I know very little about the Eagletons – although I do have a kind of personal genealogist in Ireland who supplies me with information about the family – but they were mostly rebels in the later nineteenth century. There's a radical gene. One of my ancestors, a priest, Fr Mark Eagleton, denounced the local landowner from the altar and got moved by his bishop. And this local landowner, to add a deliciously ironic twist, turns out to have been of the family of Aisling Foster, the wife of the anti-republican historian Roy Foster, an old sparring partner of mine. So history has repeated itself, though I hope not as farce. There was also a Dr John Eagleton, who died of typhoid, which was of course the disease associated with famine, when attending the poor in his twenties. He was turned down for the chair of medicine at University College, Galway, on palpably sectarian grounds, because he wasn't a Protestant. My own chair at Galway is pleasant revenge for Dr John.

So although my father was not politically active, the Eagletons had a politically radical record. And my father did sometimes talk to me about politics. He used to say, 'I think Jesus Christ was a socialist.' In those days, at the time of a highly autocratic Catholicism – and he was nothing if not an utterly orthodox Catholic – that was quite a surprising thing to say. He was a quiet and thoughtful man, who thought a lot about social injustice, I think, but had great difficulties in articulating himself. He hated every second of his job in the factory.

What about brothers and sisters? In your memoir, The Gatekeeper *(2001), you talk about the ones that died as infants, but you don't mention the others.*

I have two sisters, one older, one younger. My older sister, Annie, was the first in the family to go to university. She went to Liverpool to read English, but when my father died my mother needed her to help in the shop, so she had to transfer to Manchester University, where she was only allowed to take a general degree. She is a fiercely and brilliantly intelligent woman, a great wit and impersonator and raconteur, who could easily have been a novelist or a great literary talent; but, alas, there was no real outlet for that. The mantle then as it were passed to my younger sister Mary, a feminist critic, who is now reader in English at Leeds Metropolitan University. So we all turned out to be literary types. This was slightly surprising, because my father had no understanding or indeed sympathy for that. That led to some conflict between him and me as I reached adolescence. And I think that the fact that he died so prematurely meant that this conflict was not resolved, that I couldn't really work it through.

So can you describe the domestic culture that produced these three highly literate children? Were there many books or newspapers at home?

No. I remember a book with the rather sinister title of *Catholic Marriage, by a Priest and a Doctor*. That was the height of our literary culture. God knows where even that had come from. I tell the story in *The Gatekeeper* of getting my mother to buy me a second-hand collected Dickens, which she bought on hire purchase. I don't know where I got that idea from.

There's oddly little about reading in The Gatekeeper. *It's not clear where it emerges from, that impulse to read.*

There was for some reason a very old and tattered book, a sort of history of English literature, which nobody read. I don't know where it had come from. I did read it; I remember reading it through. There were sections on Thackeray and Dickens. I remember thinking that these were important names. And so I suppose this was the impulse behind buying the Dickens set.

I was a sickly child. I had quite serious asthma from the age of three to about fourteen, in the days when there was really no palliative for it. I was a cause of constant anxiety for my parents. They were at their wits' end to know what to do. I imagine that I came close to death's door a couple of times without knowing it. That meant that I had long stretches off school, and I was such a conscientious little angel that I used to get my poor parents to go in to school and fetch my books. I suppose that was all part of getting out of the situation. I was planning ahead. So I used to do a lot of reading in bed, and I read my way through all sorts of books that I hardly understood, like *Martin Chuzzlewit*. I got the flavour of literature, I suppose, rather than the substance.

Can you recall what it was that you liked about Dickens?

I remember enjoying the eloquence and energy, although the former was also a barrier to understanding him. I appreciated the elaborateness of his language. I picked up the humour a fair bit. I didn't understand the plots, but I liked the characterization. I suppose Dickens was my introduction to literature. I thought he was extraordinarily intellectual, being able to use all those hard words. Only later did I realize how flamboyantly anti-intellectual he was.

And can you remember what you read after encountering Dickens?

My mother remembers me saying, 'I think Thackeray is a better novelist than Dickens.' This was a) mistaken, and b) disgustingly precocious! So I think that at some point I must have read some Thackeray, probably *Vanity Fair*, though I don't remember. I don't know how I got hold of that – not from the local library, which was absolutely useless. Once when I was about eight I was reprimanded by the local librarian for bringing a book back on the same day I'd borrowed it. I was told that I couldn't possibly have read it.

Did you have relatives who had more books at home than your immediate family?

No, not at all; they probably didn't even have two books between them. But some of them on my mother's side had an oral culture of an Irish kind. They were entertainers, actors, singers, comedians, raconteurs – not all of them, but a few of them. And, looking back, I always associated my own talents, such as they are, with that culture, rather than with reading the classics. They had a knack for communication, a knack for humour, for fantasy, which I remember appreciating very much at the time. A vital breakthrough for me, as a writer, was when I discovered ways of incorporating that into my writing, which took me a long time.

So were any of these more performative relations involved in the church? Were any of them priests?

The family didn't actually produce many priests, although a cousin of mine became a priest and there were certainly one or two priests in my father's background. One of the most burdensome aspects of my own childhood was the keen awareness that my parents would have dearly loved me to become a priest. I knew I didn't want to be a priest, though I didn't know why I didn't want to be one. I was a very pious child, an altar-server and all that, and although there was a general understanding, or expectation even, that I should become a priest, I didn't want to. For one thing, I didn't think I was holy enough. For another thing, I think I realized that priests weren't really intellectuals. If I wanted to be anything, it was an intellectual – not that I would have known the word. Perhaps I've become a secular priest. And it didn't take me long to realize that my idea that priests were extremely saintly people was somewhat erroneous. I did, as I say in my memoir, take up a sort of sale-or-return, trial offer of a spell in the seminary of a very boring and undistinguished religious order. I didn't have a bad time, but this simply confirmed my conviction that I didn't want to go there.

This was when I was about fourteen. I stayed for a week and then decamped over the spiritual barbed wire.

So, if the priest wasn't the paradigm of an intellectual in the community in which you were brought up, what was?

There weren't really any. There wasn't really a model in that sense.

But you were conscious of the category, or the concept, of the intellectual?

Yes, I suppose I was conscious of whatever it was that Dickens stood for – writing, thinking. Then when I got to grammar school, certain teachers – in particular my English teacher, with whom I'm still in contact – became points of aspiration. They opened a new world to me, as schoolmasters sometimes do. But no, there wasn't a model of the intellectual. You see, in a place like Salford at that time there wasn't even a middle class. There was the doctor, and the priest, but there wasn't really a middle class. So I wasn't exposed to any experience beyond my own specific class experience. Even so, from the age of fifteen I knew I wanted to become not a train driver but a left-wing intellectual. By then I was familiar with the phrase. Perhaps this is the place to say that when you go through this kind of trek and achieve your goal, attaining a certain celebrity or notoriety in the process, you can't really enjoy it all that much because you feel that it's not real, that it's not really where you belong. It's as though it's happening to someone else.

What other culture was available in the Catholic community in Salford in the 1940s and 1950s?

My parents had no social life at all. They were very isolated; really, I should say, self-isolating. They were both deeply conscious of their lack of education; they were extremely socially unconfident in a way that transmitted itself to me for a long time. I was never intellectually unconfident, but I certainly was socially unconfident. There were hardly ever any visitors to the house. Very occasionally we sallied forth from the house. On a couple of occasions, my parents took me to the Salford Palace or the Manchester Palace to see variety artists and conjurers, the inheritors of the music-hall tradition. I was utterly fascinated, though it wasn't quite a case of smelling the greasepaint and wanting to go to RADA [the Royal Academy of Dramatic Art]. Albert Finney, who lived down the road, did precisely that. He was a bit older than me, a Salford Grammar School lad, the son of the local bookmaker – I think my mother went out with his uncle. Albert made it to RADA and that was a great event. He came back to Manchester to play Luther in John Osborne's play of that name, and I went to see that. I also knew Ben Kingsley a bit, another actor who came out of Salford, though he wasn't called Ben Kingsley then. Anyway, I can recall two or three occasions when my parents took me to the music hall – possibly because my father worked with a guy who played the trombone part-time in the palace band. And I remember being very fascinated, especially by things like conjuring and magic. Perhaps being a Catholic made me an unusually gullible little soul.

So when did the lack of social confidence to which you've referred leave you?

Not until middle age; and a certain shyness, increasingly well concealed, is still part of me.

You do a good impression of someone who got over it a long time ago . . .

Well, it was grievously compounded by the rather negative experience of Cambridge, which in turn, I can now see, was very much shaped by my father's death. My father died as I was sitting the entrance exam, in a really rather too symbolic moment. It was a very unfortunate conjuncture. Besides, the Cambridge of those days was a deeply patrician sort of place, and I felt it as socially oppressive.

I would say that what I did unconsciously, as a child, was escape from a pretty harsh working-class environment into my head, through literature and ideas, by reading and thinking. So I succeeded in getting out of that environment and into Cambridge, but my social and emotional development then lagged behind. Intellectually, I got out of the situation; but it left me under-resourced, particularly in social skills. I was very shy – oh, for a long time, for all of my younger life. I was aware of the discrepancy between what I could be with other people and what I was. My rather emotionless family background hadn't given me the emotional resources I needed to cope with the intellectual life they had wished for me, with all its public pressures. Indeed, I suspect I developed such a rich, solitary, inward intellectual life partly as a defence against an emotionally cool environment. My intellect shot me into a kind of prominence which I wasn't socially and emotionally equipped to cope with, which was a source of psychological trouble later on.

Perhaps this is a humanistic fantasy, but one might suspect that, because of the reading you'd done, you'd in fact become emotionally rather sophisticated, even if this remained impossible to articulate.

Yes, though in a cerebral kind of way. My parents, God help them (I mean, it wasn't their fault), simply couldn't handle the emotional life at all. This was partly a working-class matter. The assumption was that 'it's a hard world out there and you've got to toughen them up'. Feelings were for those who could afford them.

But that didn't extend to prohibitions on literature?

No, it didn't. They were just bemused about that, as well as vaguely fearful for me. But there was a fear of emotional display. I was brought up in a grimly utilitarian environment, the product of a kind of working-class Benthamism. Nothing that wasn't functional for survival in a precarious world was really worth anything, which is why literature was the least important activity. So although I rebelled against that emotional deprivation, I suffered emotional and social inhibitions because of it. And that took me a long time to work through. In the meantime, however, I wrote a screenplay about Oscar Wilde, that most flamboyantly non-utilitarian of Irishmen. I suspect my interest in art and aesthetics, in things done purely for their own sake, has a lot to do with being reared in a situation in which we wouldn't have dreamt of putting a picture on the wall – except perhaps for one of the Sacred Heart.

Talking of this grim utilitarianism, did the war play an important part in your childhood? It's not something you talk about in The Gatekeeper.

No, very marginal, actually. I was a war baby, but I was born late in the war. My father – possibly because he was engaged on war work in the engineering factory – was not drafted and became an air-raid warden instead. I remember the detritus of war – the odd gas mask and air-raid shelter and so on. I remember the austerity; but then it was hard to dissociate wartime austerity from general austerity.

I want to come back to the importance of politics in your childhood. You've talked a bit about your family's political inheritance, but when did you personally start to become interested in politics? Were you aware of international events in the 1950s, such as the Suez crisis or the death of Stalin?

Yes, I was. I argued fiercely over Suez with conservative friends at school. I was aware of all those things through the radio and the newspapers. My grandfather, my mother's father, was illiterate, and I had to read him the *Daily Express* every day. He would say, 'How am I doing on the money market?' I had no more idea of what that meant than he did. As a teenager I was greatly influenced by the so-called Angry Young Men – all of them now dead, old or right-wing. It was just the intersection of art, politics and dissent I was looking for. I began to fancy myself as a bit of a bohemian, though I was actually a good Catholic boy. They were about the only role model I had before Cambridge.

But the first political influence on me was no doubt Irish Republicanism. As I said before, I was keenly aware of that by the age of about seven. I remember writing execrable Irish Republican songs dripping with heroic sentiments that would make any Irish historian squirm. I even remember putting them to Irish tunes that I knew and singing them – though I don't know exactly to whom I sang them. So a sense of political grievance came not in the first place from a class situation, but from the Irish issue. That then crystallized wider class issues for me, I think.

And did you visit Ireland as a child?

No. It was the old emigrant situation of fondly recalling the dear old land but never doing anything as drastic as actually setting foot in the place. None of my relatives did. In fact it wasn't until I was about twenty-one that I first visited Ireland; and I did so then to speak about the Catholic left, at the Aristotelian Society of Trinity College, Dublin.

What about socialist politics? When did you become a socialist?

Well, I called myself a socialist when I was about fourteen or fifteen. When I was about sixteen I joined the Stockport Young Socialists – not the Salford Young Socialists – because I had a friend who came from Stockport. This was Bernard Regan, who later became an eminent, utterly indispensable figure on the British left. The two of us, who were at school together, went along to the meetings. That was my first encounter with what you might call the far left, and I found it quite fascinating. I heard local left Labour Party councillors speak and I took part in one or two debates. I did, however, have a difficult time squaring that with Catholicism, because there had been a long tradition of papal teaching against even moderate socialism. I was an over-conscientious Catholic. Catholics famously suffer from scruples, which I always think sounds like some distressing medical condition. So I was tugged in two directions: I never doubted that what I was hearing politically was what I wanted, but I couldn't see how, as a Catholic, I could accept that. Bernard had far too much sense to worry in this way. And it was then an enormous liberation – this is a further phase of the story – to go to Cambridge and meet Catholics who said, 'What are you talking about? Of course you can be as far to the left as you like!'

So there were no individual activists that could help you to resolve this contradiction when you were involved in the Young Socialists?

No, there weren't. I used to write rather ludicrous left-wing letters, of an angry-young-man type, to the right-wing Catholic press (a tautology if ever there was one). These were on a number of issues, but particularly the nuclear issue. When I was about sixteen I got into trouble in a mild way for wearing a CND [Campaign for Nuclear Disarmament] badge both at school and in the local parish, and I remember a priest telling me to take it off. My headmaster told the school chaplain to have a severe word with me; but since this chaplain was a very young Fr Herbert McCabe, radical theologian and stout CNDer, that didn't have quite the effect he intended. I was also vaguely aware, even when I was about sixteen, that there was a group of Catholic theologians and philosophers who were opposed to the bomb, though I didn't know how to get in touch with them. Later, at Cambridge, I got to know some of them.

And did the meetings of the Young Socialists that you attended give you confidence, politically and intellectually? You've mentioned that you took part in the occasional debate. Did that prove socially crippling?

No, no. It's the old story of the shy person who instantly becomes transformed on stage. I've met a lot of actors like that, people who are quite diffident when you talk to them and then suddenly come alive in front of an audience. No, I was a fierce debater – and, of course, being a Catholic, a highly dogmatic one too. Smash your enemy into the ground! There was some rather feeble Salford grammar schools debating competition, an attempt to imitate the public schools, and one year, when I was a part of the team, we won. This was when I was coming under the influence of the Angry Young Men, and I gave a suitably irascible speech, though I'm not sure what it was about. So debating was a form of compensation for being a second-class citizen. It was also an acceptable outlet for a socially bred anger, which is probably true of my polemicism today. It was a way of asserting oneself in a controlled situation. T. S. Eliot once referred to 'the braggadocio of the mild-mannered man safely entrenched behind his typewriter' – that certainly has a resonance with me. Writing, speaking and agitating were obviously important in themselves, but they were also ways of compensating for something I'd been deprived of. They were ways of being somebody.

How did you encounter the Angry Young Men? As a teenager, were you reading working-class fiction as well as seeing plays?

I was very aware of Shelagh Delaney because she came from Salford. I knew people who knew her. And my mother had known Walter Greenwood slightly. After *Love on the Dole* [1933], he'd started to buy fancy cars, and he'd then swanned off to London, to the Big Smoke. My mother also remembered seeing L. S. Lowry sketching by the roadside in Salford – I'm not sure whether people gave him a wide berth because he was an artist or a rent-collector.

I wasn't actually aware of Ewan MacColl, who I'm now of course very interested in. Salford had quite an important working-class culture. There was a well-known agitprop theatre group in the thirties, for example. Today, I'm proud to be a Friend of the world-famous Working-Class Movement Library in Salford.

What about Alan Sillitoe, for example?

I knew of Sillitoe, partly because Albert Finney – a sort of much brasher Salfordian alter ego of mine – starred in the film of *Saturday Night and Sunday Morning* [1960]. At that time, I made the mistake, as most people did, of thinking that John Osborne was a great voice in the radical cause. I was also conscious of Arnold Wesker and Kingsley Amis and all that lot. And I somehow came across a book called *Declaration* [1959], edited by Tom Maschler, which absolutely crystallized something I needed. It was a collection of statements by people like Osborne, Lindsay Anderson, Doris Lessing and Kenneth Tynan. It must have been in the Salford Library, though that seems very odd. No doubt one of the first books I ever bought was Colin Wilson's *The Outsider* [1956], which I hardly understood but which impressed me deeply. Nowadays I understand it but I'm not impressed by it.

Could you say more about the intellectual culture at your grammar school, De La Salle College? You've said that there was one teacher with whom you remained in touch.

There was the opportunity for debating and drama, both of which I took to. And most of all there was the fact that for the first time I was in a situation where intellectual achievement counted for something. Before that it had been utterly downgraded, not by my family so much as by my working-class background in general. I suffered a lot at my primary school for being intellectual and sickly – a weed, a nerd. At grammar school, I was in an environment where the talents that I had actually counted. They could command respect, whereas previously they had done the opposite. On the other hand, I wouldn't say that in general there was a lively intellectual culture there. On the contrary, it was a philistine, autocratic religious establishment devoted to levering us into English (rather than Irish) middle-class society and getting the occasional kid into Cambridge. It was quite good at doing that. But in a typically Catholic way, like much of my home environment, it was emotionally desolate. The school was academically excellent and utterly depersonalized. So I was very much out on a limb with my interest in the Angry Young Men. At the same time I quite liked that, because it gave me something to kick against.

There were a few masters who embodied something I could aspire to. The most important was my English master, a man called Peter Grant, who I still keep in touch with, as I've said, and who was a left Leavisite, as I later came to realize. That's the way I would have been taught O-Level and A-Level English – though without any knowledge of what all that meant. He was a working-class left-winger who'd been at Sheffield under William Empson. He was my role model, if you like.

And do you think that, because it was a Catholic school, there was at some institutional level a scholastic respect for ideas? After all, it's not as though any secondary school at that time would have created the space for someone with your intellectual ambition to develop.

Oh yes, there was. That was what was good about it. Because it was a Catholic institution, with all the deficiencies that go along with that, it was a place that nevertheless greatly respected rational analysis. I've always seen that as one filament connecting Catholicism to the left. We were very much encouraged to think and argue rigorously; we were encouraged to believe that the truth was important, and had a more than abstract importance. I suppose I was also introduced there to the tradition of Catholic social thought, and there was quite a rich culture of that. I valued

Catholicism even then, and certainly today, as a culture – with all kinds of flaws and horrors, to be sure. But it was a world where ideas were taken seriously and where institutions were taken seriously. That is to say, one was taught almost instinctively to think in institutional terms, to believe that human life was institutional. And that meant that when later in life I came to encounter liberal humanism or liberal individualism I really did find it alien. That, however, was both gain and loss.

So you identified liberal humanism as an ideology rather than some simply atmospheric effect?

Absolutely. I had never been inside that ethos at all. I remember Raymond Williams talking about the problems he had when he first encountered certain ideas of individualism. I had very much the same experience. I encountered it from the outside. You were brought up in an environment where the corporate, the institutional and shared belief were vital to your identity – even if they were often pushed to autocratic or totalitarian extremes. When I got to Cambridge I realized that the ethos in which most of my fellow students had been brought up was saturated with liberal individualism or liberal humanism from the outset. It wasn't in my bones to understand it. I later came to learn a great deal about the value of liberalism, not least as a Marxist, but I had to come at it from the outside.

When you talk about the importance of truth, in relation to your education, are you ultimately referring to a spiritual truth, or to secular forms of truth, or to an intermingling of the religious and the secular?

It was essentially religious, but it spilled over, as I say, into a certain intellectual approach that valued the analytic. For example, this approach didn't assume – and this is straight Aquinas, though I didn't know it then – that there is any given limit to rational enquiry, even into mysterious matters. In a certain way, it carried its religious zeal over into secular affairs. Mind you, that went along with a high defensiveness about what they would call 'the world' – the secular world. If I hadn't gone to a Catholic school, for example, my parents would have been excommunicated. But they had no fear of the secular intellect, no fear at all. There were one or two hairy moments, as when I was due to be given some prize books on speech day for my O-Levels. At that time there was a Penguin philosophy series, including Hume and others, and I asked for a few of these. I was told that, sadly, they were on the Index, the Catholic list of prohibited books, and I was given a book by some Jesuit instead. But that wasn't typical. They did that more regretfully than aggressively. They were quite prepared to let you roam about as long as the truths of Catholicism were ultimately safeguarded.

What literature were you studying at secondary school?

Well, we did a range of fairly familiar classics for O-Level, including Shakespeare and Milton. I remember my English master being very anti-Milton, which I now see would have been part of his Leavisite background. I read some Thomas Gray, and got some sense of Wordsworth. But at the same time Peter was so enlightened that he was smuggling in texts like *Waiting for Godot*, and Auden and Isherwood's dramas, that sort of thing – presumably convincing the extremely autocratic headmaster that these were necessary or valuable. I remember one occasion when he was rehearsing us in a production of *Julius Caesar* – I was Mark Antony – and some of these texts were lying around in the wings so we just started spontaneously to read them together as a group. We read *Waiting for Godot* out loud totally off the cuff, and Peter came along and took a part. I was fiercely convinced then that culture was crucially important, and that it was everything I wanted.

Can I ask about the work that you did as a teenager? What was your experience of the workplace?

I worked I think in three or four different places. I worked in a Manchester accountancy firm as an office boy. I think I was paid something like £2.50 a week – a munificent sum! And in my final year at Cambridge I worked in Marks and Spencer in Manchester, cleaning the floors and doing warehouse work. As I say in my memoir, I was reading ferociously for the Finals paper on tragedy at the time, and the other workers were absolutely stunned that somebody could read that many books. I also worked in the Cussons soap factory in Salford for a while. Nothing stands out about any of those experiences. In Cussons I ran across a few of my mates from primary school. I was there for a month and they were there for life. The most interesting job was teaching for almost a year before going to Cambridge, in a pretty rough local secondary modern school. I taught the top class and spent much of my time trying to hide from them the fact that I was only a year older than they were. It was my first experience of teaching and I realized I had the knack of being able to make it entertaining. Shades of the Salford Palace perhaps . . .

So how did you conceptualize your relationship to the working class – as a corporate entity so to speak – at the time you left home and went to Cambridge?

It was a complex one, because all of my political sympathies lay in that direction by then, but at the same time I was a classic scholarship boy who had invested a lot of energy in trying to extricate myself from that milieu. Reading Dai Smith's excellent biography of Raymond Williams, I've been struck by something I didn't know about Raymond; namely, that his father was not only a rather idealized figure for him, but also somebody with whom he tangled quite a bit, because he felt his father was pushing him out. I certainly had the same experience. There's a classic overlay here of a social contradiction with an Oedipal ambivalence. It was much the same in my own case, which was complicated by the early death of my father and, consequently, the unresolved nature of these conflicts. Certainly it was very strange to know that there were forces at the centre of the family that were trying to push me away. Paul Morel has the same problem in *Sons and Lovers*. It wasn't just a matter of my trying to extricate myself. In extricating myself I was trying also to be obedient, to conform, to embody some of the values of the family. That was what you had to do: you had to go. Those paradoxes are very hard to handle in psychological terms. I imagine that part of my drastically negative experience of Cambridge was really owing to that. It's an impossible psychical situation – not just for me but for Raymond and for many others – of investing your identity in and championing the people that you're simultaneously leaving behind, and who are telling you to go for their sake as well as for yours.

The narrative of Williams's life undoubtedly seems more ambiguous as a result of the account in Dai Smith's book; but the impression one nonetheless has is that, emerging from a rural working-class background, he was shaped by a less complex, a less contradictory social situation than you were.

I'm not sure it was any less complex, but it was different. Raymond had sprung from a working-class background that was unequivocally supportive and emotionally congenial, which certainly wasn't the case with me. So there were in my case emotional reasons for me to detach myself, whereas with Raymond the emotional bond was very strong. But now it does indeed seem that there were complexities within that which I hadn't been aware of. There's a missing mother-figure in Williams, for example. But I've certainly always thought that Raymond's peculiarly privileged background – in one sense of the word – gave him a sort of stability, a rootedness and self-assurance, and an almost magisterial authority, which were lacking in my own case. Perhaps that's part of my own idealization of a father-figure, which he certainly was to me. But I also think it's true.

I wanted to ask you in more detail about the moment when you travelled to Cambridge to do the entrance test and were told by the English tutor at Trinity that your father had died. That must have been a pretty disjunctive experience, emotionally, intellectually.

Yes, the experience of having to come by oneself to Cambridge for a week and find one's way around the colleges and sit exams was in any case intimidating – not just for me but for other people I met there. And then, on top of that, there was the interview with the tutor. In one sense the blow was eased by the fact that I'd expected my father to die. I hoped he wouldn't die when I was away, but it was on the cards that he would. It was also eased by an awareness of how dreadful it was for my tutor to have to tell me this. He was not a man accustomed to this sort of thing at all. Indeed, with his impeccably correct English-upper-class manner, he made my parents look like emotional spendthrifts. I didn't experience any immediate violent feeling. It was rather that something I needed to work through had been peremptorily cut off, and I would suffer from the consequences of that later.

Then I had to go back for the funeral. As I say in the memoir, I verbally assaulted my headmaster at the back of the church. I was angry in a general, dishevelled way, and needed to take it out on somebody. He was the man who made the decision to bring me home. My mother wasn't in a state to make a decision. I thought he was wrong. I still think he was wrong. It seemed to me to be dreadfully ironic that he was depriving my father of the university place he had wanted for me, since I hadn't finished the exam. Then I think I just survived in a state of limbo until I received information that I'd been given a place at Trinity. I was genuinely surprised. I think I had only done two papers out of six or seven, and I thought, you know, that the tutor was not the kind of man to take the risk – as indeed he wasn't, normally.

And did you feel when you did go to Cambridge that you were abandoning your mother?

In a sense, yes. It was a bad time in that respect, because she was struggling to keep up the shop, in an area that was being rapidly depopulated. Unable to mourn, deferring her mourning, she was full of grief and anxiety. It was just a bad scene all round. But I was suspended between two lives. I'd turned my back on the family, in a sense; and yet, because I felt deeply alienated from Cambridge, I had no point of identity. I think that one reason for my involvement in the Catholic left, soon after this, was that in a certain sense it spanned both worlds. It was an intellectual version of what I had been brought up with.

Before arriving at Cambridge, what was your conception of the ruling class?

It was very much an image, because as I say there wasn't even a middle class in Salford. I was deeply opposed to the ruling class even before I met any of its representatives. Encountering them merely reinforced my prejudices. Even when the situation was fairly abstract, when I was a sixth-former, it was almost a sense of personal grievance.

A ressentiment*?*

Yes, very much so. This then became a little more of a rational opposition when I actually began to understand more about class society. But certainly I had fierce and fairly primitive class instincts when I arrived at Cambridge. Reason only intensified my antagonism – which is not exactly the liberal version of reason.

You were obviously opened up to more sophisticated intellectual, political and religious influences at Cambridge, but these visceral class feelings presumably continued to shape you.

Oh I think they did. They still do today. I was always interested in the fact that Raymond's did as well, although he would not have been so ready to admit it. Raymond was acutely aware that he needed all the rational intricacy he could muster in order to be convincing in arguing against the establishment. But it wasn't only that he was voicing at a far more sophisticated level what I felt. He was also feeling at a quite primitive level what I felt as well. To a certain degree, I think, he was masking that. He was pretty canny, and he was a survivor. But I was gratified to see, in various odd moments of revelation, that these feelings could survive in somebody who to me seemed very old. He was absolutely unreconciled – it's just that it was harder to see in him than it was in me.

Stuart Hall once talked about identifying with Williams's situation in Cambridge. He referred to experiencing what he called 'that way in which the bright young lad from the "periphery", coming to Oxbridge as the idealized pinnacle of an intellectual *path, first experiences the actual* social *shock of discovering that Oxbridge is not only the apex of official English intellectual culture, but the cultural centre of the class system.' Williams went to Cambridge in the forties; Hall went to Oxford in the fifties; you went to Cambridge in the early sixties. Is that how you'd describe your initial experiences of the place too?*

Yes, pretty well. In terms of that little narrative, though, my moment was perhaps one of the last in which all of that was blatantly obvious. I mean that what I then experienced when I stayed on in Oxbridge as a tutor was a gradual, superficial democratization, so that the whole tone of the place was considerably altered. Old Etonians would suddenly appear with studs in their noses and Liverpudlian vowels. I got in pretty much on the tail-end of the sort of aristocratic dominance that Stuart and Raymond also experienced. I ended up at Trinity, which didn't help, because it is one of the most aristocratic of colleges. The staircases in Trinity were full of Hons. Even the Labour Club – which I had something but not much to do with – was largely dominated by public-school socialists, some of whom seemed to be blatant careerists. There was a paltry percentage of working-class students at the college. We were very defensive and we hung together in a clubbish kind of way.

But reading English there was much more exciting than Oxford, for instance?

It was much more exciting than Oxford, which was dominated at the time by medieval scholarship. Indeed, it may be that the suspicion with which I was greeted when I moved to Oxford, which I thought was because I was a Marxist, was because I came from Cambridge. They'd just about heard of a rather nasty little man called Leavis, and they were certainly not going to welcome any of his disciples, which was probably how they saw me. When I was an undergraduate in Cambridge, and later as a research fellow, there were Williams, Denis Donoghue, George Steiner, Jeremy Prynne, Donald Davie, Tony Tanner, and the tail-end of Leavisism. L. C. Knights arrived not long afterwards. There was a glittering galaxy of people, and they were all busy staking out positions and fighting their cases. It was an abrasive but exciting climate.

So it wasn't simply a case of you and a small group of working-class students in Trinity feeling embattled. There was a fairly vibrant intellectual culture in which you could participate, at least potentially.

There was, yes. The abrasiveness of it all suited my partisan, polemical side. Cambridge dogma reflected Catholic dogma in my case. Partly, I think, I picked it up from there; but partly I had it already. There was a deep conviction that literature and culture really mattered. There was of course an inflation of that conviction, particularly with the Leavisites. Howard Jacobson, the novelist, who came from near me in Salford, was a fervently evangelical Leavisite. I remember him getting into a fistfight with somebody in Downing College, possibly over the relative merits of Jane Austen and George Eliot. It was that kind of ethos, all very solemn, intense and high-minded. My friends and I were never actually evangelical about it, and I wouldn't have called myself a straight-up Leavisite, though I was certainly interested in Leavis. Nevertheless, there was a sense that there was something important here – something that, as Perry Anderson has pointed out, perhaps stood in for certain missing political commitments.

The man who'd informed you about your father's death, and who subsequently became your tutor, was Theodore Redpath. What kind of an intellectual role did he play in your life as a student? I suspect that it wasn't completely negligible . . .

No, I wouldn't say that at all. He was a surreal sort of figure. He had wanted to be a Tory MP, and I imagine he would have been quite a right-wing one. I think he had been a lawyer. But he'd also been an outer member of Wittgenstein's circle. The last thing he wrote was a memoir of Wittgenstein. The only mention Wittgenstein made of Redpath was a hypothesis involving boiling his head, which I suppose might illustrate the claim that any publicity is better than none. He suddenly got married, quite late in life, to a painter, and had a few children. And then he became a wine-merchant, so little vans with the name 'Redpath and Thackeray' were running around Cambridge. It was all a bit strange. Even his business partner had a literary handle. No, I learned a lot from him, although not in terms of doctrine.

We would spend our supervisions arguing about anything and everything. It was a classic case of following the argument wherever it led, and being blissfully free to do so because no argument would ever shake the walls of Trinity. We argued about Lenin, we argued about religion, we argued about philosophy. He seemed to know everything; he didn't have a clue what to do with it, but he knew everything. It was a very valuable introduction to that kind of upper-class academic mind. For example, I took it for granted that relationships with people were what was important, and I discovered that he didn't take that for granted at all. Absolutely not: he thought that was a gross presumption on my part. So I said to him, 'Sir, what is important?' and he said, 'Well, objects, ideas.' I think he even murmured something about herbaceous borders. This sort of thing was a revelation to me. It was funny and momentous at the same time. He once told me he believed in benevolent dictatorship. It was all a long way from the Stockport Young Socialists.

Presumably he didn't know what to do with all this knowledge because he didn't need to do anything with it.

No, he didn't. I think his father had been one of the great engineers of the empire, a great bridge-builder and so on. Redpath himself had been to one of the Cambridge public schools – ironically, the school that Leavis attended. He knew Leavis. But he didn't need to do anything with his knowledge because he was so supremely secure in his position. I could throw anything at him and he wouldn't flinch. So on the one hand there was a high degree of intellectual liberalism. Essentially, his attitude towards ideas was that of a wine-taster, which is more or less what he later became for real. He could sample a great many of them and not see the need to make too hasty distinctions or hierarchies. I'm sure that's what he had against Leavis. But on the other hand this intellectual *laissez-faire* was combined with the most extraordinary meticulousness in terms of actual behaviour. There was an obituary of him in the *Independent* by Adrian Poole, who recalls that at certain times he wouldn't shake hands with you because it was not out of term, or wouldn't talk to you because you weren't wearing a gown. He was pathologically committed to social order – I mean, almost to the point of insanity. I remember arguing with him about the ridiculous proportions of public-school to grammar-school students in Cambridge, and he said, 'Well, I think it's just about right.' Being taught by him was an education, but not in the usual sense.

*Ironically, your intellectual interests and those of Redpath overlapped:
he'd written about Shakespeare and you've published two books on
Shakespeare; he'd written about Wittgenstein and you've discussed
him in a number of books and articles, in addition to collaborating on
Derek Jarman's film about him; he'd written about tragedy and you
discussed the matter extensively, both in your theological writings and
your later monograph on the subject,* Sweet Violence *[2003]. Was
there a sense in which, unconsciously, you conducted an Oedipal battle
with him, and on territory that he'd demarcated himself?*

I hadn't thought of that, but it is striking. The interest in Wittgenstein
is perhaps coincidental, because my introduction to him came
from the Dominican Order and from Catholic intellectuals. But
Redpath would have known people like Elizabeth Anscombe and
Peter Geach, who were Catholic Wittgensteinians. Tragedy was
a bone of contention. I didn't consciously write my tragedy book
against Redpath, but parts of the ideology he represented certainly
came into it. We talked about tragedy, and we met in the wake of
one.

What we did have in common, really, was an interest in ideas. For
example, he taught me the so-called Moralists paper. I remember
studying everything from Saint Augustine to John Stuart Mill
with him, and he knew a tremendous amount about it, though he
didn't take up any positions. He once told me about some very rich
friends of his – he wasn't of course boasting as he would never
have boasted – and added, to my surprise, that 'you, Terence,' as
he called me, 'might find them rather predatory.' God knows what
they were like if even he could use that word. 'But,' he said, 'there
are times when I think to myself, well, it's a vigorous flourish of
life . . .' I think that this rather Paterian idea was crucial to him
– the idea that it was good to have a lot of life around, without
enquiring too much into which bits of it could be justified. So we
shared an interest in ideas. And – shades almost of Raymond – we
talked a lot about Ibsen in particular. I once wrote him an essay
on Ibsen that must have been based on twenty plays, and he sent

it back saying, 'You seem not to have read them all.' Try doing that today! So on all of those levels we were, in a curious way, well adapted to each other. He probably found it rather piquant to argue with a truculent prole like me, and I felt the kind of mixture of alarm and fascination one might feel when talking to an extra-terrestrial – though without the stench of sulphur.

Incidentally, when did 'Terence Eagleton', the name under which you first published, become 'Terry Eagleton'?

When I published *The New Left Church* [1966], ridiculously I used the name Terence, because that was the name on the contract. I was only in my early twenties and I thought I had to do that. I had been called 'Terence' by my family, perhaps up to early adolescence, and at that point I decided I wanted to change it to 'Terry' – so I did. My second name is my father's name, Francis, because Catholics in those days had to take a saint's name and it's not certain there was a Saint Terence. 'Terence' in Ireland, where the name is more common, is 'Turlough', which also means one of those small lakes that evaporate from time to time. I note that for anyone eager for completely useless knowledge.

Apart from Redpath, and of course Williams, who I want to discuss in some detail, were there other teachers who shaped your intellectual development?

I wasn't actually supervized fully by Redpath until my third year, by which time I had fallen under the influence of Williams. Redpath wasn't keen on that at all. Before that, I was taught by a motley group of people who were less interesting. My general experience of reading English at Cambridge was of knowing that I could do it, but not knowing what it was I was doing, or supposed to be doing. So when I got a first in prelims at the end of the first year I was of course very glad; but I was also surprised, partly because in the tutorial system you had no sense of testing yourself against anybody else. I suppose it was when I encountered Williams that I began to raise questions like 'What's the meaning of this?' and 'What am I supposed to be up to here?' He allowed me to pose some meta-questions, so to speak.

Reading

Anderson, Perry, 'Components of the National Culture', in *English Questions* (London: Verso, 1992), pp. 96–103.

Eagleton, Terry, *The New Left Church* (London: Sheed & Ward, 1966).

Eagleton, Terry, *The Gatekeeper: A Memoir* (London: Allen Lane, 2001).

Eagleton, Terry, 'Roy Foster', in *Figures of Dissent: Critical Essays on Fish, Spivak, Žižek and Others* (London: Verso, 2003), pp. 230–33.

Eliot, T. S., *To Criticize the Critic and Other Writings* (London: Faber & Faber, 1965).

Hall, Stuart, 'Politics and Letters', in *Raymond Williams: Critical Perspectives*, ed. Terry Eagleton (Cambridge: Polity Press, 1989), pp. 54–66.

Redpath, Theodore, *Ludwig Wittgenstein: A Student's Memoir* (London: Duckworth, 1990).

Smith, Dai, *Raymond Williams: A Warrior's Tale* (Cardigan: Parthian, 2008).

CHAPTER TWO

New Left/Church

When did you first encounter Raymond Williams, and in what context?

We arrived in Cambridge in the same year, 1961, but I probably didn't go to his lectures until my second year. Having been through the same mill himself, he gave lectures on a great variety of subjects – the moralists, tragedy, and so on – but these lectures were rather peripheral, physically speaking, to the faculty, as they were out in various halls. I remember him giving a fascinating series of lectures on the seventeenth century, which is not a period one would normally associate with him, on topics like linguistic change and the connection of that to social change. I even heard him lecture on Restoration drama.

It was a strange experience for me. Here was somebody talking what I knew was a vitally important language, which I hadn't heard used before, one that I was intellectually ready for, and yet I found it hard to pick up. This was partly because of Williams's characteristic abstractions and obliquities, but partly because it was in the nature of the language anyway. And so with a couple of other disciples I faithfully went to all his lectures. I think it became a bit of a joke actually – he would always see us at the back of the hall, like familiar groupies at a rock concert, and tip us the wink.

And who were these disciples?

Apart from me, there was John Barrell, now a distinguished eighteenth-century scholar, who was my supervision mate for a while, and a couple of working-class guys. Then, in our third year, John approached Raymond and asked if we could sit in on a seminar on the novel that he was running for his graduate students, and he said we could. So a few of us, including the Pre-Raphaelite scholar Jan Marsh, attended the classes. That was a very important experience for me, because I was able then, as only a third-year undergraduate, to listen to highly sophisticated discussions about literature and society. We just listened, as we didn't have the courage to say anything, but Raymond was very kind to us and would chat to us. But, although there was a general respect for him, he didn't have much of a following when I was an undergraduate. He was after all pretty new himself, and the Leavisites were still powerful. A few years later, by the time I was a young research fellow at Jesus College, there were a number of renegades around him: Stephen Heath, Stan Smith, Bernard Sharratt, Pat Parrinder, Pat Rogers, Charles Swann, and Gareth Jenkins (now a leading left activist). There was also Mike Long, who was the son of a London shop steward. He was in the Communist Party, but he moved to the right and became a fellow of Churchill College (not a great distance to travel, some might claim). In the end, we probably burgeoned to ten or a dozen people, but we weren't a self-consciously coherent group. We were, however, all male.

By this time *Slant*, the Catholic left movement, had got going. I asked Raymond to write a note of introduction to the first issue of *Slant*, which he did. We thought it was, understandably, rather cautious; he thought it was rashly generous. At that time he was English correspondent for *The Nation* in New York, and his editor asked him to write an article on a prominent Catholic theologian called Charles Davis, who had caused quite a stir because he'd left the Church. So Raymond chatted to us *Slant*ites about this. We also asked him to speak to a university group called the Aquinas Society, which we had effectively taken over. I can't remember much of what he said, but he did say that he was aware that religion was an absence or silence in his own work. He was quite keen on a kind of alliance with us. He wrote a long review of a book we did called *The Slant Manifesto*. After that sort of contact, he called me to his office after my final exams and offered me a research fellowship at Jesus. It wasn't as though I knew him that well, but there was a vacancy and he had obviously decided that it was me that he wanted to teach his undergraduates. So I started university teaching when I was twenty-one.

Stephen Heath once remarked that, to your satisfaction, the college elders at Trinity detested you. He also said that, because Williams wanted to distance himself from undergraduate teaching, you became the key English teacher at Jesus. Is that right?

I was the only other main English teacher, so I did a fair bit of the teaching. It wasn't exactly that Raymond shucked all or even most of his teaching onto me – he wouldn't have been allowed to because you had to do a certain quota – but he wasn't particularly interested in it. So I suppose I found myself picking up the pieces. At one point there was a small, rather angry delegation of students who came to me and demanded that Raymond teach them. He once said in defence of his reluctance – and Raymond was not a man who easily admitted to any faults – that if they had only known what a bad teacher he was they wouldn't have been so eager. I remember Stephen hectoring Raymond at a party because he had suddenly decided to teach the students in groups instead of individually, and Stephen had been looking forward to some face-to-face contact. Raymond wasn't at his best in face-to-face academic situations. He was far better as a lecturer or seminar leader, and as a public figure.

There's an anecdote that I want to invoke in this context. In Politics and Letters *[1979],* Williams is asked about the genesis of The English Novel from Dickens to Lawrence *[1971], which had started life as a lecture course in the 1960s. In his response, he emphasizes that lots of the ideas for that book occurred to him in the process of actually delivering the lectures. And he says: 'I remember for example the moment when I linked the analytic composition of* Middlemarch *to George Eliot's loss of her earlier social perspective – a connection which hadn't occurred to me till then. Terry Eagleton, who was sitting in the front row, sat bolt upright because he was so inside the argument – we talked all the time – that he could see immediately the shift of judgement that had just come out of the logic of the argument.' Do you remember that incident?*

I remember Raymond writing that, but I don't remember it happening. I'm wondering whether that's a phantom memory. I never sat in the front row; I lurked at the back. I certainly don't remember the point about George Eliot, and it's stretching the truth to say that we talked all the time about such matters. Raymond wasn't a man for intensive discussion into the small hours. He was better on the whole at monologue than dialogue.

But there was nonetheless a pretty close dialogue between you at this stage, intellectually and politically, and he wouldn't presumably have helped to procure the job for you at Jesus if that hadn't been the case.

That's absolutely right. I remember him implying, when he asked me to take up the job, that he knew there would be some negative aspects to it for me. He felt a certain responsibility for that. When those negative aspects came out – roughly speaking, when I wasn't putting in enough hours at High Table or pulling my weight on the Wine Committee – he felt rather bad about it. But he gave me my start and was remarkably patient with my personal difficulties at the time.

And what was it that was inspiring about the lectures that he gave, in contrast to the tutorials and supervisions?

There was the sense both of a strenuous intellectual adventure and of considerable subtlety. He combined rebarbative abstractions with – 'genial' might be too strong a word for it – a companionable, humane, ordinary style. It was a rather slow, measured, slightly ponderous register perhaps; but it was the style of somebody who was talking in a human voice – a phrase that Raymond would often use – and talking to people. It was really rather a striking performance. He was talking in his customary abstract, rather convoluted manner, yet imbuing this with a human touch and a subdued emotional intensity. His lecturing style embodied a combination of moral commitment and rational inquiry, properly partisan yet admirably judicious. His ideas sounded both eminently reasonable and quietly subversive.

It sounds as if the lectures were a little like supervisions, in that there was a certain sense of intimacy to them – though in making that assumption I'm no doubt influenced by his false memory of you in the lecture on Middlemarch.

He was a public figure who was at ease on a public platform, and the platform brought out his formidable rhetorical resources. Even his personal presence had an implicit public dimension. When I say that he spoke with a human voice, 'intimate' is perhaps not quite the right word. Raymond was relaxed, companionable, genial; but he always had a certain distanced, impersonal authority about him, which was in a strange way part of the attraction. He was magisterial but not in the least pompous. He wasn't exactly Wildean in his wit, but there was a coolly sardonic streak in him.

Did you see him and Joy Williams socially at all?

Yes, I did; at least, once I'd joined him at Jesus. He was quite good at giving parties for his undergraduates. He several times invited me out to his cottage. Sometimes he might just take me, sometimes his Jesus student Charles Swann might be there too. He'd take us across to the pub opposite, and with extreme tentativeness and an air of suppressed alarm he'd offer us a half-pint of bitter, monitoring us anxiously as though we were about to fall over. In both our cases this was particularly ironic. Occasionally he would have a party of Cambridge left-wingers: Bob Rowthorn, Martin Bernal, Brian Jackson, Joan Robinson, people of that kind. So I got to know a few people like that.

Also in my time at Jesus he established something called the Tawney Group. Its purpose was simply to get together various radical dons, and there were meetings addressed by people like Isaac Deutscher. I remember a great moment when the young Noam Chomsky, hotfoot from the anti-war movement, addressed the Tawney Group. He spoke without notes for an hour and a half about the situation in the United States and about how important he thought the student movement was in bringing the war to an end. The war was still going on, but it was almost at an end. We were acutely aware of events in the States.

Were you reading Marx, Lenin and Trotsky as a student?

I probably didn't come to Trotsky until later, when I moved to Oxford. I must have read some Marx as an undergraduate, because I argued with Redpath about him. Then I must have read him more intensively, partly as the background to my doctoral work on Edward Carpenter. I think I taught Marx, too, on the moralists paper. I'd read some Lenin, and had begun to read my way through Western Marxism.

In those years we also established the Cambridge Left Forum, a little-known but I think quite interesting institution. Bob Rowthorn, some other left economists and myself established a kind of town-and-gown connection. We held public meetings in the town and the speakers included some shop stewards. We managed to bring together shop stewards in the town who had been working in isolation from one another. So that was probably my first experience of town-and-gown political activities. I repeated it when I joined the Workers' Socialist League in Oxford, because the group was very active around the factory and in community issues. I felt quite strongly that there should be some kind of a hook-up between the university and the city, rather than having people like me working in isolation at one end and the car plant shop stewards at the other.

Looking back at that period, what kind of an intellectual impact do you think Williams had on you and other people? And to what extent has it continued and been extended? In the memorial lecture you gave after Williams's death, which was subsequently published in New Left Review, *you use the phrase, 'He had got there before us again'; and in a recent article in the* Guardian, *too, on the tenth anniversary of his death, you implied that he had created a new horizon for you and for others on the left. I understand 'horizon' here in the sense used by Roland Barthes, meaning both a limit, albeit one that might be exceeded, and a kind of perspective.*

Looking back, I think that what Raymond achieved was pretty staggering, and I'm not sure that I was directly aware of it at the time. I've often stressed the single-handedness of his enterprise. I mean, he had very little going for him – a Stalinized Marxism, a Leavisism that was increasingly reactionary and elitist – so I still marvel at the way that he spun so much seemingly out of his own guts at a moment when it was vitally necessary. It wasn't of course simply an isolated enterprise – there were all those forces that went into the early New Left that he was in touch with. But he was a remarkably inventive, self-sufficient and pioneering figure. Leavis was never more wrong than when he said dismissively of Raymond's work, 'Queenie did it all in the thirties.' Not in the least. In Cambridge at that time he seemed absolutely central, intellectually; and at the same time, in the perception of most people at the university, rather marginal and misplaced. They didn't really know what he was up to, and in that sense he was very isolated. But he was used to being isolated, and there were a few of us around him, which was enough for him to be going on with, because of the massive self-sufficiency he exuded. Perhaps isolation suited him temperamentally.

What I realize now is that Raymond was himself aware of his isolation. He made this clear in the interviews in *Politics and Letters*. It was very much the effect of a counter-public sphere failing to come into existence. I was struck by the way he talked in very distantiating terms about his earlier work in *Culture and Society* [1958], because he identified the political moment as being for him very negative. What then happened, as the sixties and seventies drew on, was the emergence of new political developments in which he was involved. Certainly the resurgence of the New Left around the peace movement and the various kinds of interventions during the period of the Labour government of the sixties were part of this. So he had this history of involvement, but I think that at the same time the sense of the earlier dissociation remained, and proved to be something he could never truly get beyond. Yet I think it's interesting to put the problem not only psychologically, but also in terms of the failure of the emergence of the material conditions that could have made Williams an even more influential figure than he has been.

Did the Raymond Williams revealed in Politics and Letters *surprise you?*

Part of Raymond's political isolation, and his isolation in the academy, was the result of what one might politely call a rather Byzantine or enigmatic discourse. He was somebody who spoke, and for a long time was forced to speak, a language that was not popular, that could easily be misinterpreted, and that was also to some degree a language of self-protection. As I implied in my critique of him in *Criticism and Ideology* [1976], there were ways in which his very style of discourse was related to that isolation. I was therefore struck by the way that, of all his work, *Politics and Letters* is the one in which he is most candid – where, in the company of comrades, so to speak, he talked openly about his career.

I think it is a mistake to search, as many people have done, for the private person behind the public persona, because he was always someone who saw his life in historical terms and often in quite distantiating ways. If there were losses in that, there were also some gains. Williams was able to solve or negotiate certain problems by seeing them as historical necessities, while never being fatalistic. One of the other important things about his work as a whole, although it often had a steely realism about it, is that he never succumbed to the various tides of fashionable post-Marxist pessimism that from time to time drift around our societies. In the deepest sense, he had hope – which is not of course to be confused with some brittle optimism or doctrinaire progressivism.

Since his death Williams's reputation hasn't perhaps been revived as much as it might have been expected to, given the range of interests he had. His interest in a social ecology, to take a single example, might well have led to his work being popularized in ways that it simply hasn't.

That's right, it hasn't. It may still happen, but it is somewhat dismaying that to a certain extent he has retreated into the past as an *éminence grise*. He's respected, but he's seen as very much part of a previous era – and there's some truth in that, as I've implied, because the political situation has changed so much since Raymond's work was published. That doesn't make it any the less relevant. In fact, almost all the problems to which he brought his political wisdom have worsened since he wrote.

I would say that there was a time, certainly in the seventies, when his influence – not just at Cambridge but more generally – was considerable. But that has changed. Before I wrote the piece in the *Guardian* that you referred to, someone on the paper asked me if I had anything in mind to write about. So I said, 'Well, Raymond Williams's anniversary.' To which, after a brief pause, he replied: 'Remind me . . .' This journalist isn't a literary person, but he is a kind of leftist. Of course, politically speaking, the times have changed radically since Raymond's zenith, and indeed since his death. He would, for example, have only just recognized the term 'postmodernism'.

You said in the piece on Williams *published in the* New Left Review *after he died that his first and most persistent interest lay in writing. There's a sense in which that claim applies to you, too. Did you inherit this commitment to writing, in part at least, from Williams?*

No, it predates him. One of the things that strikes me forcibly about Dai's biography is that what Raymond was doing most of the time was writing drafts of novels, and either revising them or discarding them, publishing them or not finishing them. That book brings out how central that was to him, which I hadn't really realized. I always knew his fiction meant a great deal to him, but I can now see that he used it to negotiate conflicts for which it seemed the only appropriate form. Fiction was the form he needed in order to articulate his experience – rather as Richard Hoggart, in *The Uses of Literacy* [1957], veers towards fiction, towards literature, in bringing alive certain working-class scenes. On the other hand, I think Raymond and I were very much alike – you're quite right – in that we were basically both writers. But Raymond's fiction was not as vital or valuable to me as it obviously was to him. It's not what I primarily valued about him.

As a writer I'm more promiscuous, so to speak, than he was. I write in – and enjoy writing in – a variety of genres. Raymond was not quite as diffuse or opportunistic as that. He wasn't a particularly good journalist or popularizer. Barthes uses the term *écriture*, in opposition to *écrivance*, to mean the act of writing for its own sake; and I've certainly felt for a long time that what I write is probably less important than the fact that I write. At the time of my first encounter with Raymond this would have taken the form of poetry. One of my few achievements at Cambridge, in a situation where I felt very crushed and cowed, was to publish some poetry. I published it in *Granta* and I knocked around a bit with some of the left literati, as I suppose you could call them. That was tremendously important for me. But at the same time writing poetry was always quite difficult for me. I discovered that writing criticism was equally creative but easier. For twenty years or more I regularly reviewed poetry for Jon Silkin's magazine *Stand*, and found it by far the most difficult kind of writing I've ever done.

So what kind of poetry was it that you published? Who influenced it?

It was sub-Thom Gunn. It was iambically straitjacketed and rather austere, somewhat gaunt and tight-lipped. Looking back, I can see that it was very much concerned with breaking out of restraints – though I was utterly unconscious of it at the time – and the loss as well as the gain of that. The idea of constraints that are nonetheless creative is lurking there somewhere, and re-emerges in my later work. A lot of my concerns run back to very early days and simply get rearticulated. There are shifts in my work but no dramatic breaks.

But formally the poems were restrained?

They were very buttoned-down, as indeed I was myself. But there was something struggling to get out. And there was at the same time a valuing of form, or settlement, or limits; along with a sort of fear-of-freedom motif.

Aesthetically, were you defining yourself against, or distancing yourself from, Williams's realism?

Well, not deliberately; and anyway I'd written and published poetry before I came to Cambridge. But there were those differences between us nonetheless. Poetry was not Raymond's genre, and he does notoriously treat it rather like a form of documentation in books such as *The Country and the City* [1973]. I was quite surprised, though, in reading *Politics and Letters*, to realize that his earlier interests when he was a Cambridge student were not mainly realist. They were avant-garde, Bolshevik and experimental. That didn't really sit with the man I knew at all. My interests then were more like his previous ones, and certainly I think I was more enthusiastic about modernism than Raymond was. I remember that one of the most interesting seminars he gave, in his series on novels, was on Lukács, specifically *The Historical Novel* [1937]. At this point, Raymond clearly found this realist aesthetic very congenial. I think his work had, unconsciously, followed certain Lukácsian patterns. As for me, it was the first time I had heard this critic's name. He was my first introduction to Marxist criticism.

I'd like to come back to Lukács in connection with Exiles and Émigrés *[1970]. For the moment, I'm keen to move on and ask you about* Slant. *Of course, since your recent 'metaphysical' or 'theological' turn, as you call it in* Holy Terror *[2005], this is of more than merely antiquarian interest. So perhaps you could start by saying something about the origins and emergence of the December Group, in the climate of the Second Vatican Council.*

I've already said that, looking back now, I can see that the *Slant* movement was just what I needed to bring together my background and my new intellectual world. It was in that sense another extraordinary moment of liberation. The idea that one could carry on being a Christian and be a socialist, a left-wing socialist, was enthralling for me. And of course that was also a coded way of talking about leaving one world and going into a new world, but not leaving the old world entirely behind.

The December Group had originally been founded by Neil Middleton, who ran the Catholic publisher Sheed and Ward. It was a casual group of left-wing Catholics who, before the Vatican Council, stuck out like sore thumbs in the Church. Then, in the wake of the Council, it came into its own. It was our ephemeral but euphoric moment. The journal *Slant*, which Sheed and Ward published, very much belonged to that moment. It began, almost fortuitously, in a Cambridge pub. A handful of us, mostly ex-working-class Catholics, were aware that the Vatican Council, for all its gains, was very much a middle-class, liberal-progressive phenomenon, and we saw that there was a need to politicize that. This was before liberation theology, so we didn't have much to go on. It also pre-dated – just – the Northern Irish Troubles, which might have lent this rather cerebral project a more practical context. The vital figure then was Laurence Bright, a Dominican theologian. Along with Raymond, he was the vital figure in my life at the time. Laurence himself had come into the Church from an atheistic position (he had been an Oxford nuclear physicist), and he was something of an outsider still. There was an utter clash of cultural styles between us, as he seemed to have stepped right out of *Brideshead Revisited*. Not only was he a rather languid, foppish, patrician figure, and a Dominican priest to boot, but he was also telling us we could be as left-wing as we wanted. He was very much conscious of his mentoring role in that respect. I discovered for the first time an intellectually reputable form of Christian belief, as well as a politically resourceful one.

So *Slant* began as a local Cambridge journal. Then Sheed and Ward stepped in and took it over. I think finally it might have reached a subscription list of a thousand. But it was almost as important simply as a phenomenon, a journal to be read about as much as to be read, because it established a certain possibility to which many people then looked with hope. And it burgeoned as a movement throughout the sixties. We had a network of *Slant* reader groups, rather on the lines of the New Left clubs. We had lots of meetings, we agitated for reform, leafleted churches, ran a petition against the Vietnam War, and took over the December Group.

In an editorial for Slant, *you once described the December Group as a 'counterculture', in a deliberate nod to the cultural politics of the late sixties. But wasn't it more like a counter-public sphere?*

Yes, it was a counter-public sphere right enough; and yet it was also somewhere I could belong, at a time when I didn't really belong anywhere because I was strung out between these two different milieus. One of the sources of *Slant* was Catholic CND, which marched under its own banner on the Aldermaston marches, and some of us had been members of that. There was also a Catholic anarchist or libertarian tradition that people like Dorothy Day came out of, in particular the Catholic Workers' Movement in the States. So there was a medley of different sources. But we were conscious at the time that we were very much part of the sixties ferment – that's not just a retrospective reading of it. We were aware of trying to be a wing or dimension of it. So when the May Day Manifesto Group or some such organization held a conference, they would say, 'Oh, we must have the *Slant* people along.' We came to occupy a certain niche. '*Slant* people' sounded faintly perverse, and indeed the name was finally taken over by a porno magazine, which I suppose is how some right-wing Catholics had regarded us in the first place.

The other figure that's important in this context is Herbert McCabe, who died quite recently. Can you say something about him?

Herbert kicked around on the fringes of the *Slant* movement; he wasn't an architect of it in the way that Laurence Bright was. He was, however, probably the most creatively minded theologian of the time, and I learned an enormous amount from him. There were also similarities – in our backgrounds and in our temperaments – that made Herbert a very good friend of mine. He was one of my closest friends throughout his life. Herbert's whole temperament was one that was congenial to me, and there were strange similarities of style between us. I admired the boldness and paradoxicality of his ideas; and also the fact that he was absolutely the reverse of fashionable: he was a radical because he was a traditionalist. He was razor-sharp, outrageous, ferociously satirical, steelily committed and hilariously witty.

During this period Herbert McCabe was briefly suspended as a priest, and dismissed from the editorial chair of the Dominican journal *New Blackfriars*, for writing that the Church was corrupt. This was a bit like being sacked from an English lectureship for announcing that D.H. Lawrence was sexist. There was a tremendous furore, in which I was actively involved, and Herbert was finally reinstated after some years in the cold. He began his next editorial with the words, 'As I was saying before I was so oddly interrupted . . .'

And what were the theological influences that informed him and Laurence Bright? Where were they coming from?

They came from the Dominican order – which, not insignificantly, had for some time been the intellectual maverick of the Catholic Church. The Dominicans weren't characterized by the *sancta simplicitas* of the Franciscans or the genteel asceticism of the Benedictines. And they weren't the suave intelligentsia of the establishment, like the Jesuits. You might almost say that the Jesuits were the traditional intellectuals and the Dominicans were the organic ones, though that's stretching it a bit. Their brief – ever since Aquinas, I suppose, their greatest member – was to interpret the gospel in the light of contemporary experience, to bring contemporary ideas to bear on the gospel. Aquinas applied Aristotelian and Platonic ideas. But in the forties quite a few of the Dominicans had been Jungians, and there had been Freudian Dominicans as well. They also had some very important contacts with Wittgenstein: the man who taught Herbert and Laurence, Cornelius Ernst, had been a pupil of Wittgenstein. Then in the sixties the Dominicans became interested in Marx. Some of them also became interested in Marcuse and the counterculture and so on. Despite all this, as I say, they weren't in the least modish. For the most part, they were utterly dedicated men.

In the introduction to The Slant Manifesto, *which appeared in 1966, Neil Middleton says that it was 'more by accident than by design' that the people around* Slant, *and around the December Group, were Roman Catholics, and he goes on to mention a significant intellectual debt to the* New Left Review. *Was it more by accident than by design? It seems implausible.*

No, it wasn't really by accident. Certainly the December Group, which met in a Dominican priory, was more or less exclusively Catholic. Both groups would very much have seen themselves as the radical wing of Catholicism. At the same time there were members of both organizations who weren't Catholics. But I would say that they were both radical Catholic organizations in the main.

What was the reception of The Slant Manifesto, *among Catholics on the one hand and socialists on the other?*

We were always a source of both hope and horror for Catholics. In Holland or Germany, where the most radical theological developments were happening after Vatican II, the *Manifesto* probably wouldn't have caused such a stir. But in Britain the editors of the official Catholic press gave orders that we were not even to be mentioned. We heard vague, distant rumours that the bishops were fluttering and flapping; but because we were a lay enterprise they couldn't touch us. The clerical members had to keep a low profile in that respect, in case they were fingered. On the other hand, there was hope. For many Christians the very fact that such a position could be staked out was encouraging – even if they had very little first-hand contact with it. The response of the non-Christian left was surprisingly welcoming, although it was obviously one of some bemusement as well.

Can you describe the Slant *symposium of 1967? The New Left was an important presence at this event: Stuart Hall and Charles Taylor both gave papers, and Williams contributed to the book.*

I think David Cooper was there, too, though he may not have given a paper. It was our modest papist equivalent of 'The Dialectics of Liberation', the famous London Roundhouse meeting with Ernest Mandel, R.D. Laing, Stokely Carmichael and so on. It absolutely shot out of its particular historical moment. Among other things, it was an attempt to build bridges with the non-Christian left. Chuck Taylor was brought up a Catholic, and has since returned to the Church, but he wasn't particularly close to it then. And there were various other people, like Cooper, who were certainly not Christians. But it was a landmark moment. Raymond was supposed to address the conference and pulled out at the last moment, which was a source of some disappointment. He was getting rather sedentary in his ways, but he was kind enough to do the interview with me that resulted in the topping and tailing of the book. His piece hardly needed any editing at all, as he always spoke in perfect syntax. It was a moment that marked the arrival of *Slant* as a relatively serious group that then became known to non-Christian groups. But only three years later we folded. We wouldn't have predicted that at the time.

Why did it fold in 1970?

It folded for a number of reasons. We were all getting university jobs in different places, so the coherence of the group had gone. We were a financial burden on Sheed and Ward, and the auditors told them in no uncertain terms to get rid of us – they were only publishing us out of political solidarity really. More significantly, there was no longer really a consensus as to what we were doing. And that was partly because we weren't making political headway. In any case, the tides of Vatican II were rapidly ebbing, and they left us pretty high and dry. The journal folded quite unacrimoniously.

There was a feeling that we had done a specific job and that that was it.

The papers from the Slant *symposium ended up in the book* From Culture to Revolution *[1968], a collection that you and Brian Wicker co-edited. One of them, 'A Note on Violent Revolution' by Middleton, starts by arguing, in opposition to the usual political assumption, that it isn't necessarily the case that there'll never be violent insurrection in Britain. By the time it was actually published, the May events had taken place all over Europe. So in one sense it was prescient and in another sense it appeared to have been left behind by historical developments. What was the relationship of* Slant *to the counterculture, and to far-left politics specifically, in the late sixties?*

I would say that by the end of the sixties, by the close of *Slant*, we regarded ourselves as political revolutionaries. Certainly a year or so after the end of *Slant*, one or two comrades joined the International Marxist Group (IMG).[1] I left *Slant* and joined the International Socialists (IS).[2] Some members stayed in the Church, some left for secular politics, and others led a twilight existence between the two. One of the questions we were asking ourselves – and couldn't really resolve – was: what difference to being a leftist did being a Christian make? When *Slant* broke up and went in its various directions, some people – Neil, myself and a few others – moved into secular political activity. Others continued in some way within the radical activities of the Church. Because we had aimed for a pretty high level of abstraction, it was hard to hold this synthesis together. So there was a sort of parting of the ways. As

---

1   International Marxist Group: the British section of the Trotskyist Fourth International, founded in 1968; its leading figures included Tariq Ali, Robin Blackburn and Peter Gowan.
2   International Socialists: a Trotskyist tendency formed by Tony Cliff in 1962, after the Socialist Review Group had been expelled from the Fourth International. Its leading figures, apart from Cliff, included Chris Harman, Nigel Harris and Mike Kidron. It renamed itself the Socialist Workers Party in 1977.

the old cliché goes, we were in the wrong place at the wrong time. If we'd been in Northern Ireland, and certainly in Latin America, it would have clarified the mind wonderfully.

Can I briefly go back to Williams's relationship to Slant? *There is something a little slippery about his editorial for the first issue of* Slant. *He praises 'the seriousness and energy of the Christian enquiry into contemporary politics'. Then at the end, in slightly lukewarm tones, he states that 'if we cannot learn from this, we can take heart and fellow feeling' from it. Was there a tension between his atheism and your Catholicism?*

'Those of us who are not and cannot be Christians . . .' is another phrase he uses there. Yes, he was properly somewhat wary of us, partly perhaps because he didn't know that *Slant* wouldn't fold at the first issue, like many a student journal. On the other hand, as I say, he was very generous with his time, despite his circumspection. He contributed a note to *From Culture to Revolution*, and wrote about the *Slant* movement in his regular column in *The Nation*. As I've pointed out in print, he believed deeply in diversity and plurality long before the words were fashionable, and he would have seen his relationship to us as part of that. He was worried about getting labelled as a Christian-lover; but we tried not to compromise him in that way, and I think it worked out all right.

Do you think he rethought the 'Culture and Society' tradition in the light of his dialogue with Slant? *He did after all concede that he had rather neglected the religious dimension of that tradition.*

It was a fairly token concession. I think *Slant* opened his eyes to the fact that there could be something interesting and congenial in Christian thought, but I don't think it made any other difference. Of course, by the time of the *Culture to Revolution* book, he himself had moved pretty far from *Culture and Society*.

Can you say something about the theological role of the liturgy for the December Group? As someone who's not from a theological background at all, I find the emphasis on it in Slant *and the publications associated with it extremely striking. In a book called* Culture and Liturgy *[1963], Brian Wicker makes this interesting but — to me — slightly tenuous connection between literature and the liturgical, both of which seem to function for him as rituals that mediate between the ordinary and the transcendent. What kind of symbolic role did the liturgy play for you?*

When Raymond spoke to the Aquinas Society at Cambridge we asked him to speak about Brian's book, and he gave a kind of running critique of it. One of the sources of Vatican II was liturgical reform, and that was much in the air. It was a matter of converting the Mass from a rather Byzantine ceremonial, spoken by somebody with his back to you, into something that looked more like a communal event. So in a sense the liturgy was a way of fleshing out in practice a lot of the ideas we were talking about — ideas of community and solidarity and so on.

So it was in terms of liturgical reform that you created a dialogue with Catholics who weren't explicitly on the left?

Exactly: it was a point where we could connect with the progressive brigade, the liberals, the Vatican II-ites. That was very much what they were intent on, and our role was to draw out certain political implications of this. It was at once a theoretical or theological affair and a practical one, and it was very much the centre of concern for liberal Catholics. Of course, it caused a lot of conflict — not least, for instance, around the vernacularization of the Mass.

But any attempt to democratize or communalize liturgical ritual surely runs up against ingrained institutional hierarchies and structures that either lead you to question the Church or to question organized religion itself . . .

Yes, or to some uneasy coexistence or compromise – which is what *Slant* embodied really. This is the position the radical Catholic movement in general was forced into eventually. Of course, reforms to the liturgy were made, much to the horror of the reactionaries. Certain issues, like replacing Latin with the vernacular, were real hot potatoes – I think people left the Church over that. But it became quite clear that the wider power situation wasn't changing, and that we weren't winning the argument that the liturgy only made sense in terms of the Church as a radical movement in the world.

At the end of the sixties, were you less of a Christian than you had been at the beginning?

Yes, though I don't know what kind of a Christian I was even during the period of *Slant*. What strikes me, looking back, is that *Slant* was actually a very impressive intellectual venture. It was high-powered stuff, it quite often produced highly original material, and we were working very much against the grain of conventional wisdom. But what also strikes me about that now is a certain kind of callowness, a certain intellectual overdevelopment. I don't know if any of us at that point in our early twenties had experienced enough, in terms of ordinary living, to be able to cash out some of these ideas in reality. So in a sense I was a Christian of a cerebral kind at that point, because it was all so intellectually exciting. But by the end of the sixties or the beginning of the seventies I was fairly disillusioned. The *Slant* venture seemed to have failed, although I had taken an enormous amount from it. Joining the International Socialists was probably a sign of turning away from all that. And I would say that in my Althusserian phase I was at my furthest from Christianity. It was at this point that I ceased to have active involvement in the Church. I have retained an interest in Christianity, as my recent work testifies; but it was then that I stopped calling myself a Roman Catholic, even though I continued to value aspects of that cultural context and tradition.

As George Steiner once said about being a Jew, it's not a club you can easily resign from, culturally speaking.

No doubt this is a naive question, but how important was God to you in the mid-sixties?

Well, I suppose that God was the lynchpin of the whole project; but at the same time I don't know that God was important to me in any personal way. It's hard to say, because of course one was inheriting a Catholicism in which the idea of the personal was rather suspect – in which the whole idea of personal experience was problematic and, at the worst, Protestant! I've talked already about the impersonality, the lack of emotion, which was there in my whole background. That might in the first place have been working-class utilitarianism, but it was certainly underscored by Catholicism. So questions of personal belief – questions so vital to Kierkegaard for instance – weren't central to us. Rather, we were engaged on a political and intellectual project of great excitement.

I wanted to ask about the relationship between Slant *and socialist humanism, which was an important phenomenon at this time. At an international symposium on it in 1965 the speakers included Ernst Bloch, Erich Fromm, Lucien Goldmann, Herbert Marcuse and Galvano della Volpe. Were you conscious of the debates taking place in Europe?*

Yes, I would say so. We were conscious of the Frankfurt School, we were conscious of the international counterculture, we were conscious of Gramsci and so on. And I think humanism was a bridging term in our dialogue with Williams, and through him the wider left, in that whereas one might naturally associate the ideas of socialism and humanism it was much less acceptable to be trying to develop a kind of Christian humanism. Humanism was not exactly the term one would associate with orthodox Christianity.

So humanism was a rather more explosive idea in the Christian context than it was elsewhere. It had far more radical connotations. We took seriously the fact that Christ was a man.

So how would you have identified yourself at this time? Jürgen Moltmann described Ernst Bloch as 'a Marxist with a Bible in his hand'. Did you see yourself as a Marxist with a Bible in your hand, or as a Christian with a copy of the Communist Manifesto *in your hand? Or is to formulate the question in those terms to make a category mistake?*

No, I don't think so, because it was a question that was often asked of us, the question of how we designated ourselves. I suppose we sometimes used the phrases 'Christian Marxist' or 'Catholic Marxist' – though it sounded like a hell of a lot of belief, a positive surfeit of faith. I think that by the time we folded we thought of *Slant* as part of a Marxist project. On the other hand, there were certainly individual members of *Slant* who were more in the anarchist tradition, and others who were left-wing socialists. These people probably wouldn't have accepted the Marxist label, but in general I think it was pretty much current. I think the line would have been – and this again was very much in the Dominican tradition – that in every era the gospel has to be spelt out anew in some humanly intelligible terms, that its revolutionary character has to be translated and remade in contemporary language and action. In our situation, Marxism and other forms of leftism were the language for that.

Erich Fromm argued at roughly the same time that 'authentic Marxism was perhaps the strongest spiritual movement of a broad, non-theistic nature in nineteenth-century Europe.' Was there a sense in which for you, in the sixties, it was also in some sense a non-theistic spiritual movement? Or was the attraction of Marxism in part precisely that it refused the spiritual?

Well, it properly resituated the spiritual in mundane, material terms. I remember one *Slant* member writing that there is nothing in the Marxist critique of God that a Christian shouldn't agree with. I think that this was certainly a shared position, that the idolatrous or Satanic notion of God needed to be demystified. I think that for somebody brought up with a Catholic idea of spirituality, or what I would now call a Judaeo-Christian idea of God, spirituality is not a separate or sealed realm or refuge but a particular form of conduct. It is a particular kind of relationship, involving a particular kind of body.

It's a kind of ethics, in other words?

Yes, that's traditional Catholic teaching. The Catholic tradition is of course riddled from one end to another with bogus conceptions of spirituality, in which spirituality is a reified realm in itself; but the mainstream Catholic tradition could recognize itself in the Marxist humanist conception of spirituality as simply quotidian meaning, value, communication, relationship. There was a certain earthbound quality, I think, to both ideas. Both regard spirituality as inherently relational and institutional.

Let me ask about the role of humour at this time. It's not characteristic of Slant; *and my impression is that it's not something associated much with Raymond Williams either. But in the* Festschrift *that Stephen Regan edited for your fiftieth birthday, in the inaugural issue of* The Year's Work in Critical and Cultural Theory *[1991], Adrian Cunningham says that 'working within a religious hegemony in a capitalist-dominated world, we were often saved from either gloom or hubris by the sheer improbability, if not ludicrousness, of what we'd undertaken.' That sense of ludicrousness doesn't communicate itself much in the articles in* Slant . . .

The journal was absolutely ripe for parody. When David Lodge talks about *Slant* in his novel *How Far Can You Go?* [1980], he doesn't do the kind of parody that he could have done – not that he was very approving of it either. Yes, in one sense it was a ridiculous enterprise, like 'Trotskyist mystics' or 'Leninists for St Teresa'. There was something rather wacky about it. In a sense it was part of the inspired madness of the culture of the late sixties. But you're absolutely right: you would never have guessed that from the very solemn, male-intellectual tone of *Slant*. I did, however, attempt to insert a bit of satire into it. I wrote a satire in *Slant* of the anti-psychiatry movement, which I called 'anti-medicine'. It was all about the liberating effects of disease. That was a rare sort of thing, though. We had a single column devoted to quoting examples of absurdities taken from Catholic sources, but we weren't quite aware of how absurd we must have looked ourselves.

The obverse of this was an impressively precocious intellectual sophistication.

We were very clever – with all of the strengths and limits of the word 'clever'. We just hadn't lived through enough.

You published The New Left Church *[1966] when you were in your early twenties. As its title suggests, the book attempts to splice together radical Catholicism and humanist socialism, ideologically speaking. Methodologically speaking, it combines theology and literary criticism. Did you deliberately set out to synthesize these discourses, or were you doing it without having to think about it?*

That was something I was spontaneously doing at the time. The book came out of lectures and talks given to various groups associated with *Slant*, so it wasn't really planned as a whole. It wasn't so much a deliberate synthesis as the way I was thinking in that period. I began speaking in public when I was twenty-one and still haven't shut up.

There's an obvious interest in ethics in this book, and that's something that's been woven through all the texts you've produced, but has

reappeared especially forcefully more recently, most explicitly in
Trouble with Strangers *[2008]. One example of this in* The New Left
Church *is your interest in tragedy. Your argument, which is evidently
influenced by Williams's conception of it in* Modern Tragedy, *also
published in 1966, is that tragedy is ordinary. You conceive it there, as
you do in* Sweet Violence *[2003], in terms of everyday conflict in the
conditions of modernity – between the idea of the common life and the
idea of intensity, as you call it, between collectivities and individuals,
between the exterior and the interior, between subject and object.*

That's interesting because, although they appeared in the same
year, my book must have just predated Raymond's. I'm not aware
of having read it at that time. It wasn't influenced by *Modern
Tragedy* itself, but it was almost certainly influenced by Raymond's
lectures and by general talk with him. Tragedy was my first way
of thinking about the problem of the common and the special.
Charles Taylor claims in *Sources of the Self* [1989] that Christianity
invented the idea of everyday life, the idea that the everyday was
the vital arena. But Christianity also of course revolves around
tragedy in the sense of extraordinary events. So perhaps what I
was groping towards was the idea that Christianity involves an
interesting realignment of the ordinary and the extraordinary.
One way of putting that might be to say that the New Testament
presents Jesus as tragic, with all the intensity that involves, but not
as heroic. It is indeed an anti-heroic document in many ways. I was
interested as early as *The New Left Church* in the reconciliation of a
certain personal intensity or authenticity with social relationships.
It's an idea that also lies at the root of *Shakespeare and Society*
[1967]. There were existentialist overtones to the argument at the
time – Sartre was a key figure for me – but I think the question
survives that particular context.

One of the things I find interesting in The New Left Church *is your
discussion of 'recklessness' or 'not recking the cost', as you put it. You
effectively advocate an ethics of use value. What you refer to as 'a*

spontaneous life of grace' is premised on a refusal of exchange value;
the theological category is predicated on the logic of value. And so
grace gets transmuted into gratuitousness. Do you think this still has
valence?

Yes, it's run as a thread through my work, and it's come back,
partly with the book on tragedy, partly with the book on ethics. It's
also there in my work on Shakespeare, because he too was clearly
concerned with the idea of mercy or forgiveness as gratuitous,
as lavishness, as rupturing the circle of exchange value. He was
also keenly aware of a potentially dangerous form of excess.
There's a creative kind of surplus and a rather more negative one.
There's a recklessness which is about simply not giving a damn, a
recklessness which is really deeply aligned with cynicism, one in
which any value can be permeated with any other because they're
all basically bankrupt. But in *The New Left Church* I was trying
to explore the idea of a kind of creative recklessness. It's an anti-
accountants' ethic, as I think I put it in *Trouble with Strangers*. I talk
in *Reason, Faith, and Revolution* [2009] about the deliberate over-
the-top-ness of the New Testament ethics, its spendthrift, profligate
quality. Having said that, it occurs to me that it appears too in the
play I wrote about Oscar Wilde, *Saint Oscar* [1989]. Wilde was all
about creative wastefulness, anti-utilitarianism. I don't want to be
too biographically reductive here, but it probably goes back to the
rather brutal utilitarian environment that I experienced as a child,
which I reacted very sharply against. I think I've been attracted –
not in my life, particularly, but certainly in my thought – to notions
of gratuitousness, of not reckoning, of things done for the hell of
it. Nothing in my childhood was done for the hell of it.

Thinking about the biographical in relation to that point, I'm reminded
that there's a passage in The New Left Church *in which you make*
an almost parabolical comparison between two workplaces, two firms,
in order to illustrate the differences between two kinds of capitalist
management. One is an old-fashioned model, which effectively uses

coercive methods to oppress the workers; the other is a 'modernized' model of management, which uses consensual methods to co-opt them. You then contrast both of these models with a socialistic factory. Could you say something about this parable and the experiences that lie behind it?

The first one is almost certainly my father's factory as I imagined it, though I never actually visited it. The paternalistic, phony-liberal one must have been Marks and Spencer, where I worked as a student. I suppose part of the Catholic critique of liberalism was directed against a certain kind of liberal paternalism that was becoming fashionable in the wake of the Vatican Council. I reacted quite sharply against that, and I learnt quite a lot from Raymond, I think, about how to combat it. There is some excellent material in the conclusion to *Culture and Society*, which I still think is one of the most magnificent documents that he ever wrote, and much underrated. He scores a direct hit there at the process by which the state tries to incorporate its citizens but yields them no real power. Raymond was always marvellously alert to that kind of bogusness. But there was something in that anti-liberal Catholic background that made me sensitive to it as well. There are, in short, both good and bad ways of being hostile to liberalism. *Slant* had inherited from Catholicism what was by and large a bad way, but tried to turn it to good political effect.

I also wanted to ask you about the range of cultural influences in The New Left Church, *which seems to be quite considerable. In an epoch of increasing academic specialization, your books obviously seem pretty diverse, culturally speaking; but this book, ironically perhaps, appears to be almost the most pluralistic of all. In addition to detailed interpretations of Wordsworth and others from the 'Culture and Society' tradition, there are lots of allusions to contemporary drama and poetry. And there are references to more strictly popular forms of culture too: there's a discussion, albeit a brief one, of modern cinema, Antonioni's* L'avventura *[1960] and Clayton's* The Pumpkin Eater *[1964] in particular; and there's a reference to the Beatles, to the managerial politics of the band and the music industry that produced it.*

That surprises me, because my memory of my intellectual stock at the time, as it were, is that it was rather restricted, in a Cambridge sort of way – although not perhaps as narrow as the Leavisite agenda. Raymond's range was also rather narrow, and apart from the drama there's not a lot of cosmopolitan range in his work. He's very different from Fredric Jameson, for example, in that respect.

Speaking of the Beatles, the very first piece I ever published was on the group. It appeared in *New Blackfriars*, which had a special column about the visual arts – something I've never been very good on. I just thought that the Beatles were interesting, sociologically speaking, in the early 'Love Me Do' days. So I discussed the shift between them and the previous rather more dour, intense, rocker style. The piece ends with the immortal sentence: 'One member of the group is already showing incipient cynicism' – that was Lennon – 'and the end of the year might well see them off.' That was in '63 or '64! So my publishing career opened with a crashing miscalculation. Some would claim that it has continued in this mode ever since.

Have you ever written criticism of that sort since then?

Not much, though in the early 1990s I reviewed a couple of plays for the *TLS* [*Times Literary Supplement*], and even some film and television. It's a standard criticism of my work that I don't look enough at popular culture. I've done very little on the visual arts. Whereas on the one hand I feel, no doubt irrationally, that anyone with a modicum of intelligence can be a film or television critic – that it's really too easy – on the other hand I feel very wary about it. When Raymond was reviewing for the *Guardian* the theatre editor needed someone to review regularly in Cambridge, and Raymond suggested me. But it was a hair-raising assignment, because those were the days when you phoned in the review straight after the

show, and I chickened out of it. I often regret that I did, but I just
didn't have the confidence. Apart from theatre, and the screenplay
for Derek Jarman's *Wittgenstein*, I suppose I've not really been
engaged with any visual medium.

The film references in The New Left Church *are particularly striking,
because subsequently you don't seem to have discussed film at all in
print.*

I've been very chary of it, for reasons that I don't quite understand.
Again, I feel that writing on film and television is too easy, though
certainly not writing on Raphael or Courbet. I deeply admire the
work of T. J. Clark, and think him one of the finest stylists writing
in English, at once easy and elegant.

*This sounds suspiciously like an Adornian suspicion of popular culture.
Doesn't the ideology of popular cultural forms interest you?*

No, it's not an Olympian distaste for the popular. For example,
I was actively involved for years in traditional Irish music. I still
enjoy singing and listening to it.

Have you gone on watching films?

Moderately, although increasingly things like *Harry Potter* with
small children. They say that the Irish have very little visual sense,
so that might be one highly disreputable explanation for this. Or
perhaps it's just the British who say this – I mean, people who also
say they're lazy and smelly. The visual arts in Ireland were very
underdeveloped, partly because they need so much infrastructure,
and it wasn't a rich enough country to provide it; partly because
when the Irish looked at a beautiful landscape they saw poverty
and politics. The Irish are normally thought of as being fine at
writing and music, but not so much the visual arts. So there's my

ethnically essentialist self-defence . . . Of course, that's traditional Ireland; postmodern Ireland is an intensely visual place.

In spite of the reference to Antonioni, the aesthetic commitments of The New Left Church, *if I can call them that, seem strictly realist . . .*

There's probably a dash of Williams in that realist tendency. There was certainly a strain of what I would call Cambridge moralism in some of my earlier work. A later instance of it comes in *The Rape of Clarissa* [1982] when I tick Lovelace off for being emotionally immature – or some such dreadful schoolmasterly phrase. That's probably a lethal combination of Catholicism and Leavisism.

There's one rather moralistic passage in The New Left Church *in which, intriguingly, you criticize Lewis Carroll for reifying language. You compare his reification of language to the fetishization of the sacraments by contemporary Roman Catholics of a certain stripe: 'When the idea of real presence becomes over-physical, the damage done to the sacraments is parallel to the damage done to language in Lewis Carroll's nonsense verse.'*

One of the interesting points about *The New Left Church* is the presence of semiotics there, more or less *avant la lettre*. This is because aspects of the theology of the sacraments that people like Herbert McCabe were developing belonged to a Wittgensteinian, phenomenological or semiotic tradition. That was one way in which *Slant* came into the arguments over literary theory: I'd been prepared for them by this highly unusual route into the subject. 'Sacrament' doesn't mean 'sacred', it means 'sign'.

As its title of course indicates, The Body as Language *[1970] is especially proto-semiotic in its concerns.*

I always maintain that the postmodernist body cultists all jumped on my bandwagon. You have to have the word 'body' in your title to get published these days. In my day it was 'dialectics'. Postmodernists are very selective about their bodies, though – sexual ones are fine; sickly, suffering or labouring ones aren't quite so fashionable.

You've mentioned that existentialism was in the air in Cambridge, but in other contexts you've been quite dismissive of its influence. In both The Gatekeeper *and* Reason, Faith, and Revolution *you've said that it was a mere flirtation, an 'ontologically imposing' way of saying that you were a depressed late adolescent; but in* The New Left Church *you quote* Being and Nothingness *and engage quite seriously with Sartre's ideas.*

Yes, it's far too glib to say that it was just a way of feeling blue, and that later on this attitude came to be called post-structuralism. A certain glibness or facetiousness is a familiar defect of my work. I think that I'd forgotten – underplayed in my own mind – the influence of existentialism on me at that time. It was pretty strong. Certainly in Cambridge there were students who were running some sort of synthesis of existentialism and Marxism. I was very taken with the idea that living was a question of constant self-definition, perhaps because I didn't seem to have much definition. I read quite a lot of Sartre at the time. I also remember being very excited by Heidegger's *Being and Time*. It's an influence that was strong but that seemed to fade fairly rapidly – as it did in the general culture. But in Cambridge in the early sixties existentialism was certainly an important language. Someone even argued that the Cuban revolution, which had recently taken place, was an 'existentialist' revolution. I don't know what Castro would have made of that.

And did Sartre provide an attitudinal model, so to speak, for the politically committed intellectual?

I suppose so. He was important as a hybrid figure who combined literature, politics and philosophy, and whose philosophy made rather more political sense than J. L. Austin's.

The other thing that's striking, going back to The New Left Church, *is your prose style. One might expect it to be typified by the piously serious discourse of the aspiring male intellectual, which you've gleefully mocked a good deal since the late seventies, but important aspects of your later style are apparent. In one sentence, for instance, you invoke Sartre and De Sade, in a characteristically alliterative comparison. In another, you conjugate high and low culture in an allusion to 'Kierkegaard and the Kinks'. Were you conscious of trying to develop a distinctive rhetorical style at this time?*

No, I wasn't, although there might be something significant in the fact that *The New Left Church* is stylistically distinct both from typical *Slant* writing and from the more technical stuff I wrote, which people found much more rebarbative. One of our sample readers once said, 'I don't read *Slant*, I study it.' From what I remember *The New Left Church* is by comparison fairly lucid, perhaps because primarily it came out of lectures and talks on the Catholic left circuit. In some ways it's what you might call a Sixties style: urgent, exposed, buoyant, rather self-consciously unpretentious.

One of the silences in The New Left Church, *from my point of view, concerns the Marxist critique of religion. Although you were obviously immersed in it – and you've said that the* Slant *lot thought it was an important dimension of de-fetishizing the sacraments – you don't specifically address it. You cite Marx's discussion of alienation at one point, and you even quote passages that use Feuerbach to ground this discussion, but you don't appear to acknowledge that Marx is critiquing religion too.*

That's entirely a matter of taking it for granted. I think in those theological circles it was assumed that we all agreed with Marx's critique of religion and that we didn't need to labour it. Religion had failed in its transformative mission and politics had taken over. Later on, when politics was felt to have failed in its turn, something called culture would step vaingloriously into the breach.

I have one further question about The New Left Church. *Both there and in* Shakespeare and Society *[1967] you criticize John Stuart Mill, as a representative of the liberal tradition, for failing to reconcile Benthamism, which comprehends the world, and Coleridgean Romanticism, which comprehends the self. Analogously, I wondered how you yourself avoided replicating the same kind of split between Marxism as a mode of comprehending material life and Christianity as a mode of comprehending spiritual life. Perhaps this is a mistaken question because my conception of Christianity is unconsciously a Protestant one . . .*

Catholicism certainly didn't mean personal interiority to us, so for several wrong reasons I don't think this was a problem. We perceived both Marxism and Christianity in practical, institutional, world-transformative terms. I was, however, much too hard on the mighty Mill. We were far too one-sidedly anti-liberal, because liberals, particularly Christian liberals, were the audience we were addressing and also the enemy. It was the familiar young-radical syndrome, and later I came to appreciate the great riches of the liberal tradition. The other criticism is that we ourselves were, on the contrary, too anti-dualistic, too compulsively monistic. We were hunting for syntheses. And because of the extraordinarily damaging influence on Christianity of Cartesian dualism, 'dualism' was a dirty word in theological circles. I think that that led us, with a certain youthful triumphalism, to want to merge and to override the inevitable conflicts between things. The irreconcilable was not part of our vocabulary. There is no reason why, when one spots an antithesis, one should seek to resolve it; but we didn't really see this.

Reading

Barthes, Roland, 'Outcomes of the Text', in *The Rustle of Language*, trans. Richard Howard (Berkeley: University of California Press, 1989), pp. 238–49.

Cunningham, Adrian, and Terry Eagleton, eds., *Slant Manifesto: Catholics and the Left* (London: Sheed & Ward, 1966).

Cunningham, Adrian, 'The December Group: Terry Eagleton and the New Left Church', *The Year's Work in Critical and Cultural Theory* 1:1 (1991), pp. 210–15.

Eagleton, Terry, 'New Bearings: The Beatles', *New Blackfriars* 45 (1964), pp. 175–8.

Eagleton, Terry, *The New Left Church* (London: Sheed & Ward, 1966).

Eagleton, Terry, *From Culture to Revolution: The Slant Symposium 1967* (London: Sheed & Ward, 1968).

Eagleton, Terry, *Criticism and Ideology: A Study in Marxist Literary Theory* (London: New Left Books, 1976).

Eagleton, Terry, 'Interview with Terry Eagleton' (with Andrew Martin and Patrice Petro), *Social Text* 13/14 (Winter/Spring 1986), pp. 83–99.

Eagleton, Terry, 'Resources for a Journey of Hope: The Significance of Raymond Williams', *New Left Review* 1:168 (March-April, 1988), pp. 3–11.

Eagleton, Terry, review of Sean O'Casey's *The Plough and the Stars* (The Young Vic), *Times Literary Supplement* (17 May 1991), p. 16.

Eagleton, Terry, review of Bertolt Brecht's *Resistible Rise of Arturo Ui* (Olivier Theatre), *Times Literary Supplement* (16 August 1991), p. 19.

Eagleton, Terry, review of Harold Pinter's *Party Time* (Almeida Theatre), *Times Literary Supplement* (15 November 1991), p. 20.

Eagleton, Terry, review of John Le Carré's *A Murder of Quality* (Thames Television), *Times Literary Supplement* (12 April 1991), p. 16.

Eagleton Terry, review of Bruce Beresford's *Black Robe*, *Times Literary Supplement* (31 January 1992), p. 20.

Eagleton, Terry, *The Gatekeeper: A Memoir* (London: Allen Lane, 2001).

Eagleton, Terry, 'For Pat Hanrahan', *New Blackfriars* 83 (July 2002), p. 346.

Eagleton, Terry, 'Irony and the Eucharist', *New Blackfriars* 83 (November 2002), pp. 513–17.

Eagleton, Terry, *Holy Terror* (Oxford: Oxford University Press, 2005).

Eagleton, Terry, 'Culture Conundrum', *The Guardian*, 21 May 2008. (http://www.guardian.co.uk/commentisfree/2008/may/21/1?gusrc=rss&feed=networkfront)

Eagleton, Terry, *Reason, Faith, and Revolution: Reflections on the God Debate* (Yale: Yale University Press, 2009).

Fromm, Erich, ed., *Socialist Humanism: An International Symposium* (London: Allen Lane, 1967).

Moltmann, Jürgen, *Religion, Revolution and the Future* (New York: Scribner, 1969).

Smith, Dai, *Raymond Williams: A Warrior's Tale* (Cardigan: Parthian, 2008).

Steiner, George, *The Death of Tragedy* (London: Faber & Faber, 1961).

Taylor, Charles, *Sources of the Self: The Making of the Modern Identity* (Cambridge: Cambridge University Press, 1989).

Wicker, Brian, *Culture and Liturgy* (London: Sheed & Ward, 1963).

Williams, Raymond, *Culture and Society 1780–1950* (London: Chatto & Windus, 1958).

Williams, Raymond, *Modern Tragedy* (London: Chatto & Windus, 1966).

Williams, Raymond, *Politics and Letters: Interviews with* New Left Review (London: New Left Books, 1979).

CHAPTER THREE

Individual/Society

Shakespeare and Society *was published in 1967, the year after* The New Left Church. *It centres on relations between the individual and the community, the self as subject and the self as object; and it attempts, as you state in the introduction, 'to show the tension in some of Shakespeare's plays between the self as it seems to man in its personal depth, and as it seems in action, to others, as part of and responsible to a whole society.' In this respect it seems continuous with* The New Left Church. *Is it in some senses a 'left-Leavisite' book, to use the formulation that you later coined in your critique of Raymond Williams? How did you relate to Leavisism at this time?*

I wouldn't necessarily have thought of the book in those terms. Even as undergraduates, when some of my friends and I occasionally attended Leavis's lectures, we had a balanced and pretty valid view of him. We learnt a lot from the tough analysis, the close reading, the intense cultural seriousness, the brave polemicism, the broad social concern, and also from the genuinely liberal anti-establishment aspects of Leavis. I'm appalled by the way in which a certain cultural left today has used Leavis as a whipping boy. This is a man who once said he was in favour of some form of communism, who was denied a proper job, and who was hated by the whole establishment. He was even interviewed by the Cambridge police for possessing a copy of *Ulysses* – that wouldn't have happened to Lord David Cecil. But at the same time we saw the élitism well enough. We saw this not only intellectually but in practice –

the chosen circle around Downing College, the sycophancy, the heterodox orthodoxy, and the exclusion of so many of the issues that Williams stood for. I think that Raymond had to work his way through all that because it was the main resource available to him. He then worked his way into a left-Leavisite position and beyond. So in a sense we didn't have to, because he'd done it already.

In the acknowledgements to Shakespeare and Society, *which is dedicated to Williams, you state that you offer it as 'an extension of his own explorations', which seems faintly ambiguous. There's an obvious sense in which the book expands the* Culture and Society *tradition into the past so as to encompass Shakespeare. And in its aspiration, in examining the relations of individual and society 'to see how the qualities of spontaneous life now available to us can be translated without loss into the terms of a whole culture', the book is manifestly indebted to Williams. Do you think that in methodological terms too it extended his work?*

Well, in the sense that I don't think it's a book that he would have written himself. It's a book that draws deeply on his work – it certainly draws on his ideas of the individual and society – but I don't think Williams himself would have taken an idea like that and worked it through in textual detail. He would have written in more general terms. So that's a break with him. It seems to me very much a one-idea book. But it's a relatively original idea, I think, and the book is able to illuminate it from different angles. I thought – and I don't think this was just youthful euphoria – I was able to see something in Shakespeare that hadn't been seen before. On the other hand, the case suffered from a *Slant*-ite excess of anti-dualism. The tensions, the contradictions between an individual and society, not to speak of all the mediations between them, are really absent. Also, it didn't look at the work as drama. As some of the critics pointed out, mainly the ones who were politically unsympathetic, it very much raided Shakespeare for ideas – the worst kind of leftist criticism. It was the beginnings of a continuing interest in him that then found expression in the later Shakespeare book, *William Shakespeare* [1986]. It rested on the conviction that the ideas I was learning from Williams and others were by no means just contemporary, and that one could construct a genealogy of them.

The book's concept of 'society' is an abstract one, conceived almost entirely in terms of the individual's relation to the community.

Yes, it remains an abstract concept, and it's somewhat un-nuanced even as that.

Were you conscious at the time of its ahistorical character?

Not particularly, though it was pretty rapidly brought to my attention. The same charge can be laid against the later Shakespeare book, which I think is more interesting, and which isn't a one-idea work. What interests me about Shakespeare are ideas that one can find in contemporary culture as well as in his particular historical situation. He really is most extraordinarily proleptic. I think this is because he lives at a historical moment when, because of what one might call in crude shorthand the early emergence of bourgeois society, ideas of value, meaning, language, exchange, relativism, norms, identity and so on have been pitched into major crisis. It's in this sense that he's 'contemporary', not just by virtue of back-projecting some fancy modern ideas onto him. Language, value and meaning are part of his own stock-in-trade as a working dramatist, and this infiltrates his very writing – I mean in form as well as content. And this – without bardolatry – is why it sometimes seems as though he's just been reading Marx, Hegel, Wittgenstein and so on. In fact, the bardolaters wouldn't approve of such reading at all.

But you could have grounded those continuities historically, in terms of the origins of capitalism.

I could have done. One of the reasons I didn't, apart from not having enough historical knowledge, was that I wrote *Shakespeare and Society* while I was writing my doctoral thesis on Edward Carpenter, and I knew that I wouldn't get the book through as a thesis. It was a matter of a carefully calculated division of labour. I decided that I would write the thesis with one hand, which didn't take that much effort to do, and the book with the other. I treated the PhD purely instrumentally, as an academic exercise, which is perhaps the way to do it – I often have to tell my PhD students that they're making too much of a fetish of it, that they shouldn't forget that it's just a passport. I could have spent four years trying to develop the Shakespeare thesis, but I was gravely in doubt as to whether I would get it through. I was already in minor ways being gunned for in Cambridge as an acolyte of Williams. He was too authoritative himself to be shot down, but they were sniping at several of his disciples. They did it later with Francis Mulhern, whose wonderful thesis on *Scrutiny* was rejected at first. He got the degree in the end, but only after a lot of manoeuvring. They then did much the same with Colin MacCabe, who was disgracefully turned down for a lectureship. I had also been turned down some years before, as I've said, and the post was given instead to a man I'd taught from his first year as an undergraduate – a splendid and brilliant man, I should add.

One of the passages in the book that I like most is the discussion of Macbeth, *which effectively revisits the idea of recklessness and its relation to use value. You discuss evil – 'the area of nameless deeds' as you call it – in terms of meaninglessness. Macbeth himself in this account is not some Promethean anti-hero but a monstrous animal, less than human rather than more than human. At the same time, there's a sense that you admire his and Lady Macbeth's 'gratuitousness', and perceive a creativeness in their 'gratuitous self-expenditure' at the end of the play.*

I think I come right out and call Lady Macbeth an existentialist, although that might be in the second Shakespeare book. She believes in endless self-achievement without inherent limit. Macbeth thinks that one has to respect limits in order to be oneself. That goes back to my poetic obsession with the interplay between restraint and freedom. So there might be a biographical element there too. But it's perhaps the first time that I write about something that has preoccupied me more and more in recent work, namely the clash between the finite, the mortal, the necessarily constrained, and the hubristic. Macbeth, in 'o'er-reaching himself and falling on the other', is precisely hubristic in character. The political resonances of that Faustian myth, the lethal belief in infinity – which is playing itself out in American foreign policy as we speak – might again come back to the distinction between use value and exchange value. Use value is limited and specific whereas exchange value is potentially endless. Today, rather alarmingly, with the work of Deleuze, Badiou, Žižek and others, the notion of infinity is being rehabilitated – not of course in an American Dream-like way, but still, I think, wrong-headedly.

The hero of Shakespeare and Society *is effectively Prospero, who according to you embodies grace in his 'fusion of spontaneity and aware responsibility'. He seems to function as the solution to all the contradictions between individual and society that you discuss in the book, though in* William Shakespeare *you are far more sceptical of his capacity for resolving the conflict.*

I'd forgotten that. Not long after, leftist critics would see him as an odious colonialist! The phrase I probably should have used about Prospero is the imaginary solution of real contradictions, which I'm getting a bit nearer to in the second Shakespeare book. Oddly, the only time I ever met R. D. Laing was when I was writing the Shakespeare book – I think he even offered to publish it through the Tavistock Press. I rather naively raised my ideas about *The Tempest* with him, specifically the idea of personal reconciliation acting as a symbol of more general reconciliation. He said something hard-headedly Scottish, like: 'You wouldn't solve the Soviet–American problem by marrying the daughter of Khrushchev to the son of Kennedy.' He deflated it, but it deserved to be deflated. I wasn't then in command of the concept of utopia, which might have been the concept to use about this enabling fiction.

I was going to ask about Laing, because in the acknowledgements to Shakespeare and Society *you express an intellectual debt to him, though you say there that you've only recently discovered his work. That debt is evidently to* The Divided Self *[1965]. You met him too, did you?*

I met him through Neil Middleton, at a meeting of Slantites. I sent him a copy of *Shakespeare and Society*, which was indebted, as you say, to the idea of 'the divided self'. The part of Laing that I was most secure with was the earlier, anti-dualistic work. I was too quickly stitching the sociality and selfhood together, whereas Laing had increasingly headed off into the interior, as it were, and had left those problems behind. By the time I sent the book to him he'd passed on to more *outré* ideas, and he wrote me a rambling, eccentric, not particularly helpful letter in response. He asked, 'What do you think about dreams within dreams within dreams?' and other questions not burningly relevant to *Coriolanus*. Laing was certainly an important influence on *Slant*, however, not least in his early fusions of phenomenology and political dissent.

The conclusion to Shakespeare and Society, *which skips on to the end of the nineteenth century, sits a little uncomfortably at the end of the book. It's rather provocative, though, because it attempts, as you put it, 'not just to show how the same problems have stayed with us, but to make the preceding study of Shakespeare fully comprehensible by an account of the contemporary experience in terms of which it is written.' How successful do you think this conclusion was?*

It's the one piece of work I've done that I'd rather take poison than have to read again. I don't know why I did it actually. It could have been the advice of Raymond, with whom I discussed the book, including its title, quite a lot; it could have been Chatto and Windus, who wanted something about the relevance of the thesis for today. I suspect that I wouldn't have written that chapter had it not been for certain pressures, though it's true that I was interested in 'Shakespeare our contemporary', so to speak, as I was in the later Shakespeare book. But it is done in such an incongruous way, more like an appendix than a conclusion — the book could benefit from an appendicectomy.

It impresses me that Chatto and Windus was prepared to publish a polemical book on Shakespeare by such a young academic.

I myself was quite surprised that Chatto, which consisted of gentlemen publishers of the old school like Ian Parsons and Cecil Day Lewis, picked it up so quickly. They wrote back to me almost immediately and said they'd take it, partly because they thought it was clearly written and wasn't full of jargon, partly I suppose because they were Raymond's publishers, although Raymond didn't particularly push my book with them. It did seem to me odd that it sat in a list of canonical critical texts. I never got a sense of how they regarded the argument or what they thought about it. I think Day Lewis put a few semicolons into the manuscript, for which I suppose I should be grateful. They turned down a later book of mine, and were quite right to do so. It was a kind of clotted, opaque early draft of what became my second Shakespeare book.

What kind of a reception did Shakespeare and Society *have?*

It was quite widely reviewed, somewhat to my surprise, although not altogether favourably. Some reviewers noted what they perceived as the originality of it. I remember a youngish Denis

Donoghue writing in the *Guardian* about its bloodless style, which hurt but which I think is true. I simply wasn't confident enough to write in a more elaborate, ambitious way. With *The New Left Church* I felt I was writing for a knowable community, whereas this was my first venture into the literary-critical dark. So there is something anaemic and inhibited about its style. But it was just one of those books where you think, 'I'm onto something' – just that one thing.

Incidentally, did you and Williams discuss alternative titles for the book?

The title I wanted, 'The Free Dependent,' which I also discussed with Charles Swann, came from *Measure for Measure*: 'I am your free dependent.' This would have captured precisely the paradox of freedom and relationality I was investigating. Chatto said it was too paradoxical, which is typical of the literal-mindedness and heavy-handedness of publishers. I'm surprised that *Madame Bovary* isn't published in English as *Mrs. Bovary*. (Even Blackwell, when I told them that I wanted to call my recent book on tragedy *Sweet Violence*, said with a mournful eye on the catalogues, 'So it's not just called "Tragedy"?') Chatto didn't know what 'free dependent' meant. 'Shakespeare and Society' was the book's subtitle and I felt quite embarrassed when this rather flat phrase became the title.

You refer to Wilde in the conclusion, specifically 'The Soul of Man Under Socialism' – though not particularly sympathetically. You argue that he tries to heal the gap between culture and society, but that he fails because when he insists that the state should make useful products and the individual beautiful ones, he effectively ratifies that gap. When did you start to look at Wilde in a more positive light?

The playwright David Hare, who was one of my first students at Cambridge, has written somewhere that he once asked me if he could write about Wilde for a mini-thesis that he was doing for his degree, and that I responded that Wilde was too minor. 'Then he goes and writes a play on the bloody guy!' Hare added with understandable exasperation. I'd utterly forgotten that incident, but I should imagine that I had a somewhat Leavisite attitude to Wilde at the time. I had no sense of his Irishness, which was one of the main things that led me to him later. Nor, I suspect, did Hare. I was, however, always fascinated by 'The Soul of Man Under Socialism', even if I'm strangely denigratory about it in that book. That was the bit of Wilde I knew and treasured, as opposed to the drama. It was lavishness and gratuitousness and for-the-hell-of-itness again. It wasn't until the eighties that I became interested in Wilde as an Irishman, and by then it seemed inevitable that I would write a substantial piece on an Irish socialist proto-post-structuralist who'd been at Oxford.

The most striking absence of the conclusion to Shakespeare and Society, *in my view, is William Morris. In your early writings you frequently imply that he is an exemplary figure in the* Culture and Society *tradition, because he attempts to dissolve the difference between society and the individual through a fusion of art and labour. Certainly it is Morris who in the nineteenth century does most to graft a Marxist commitment to the self-emancipation of the proletariat onto the anti-capitalist critique of industrialism that descends from Romanticism. But you never actually discussed him in any detail. Why do you think that was?*

I don't know. I was deeply influenced by Edward Thompson's early book on Morris – which Thompson himself, incidentally, once dismissed in my presence as his 'old polemical work'. I found it extremely useful for my work on Carpenter, not least because Thompson knew about Carpenter, which was a rare thing in those days. His Morris book was helpful to me in putting Carpenter in a historical context. I don't know why Morris doesn't crop up in that conclusion – possibly because I had nothing very interesting to say about him, even though I was a keen fan of his work. I think I probably lost a lecturing job at Cambridge for saying at the interview that Morris 'wasn't just a medievalist'. I noticed, in *Lucky Jim* fashion, that the venerable professor of medieval English literature then scribbled something ominous on his writing pad.

One figure of explicit importance to your writing from this period is D. H. Lawrence, who appears to be the really compelling remnant of the Culture and Society *tradition for you. 'Lawrence exposes the problem for us in our own time,' you state at one point. At times you even seem to talk about him as if he's still alive. Why do you think his legacy seemed so pressing?*

I'd read some Lawrence at school, but he became very important to me at Cambridge. I wasn't ever part of the Leavisite cult of Lawrence, though. There was a feeling in Cambridge at the time that Lawrence put everybody else in the shade, that the whole of wisdom was crystallized in him – this, of course, was pre-feminist – but I never fell for that. I think my attitude changed when I realized that both Leavis and Williams were in certain key respects misreading him as a humanist, and, in Raymond's case, slotting him into the end of the radical humanist lineage of *Culture and Society*. I had read some of the notably illiberal prose writings, and I became more and more convinced that although 'humanist' was true enough in some senses – he gives us a marvellous sense of human possibilities – it certainly wasn't in some others. I wrote about that in a little-known essay in a book called *The Prose for God* [1973], a collection of Catholic left essays on writers, to which I contributed a piece on Lawrence that I still think is quite useful. I tried to show the ways in which Lawrence wasn't a humanist, but was rather in some respects a deep determinist who didn't make much room for agency. I argued that he was a kind of romantic libertarian. The vital distinction for Lawrence isn't one between human and non-human, it's between fulfilled and unfulfilled. In this respect, a lizard can be ontologically superior to a coalminer.

What's interesting about your treatment of him in the 1960s is that you address him as a problem. You don't seek to neutralize his recalcitrance.

No, whereas Raymond's treatment of Lawrence in *Culture and Society*, from which I learnt a lot, is highly selective. It edits Lawrence to fit him into a humanistic tradition. But Lawrence is a lot stranger and wilder and more rebarbative than that. Incidentally, everybody who begins work on Edward Carpenter realizes in the first few weeks that he was probably a massive influence on Lawrence. The second thing you realize is that you can't prove it. Some of the more disreputable aspects of Carpenter pass into Lawrence, but Lawrence was adept at hiding his sources, so that isn't immediately obvious. I thought briefly of working on Carpenter and Lawrence after I'd done my PhD, but like almost all doctoral students the only thing I really wanted to do with my thesis once I'd finished it was forget about it.

This PhD, which was examined in 1968, was entitled 'Nature and Spirit: A Study of Edward Carpenter in his Intellectual Context'. You've already described the two-handed process by which you wrote the thesis in order to satisfy professional requirements, and the Shakespeare book to fulfil less narrowly scholarly purposes. Could you explain why you decided to do research on Carpenter in the first place?

It wasn't an entirely cynical enterprise, as I was of course interested in Carpenter. By the sheerest serendipity I found a long footnote to him in some history of English Literature, which described him as mystic, anarchist, early homosexual reformer, Whitmanite and so on. Then I discovered that in Sheffield there was a whole library of his material – the Carpenter Collection – that hadn't been much worked on. But I think what primarily attracted me was that he had so many connections in the period – Morris and Tolstoy and Kropotkin – so that he provided a marvellous mode of access to a whole fin-de-siècle counterculture. He was one of those lesser figures who were nevertheless typical by virtue of their very minor, marginal, jack-of-all-trades status. In 1920, people said that the two greatest figures in the labour movement were George Bernard Shaw and Edward Carpenter. A generation later they only mentioned George Bernard Shaw. What happened to Carpenter? Perhaps he was so fully and utterly part of the age that when that passed away, he passed away with it, until gay and feminist theories arrived to resurrect him some decades later,

When I proposed the topic to Redpath it transpired that, oddly but not uncharacteristically, he knew about Carpenter. 'Oh, the English Tolstoy!' he said, which is hyping him a bit. Redpath had written a small, very bad book on Tolstoy. The playwright Simon Gray, who was in the year above me, remarked that it was like a flea on the back of an elephant saying, 'Hmmm! Seems to be a lot of life around up here!' So the odd person knew about Carpenter. He was a classic of second-hand bookstores: I assembled most of my Carpenter books from the Charing Cross Road.

Had Williams, who supervised your thesis, read much Carpenter?

No; he'd heard of Carpenter but he hadn't read much of him. I think it's true to say that we didn't even have a supervision. He let me get on with it and then I simply tipped over the manuscript of the thesis to him. He made perhaps three marks in the margin and that was it. He wasn't the most dynamic of postgraduate supervisors, as opposed to his charismatic presence as a lecturer.

Who examined it?

Edward Thompson was the external examiner and Graham Hough the internal one. They were chalk and cheese. Hough was a sort of disenchanted latter-day aesthete. The most brilliant critical remark he ever made was that when you're in a Japanese prisoner-of-war camp with dysentery and a *Collected Yeats*, which had been true of him, you find out quickly enough which are the most valuable poems. Thompson I knew slightly, because I'd met him in Raymond's room in Jesus College through the May Day Manifesto. His first question to me was, 'Do you know who has the letters between Carpenter and So-and-So?' The answer was that he did. It wasn't the most auspicious of beginnings. I had a bit of a hard time from Thompson, because the thesis wasn't really a historical account of Carpenter. He thought that I hadn't done enough looking for original manuscripts. I was more interested in ideas, and felt that the Carpenter Collection was complete enough to be going on with. But it was fairly amicable.

Did you remain in contact with Thompson?

Well, Thompson was rather dismissive of Carpenter, as he is in the Morris book, so he had no great interest in talking about the topic with me. And not long after that he identified me as one of the dreaded Althusserians. I met him at a political meeting at All Souls, of all places, when he came to give a lecture on Marx at roughly the time *The Poverty of Theory* [1978] appeared. On that occasion his polemic against Althusser turned into a polemic against Eagleton. He had a vastly appreciative audience. I stood up and asked Thompson a question – I can't even remember what I asked him – and in the course of his response he used the phrase: 'We must oppose Terry Eagleton!' I think that he was in his most anti-Marxist phase at this time.

I then reviewed *The Poverty of Theory* fairly negatively for *Literature and History*. As it happens, I thought that some of the points in his polemic were well taken, but this book wasn't the kind of thing Thompson could do best. It's a little bit like Derrida defending Paul de Man – best left alone because it doesn't bring out your strengths. I made a reference in the review to the photograph on the book's cover, which was of Thompson with a cat on his shoulder. I wrote about the semiotics of the photograph. He's buried his head in his hands, there's a great shock of grey hair, and this small cat is looking out at the camera on his behalf. To my surprise he sent me a postcard that said, 'My cat is not small: look at the other shoulder.' And sure enough the cat's behind can be seen perkily protruding on the other shoulder. This was the last, highly intellectual exchange we ever had. He did however add that we should talk sometime about the Romantics, which he seemed to see as the chief bone of contention between us. I reviewed his book on Blake after his death, and pointed out that, though he seemed allergic to Althusserian jargon, he didn't seem in the least fazed by the highly esoteric talk of the Muggletonians and other heterodox Christian sects of Blake's time.

Sheila Rowbotham's recent biography confirms the suspicion that if Carpenter hadn't already existed it would have been necessary in the late 1960s to invent him. His socialism, his sexual activism, his vegetarianism, his mysticism, his vitalism, his 'lifestyle politics' – all make him seem in retrospect like the patron saint of the contemporary counterculture. Were you aware of this resonance in the course of researching the thesis at all?

That was never really the side of Carpenter that most interested me. When I researched on him, he was for me a purely historical figure with almost no contemporary resonance. Carpenter certainly wasn't popular when I worked on him, and I began the thesis before the sixties had really taken off. Indeed one of the reasons I studied him, as I say, was to find out why he had sunk without trace. After the thesis had been accepted I felt I never wanted to think about Carpenter again for the rest of my life. But such are the ironies of history that, at that precise moment, partly because of the emergent gay rights movement, he started to become something of an icon once more. Sheila and various others became interested in him, and a Carpenter bandwagon suddenly began to roll. He became a contemporary figure. Several small gay presses even asked me if they could publish my thesis, but I didn't want to inflict it on the world. There was no point in allowing it to bore anyone but myself.

What kind of political activism were you involved in at the end of the 1960s?

A lot of it was *Slant* activity, which seemed to take up a lot of time as we were continually being asked to address various Catholic progressive groups. I continued to be involved in the Cambridge Left Forum, and particularly the attempt to form a local shop stewards' committee. I was also in the Labour Party, which I think I joined in the mid-sixties. I attended the branch meetings of my local Cambridge Labour Party and did some election work for them. I went more or less directly from Labour to the International Socialists [IS] when I arrived in Oxford in 1969.

Like a lot of people in the Trotskyist tradition, though, I subsequently saw a new movement opening up in the Labour Party and rejoined it in the late seventies. I managed to get in by the skin of my teeth. I was rejected by the Labour Party on my first application, and then, after a long and somewhat stormy set of interviews, managed to scrape in, I think by two or three votes. I remained in the Oxford Labour Party until some time during the later eighties, and I found that it was a significant political area not so much for itself as for the kinds of connections, single-issue campaigns, forums, that it provided. In a relatively bleak period, the Labour Party in various places – and Oxford happened to be one of them – presented such opportunities. I was, for example, a member of the Labour Committee on Ireland, which was a pressure group within the national Labour Party seeking to break the bipartisan policy on Ireland. I think the East Oxford Labour Party was at that time the biggest branch in the country, and probably one of the most militant.

Can you recall the impact of the événements *in Paris in 1968?*

Very well. There were various overspills from Paris in Cambridge at the time, and I was moderately involved in them. I remember a huge demonstration in Cambridge against Harold Wilson and the

Labour government, which was in part an attempt to recreate the Parisian situation – people shouting 'Remember Che!' and so on. This was of course the epoch in which everyone was occupying, demonstrating and sitting in. I think *Slant* even occupied the Cambridge Catholic Chaplaincy for some reason – a demand for more coat pegs or something like that – though we could probably have spoken to the Chaplain about it quite easily. But in those days you didn't consider such *petit-bourgeois* tactics; you sat in. If you wanted your landlady to give you extra towels, you sat in her bath, preferably wearing a trenchcoat, till she caved in. I think my first experience of Oxford, when I was still at Cambridge, was speaking through a megaphone on the steps of the Clarendon Building, where there was an occupation. I remember the proctors coming out and sniffily rejecting some petition that they'd been handed. Subsequently, when I moved to Oxford in 1969, the immediate political demand, slightly farcically, was for a student union other than the Oxford Union. That quickly evolved into an occupation. The Schools Building was taken over and there was a sit-in that went on for at least a week. The proctors locked the doors and turned off the electricity and the heating, and some of the students were tried before a university court. I remember giving a seminar on Gramsci in candlelit darkness in the occupied Schools. I think I was the only don to set foot in the place; even the leftish dons were quite nervous of it.

What was your involvement in the May Day Manifesto *[1968], which you mentioned in connection with E. P. Thompson?*

It was a pretty limited involvement in terms of actual writing, though I wrote something in the section on monopoly capital. I was assigned certain small tasks and talked to economists and wrote the odd paragraph. Everything was very much overwritten by Raymond, as the style would suggest, and I think he altered most of it in the process of redrafting it. There is a sense in which it is very much his own personal manifesto. But there were several interesting meetings, sometimes in Raymond's cottage outside Cambridge, where a whole bunch of New Left-type people regularly converged. It served as a rallying point for the independent socialist left in the early Wilson period. Then there was an argument about whether the set-up should cease to exist, because it had effectively made its point, or whether it should carry on in some more permanent form. Wrongly, I think, it decided to carry on – even though people like Stuart Hall, and perhaps Raymond too, had seen it only as a very particular intervention. It carried on, and spawned a rather empty sort of bureaucracy that didn't seem to be to any particular political end. There was one spin-off, though, in the form of a National Convention of the Left, which took place in London. When the intellectual left has nothing else to do, it starts a journal or throws a conference. The journal usually fails after three issues and the conference is simply similar-minded people speaking to each other. All this wouldn't have been so bad, but the convention was invaded by the militant left, by Trotskyist groups, which denounced the *Manifesto* in various ways, some of them quite correctly. Only by sheer personal authority did Raymond manage to hold this conference together. I remember him giving a masterly unscripted summary of the whole conference in the afternoon, taking in every paper and almost every remark that had been made. He just about salvaged something from what was otherwise a rather unseemly event. But it led nowhere at all.

Had your politics shifted further to the left by this point, do you think?

No, I was pretty much behind the left-reformist case of the *May Day Manifesto*, though I suppose I would have positioned myself on the far left. I remember speaking at various public meetings in Cambridge in its defence. I know that I make some withering remarks about it in *Criticism and Ideology* [1976], in the section on Williams, but I wouldn't have thought like that at the time.

You visited the States in 1970. Did that shape your political trajectory?

I went to the States, believe it or not, to teach two hundred nuns.
I taught for ten weeks at a very posh place called Manhattanville
College in New York State, which was more like a finishing school
for Catholic young ladies. The Kennedy daughters had been
educated there, if 'educated' isn't too inflated a term. The college
had heard that I was a figure on the Catholic left and they wanted
lectures on everything from hell to Hegel for their people. I had
a very bizarre time. *Hair* was on Broadway at the time, so we
went, and all the nuns wanted to dance onstage. Everything was
effervescing and burgeoning and mind-blowingly hopeful. I did
almost nothing political except for going to Berkeley – parts of
which had been burnt out – in the wake of the demonstrations. I
also went to a Head Start programme for black children in a New
York ghetto, thanks to contacts who knew some Black Power
people. I had minimal political involvement, but it was directly
after this trip that I joined the International Socialists [IS], later the
Socialist Workers Party [SWP].

*And why did you join the IS as opposed to another organization on the
far left like the International Marxist Group [IMG]?*

I was for some reason more aware of the IS in Oxford, where they
had a large group, some of whom I knew already. But I don't think
I knew much about the IS's politics in any detail when I joined. It
just seemed to me the most visible and active group on the horizon
at the time. As for the IMG, I think I felt very ambivalently about
the Fourth International. When it was the leading political edge of
the student movement, and of the Vietnam Solidarity Campaign,
it seemed to me admirable, and yet to be very unrooted in the class
struggle. The International Socialists, at that point at least, were
making a concerted effort to turn the group towards the industrial
struggle, and that impressed me. I think that that went along
with various forms of workerism and, in the worst sense, anti-

vanguardism, of which I later became very critical, and indeed I left the organization in the mid-seventies.

Was it an educational experience, politically and theoretically?

It was. I read a lot of Marxist theory at the time, partly through membership of the group, partly because I had recently launched the seminars on Marxist theory at Wadham. I was doing a lot of reading and thinking. There was an intensive Marxist culture around at that point, and my seminar was quite an important part of that in the city. It drew in people throughout the university who were dissident in different ways. It mopped them up, so to speak, providing a temporary refuge for people who for all kinds of reasons didn't really fit into Oxford: Ruskin College trades unionists, overseas students, leftists, intellectual vagrants, transient professors and so on, along with the usual quota of maniacs, closet psychopaths and those who just needed a social life. It was fairly separate from my IS commitments. But it seemed to me that the IS was doing interesting work in the town which I ought to take part in. So I ended up leafleting the Cowley car plant with people like Christopher Hitchens, Jairus Banaji and a number of others. Hitchens was in the group, but he was already looking wistfully across the Atlantic, thinking perhaps that there was a bigger place for him than this rather small pond. At the age of twenty-one he was already mesmerized by the idea of America.

In 1970 you published both The Body as Language: Outline of a 'New Left' Theology *and* Exiles and Émigrés: Studies in Modern Literature. *The former is largely theological and the latter largely literary-critical, so it's as if there is a divergence of the two discourses that had converged in* The New Left Church. *Is that significant at all?*

That's true, although I hadn't thought of it that way. In a sense *The Body as Language* was the last gasp of my *Slant* career – indeed it was published the year the journal folded. Most of it was culled from *Slant*. But I think that at that point I was very nervous of what you might call a theological literary criticism. There were some people in the States developing that, but it struck me as something of a cul-de-sac.

It's quite a unified book for one that's culled from a series of essays, but I imagine that in part that's because you were writing for the 'knowable community' to which you've already referred. The interests of this book, not least the conviction that language enables human beings to transcend their biological limits, but that the result of this self-overcoming is 'tragedy and violation', are also strikingly consistent with those of later books. At one point, interestingly, you criticize Williams's Modern Tragedy *[1966] for failing to resolve the contradiction between the claim that tragedy is ordinary, that it's effectively an anthropological condition, and the claim that it can be surmounted historically. According to you, only 'the Christian revolutionary perspective' represents a route out of the deadlock, because Christ embodies both positions on tragedy at the same time. It's a neat conclusion, but isn't it also an imaginary solution to the contradiction?*

Yes, quite possibly. I think I come back to that in the later tragedy book. I did think, and still think, that I'd seen an incipient contradiction in Williams's book, and that's still a problem to be addressed. But I think this book is far too glib in the way it proffers a solution to that. Williams is talking in his book on tragedy about finding a way to live contradictions, and this is perhaps one of them: the utopian desire to transcend tragedy, coupled with the conviction that you mustn't thereby etherealize it and remove it from the common life.

Modern Tragedy *was a more or less explicit attempt, wasn't it, to take on the tradition of tragedy institutionalized in the exam system at Cambridge?*

Yes; and in particular to take on George Steiner. Steiner too was a maverick outsider in his own way, but I think that a riposte to Steiner's *Death of Tragedy* [1961] was built into that book. Steiner once said in my presence, 'Mr. Williams doesn't like tragedy.' In one sense that was simply false; in another sense it's a bit like saying, 'Mr. Williams doesn't like torture.' The ideologically bred obtuseness of highly intelligent people . . .

In The Body as Language *you also discuss Christ as a tragic scapegoat, in ways that pre-echo your account of the scapegoat in* Sweet Violence *[2003].*

I'd totally forgotten that it crops up as early as that. Incidentally, people sometimes accuse my work of butterflying about, but my own criticism would be that it's far too consistent.

You've used a series of slightly different lenses, it seems to me, to examine a remarkably persistent set of interests . . . If The Body as Language *is the last of your explicitly theological books, it is also perhaps the first of your critical-theoretical ones. It's probably the most theoretically adventurous book that you published before* Criticism and Ideology, *at least in its philosophical references, and it's a good deal more pluralistic than either that book or* Myths of Power *[1975]. It opens with a reference to Wittgenstein and it goes on to cite Barthes, Heidegger, Laing, Lévi-Strauss, Merleau-Ponty and Sartre, among others – though it doesn't bother with footnotes. In what context did you encounter Barthes, to take him as an example?*

At that point I think I only knew *Writing Degree Zero* [1953], which I suspect was the only thing then translated. I didn't really have much of a sense of how Barthes figured in a wider cultural constellation. It is interestingly eclectic, *The Body as Language*, isn't it? There are lots of sources being pulled together.

It's a bricoleur*'s book.*

Yes, and that partly reflects the fact that it came from *Slant*. It was also influenced by Herbert McCabe's *Law, Love and Language* [1968], which had been published a couple of years earlier. One of the exciting things about *Slant* as a project was that it allowed us so much theoretical free range. There is a sense in which I first learnt to be a theorist in the context of theology. You can of course accuse the *Slant* project of being too eclectic; but *The Body as Language* is the fruit of a certain intellectual liberation that was the beginning, the seedbed, of my career as a theorist. It all began from there, rather than from, say, *Shakespeare and Society*. Those early literary works are author-centred or text-centred, all the way through to the Brontë book. The theory is largely carried on somewhere else. It then in a sense enters the literary work at a certain point.

So theology provided a kind of meta-discourse, prior to the appearance of literary theory per se?

Yes, very much so. Because, whatever one thinks about theology, it raises a lot of starkly fundamental questions. It seemed to me that in default of other discourses, including literary criticism, theory needed to be invented to take care of those fundamental questions. Philosophy in Britain certainly wasn't doing so, and neither was orthodox political theory.

What about philosophy more generally? Was it effectively subsumed for you under theology at this time?

Well, I've never had any professional philosophical training, so it came to me very much through other avenues – through sociology, through theology, through political theory. I think that literary theory eventually provided the sort of opportunities for philosophizing that a somewhat desiccated philosophy – not least linguistic philosophy – wasn't providing. It was a kind of stand-in. The derogatory way of putting the point is to say that a lot of literary theorists are just second-rate philosophers. But there was a task to be done that had been reneged on by other disciplines – the task that one might classically describe as that of the intellectual. *Faute de mieux*, cultural theorists have come to fill this role in our time. As an old-fashioned materialist, I have somewhat ambiguous feelings about this.

What about phenomenology, which was obviously of instrumental importance in enabling you to develop the theory that the body is a language?

That also came out of the Christian left, as I think I've hinted. I read Merleau-Ponty and others, and I found them enormously fruitful. Herbert McCabe, who edited a volume of Aquinas's work, pointed out that for Aquinas there was no such thing as a dead body; there were simply the remains of a living one. The case was, so to speak, purely phenomenological. I became interested in those connections between traditional Catholic theology and phenomenology.

As a materialist, I've always been interested in hermeneutical phenomenology of the kind practiced by Merleau-Ponty because it's a thoroughly corporeal way of thinking. In fact it's anticipated by the very early Marx, of the Paris manuscripts, who has learned his phenomenology from the horse's mouth – Hegel – and speaks of subjects and objects and subjects-for-objects and objects-for-subjects in ways that the modern phenomenological tradition will develop. The phenomenological tradition has been extremely valuable in demystifying a certain private-property model of lived experience – the assumption that I am somehow the private owner of my joys and pains, which I possess rather as I possess a pair of suede shoes or a toothbrush. The later Wittgenstein has great fun in demolishing this Cartesian model, as when he mischievously suggests that there may be a pain in the room somewhere but it's not clear which of us is having it. It's only our deceptive grammar which tricks us into thinking that 'I have a pain' is the same as 'I have a donkey'. I don't have any special or privileged access to my own 'private' experiences, as I might have privileged access to my own bank account. The way I know myself is roughly the way I know you. Phenomenology of this kind – though not of the Husserlian kind – has helped us to understand that our bodies are not things we are 'in', as ink is in a bottle, so much as projects, centres of relation, practical orientations, ways of being bound up with a world. And this is certainly a dimension that historical materialism needs. It also, of course, needs the psychoanalytic insight that the true alterity, the real other, is oneself. And phenomenology has found some difficulty in accounting for the unconscious.

It was at roughly the time you were putting together The Body as Language *that you moved from your post at Cambridge to one at Oxford. Had you had enough of Cambridge? Had Cambridge had enough of you?*

Almost the day that Raymond arrived in Cambridge, shortly after *Culture and Society* had appeared, the editorial of the university journal ran a supercilious and savage piece under the heading: 'Mr Raymond Williams.' I think it was by Maurice Cowling, the far-right-wing historian. Raymond was very surprised at this hostility. The Cambridge establishment couldn't threaten him much, however, both because he was personally so authoritative and because he quickly established an international reputation. So they couldn't gun for him directly. Instead, they gunned for his acolytes. Raymond encouraged me to put in for a couple of assistant lectureships at Cambridge, but they were certainly not going to give me one. The writing was on the wall. I knew I couldn't stay in Cambridge, partly because the atmosphere was so unpleasant and partly because I couldn't survive financially without a lectureship. The reason I ended up at Oxford was that it became obvious they weren't going to give me a job in Cambridge.

Of two places that were fairly hostile, though, Cambridge was by far the most interesting place to be. It was where the politics of criticism were being determined.

So in 1969 you moved to Oxford, where you were appointed as a fellow of Wadham College. The interview panel included two figures that now seem almost impossibly remote, Sir Maurice Bowra and Lord David Cecil . . .

Cecil was the representative of the English faculty, which he was on the point of retiring from. Apart from him, the panel consisted of various college fellows. Bowra, who was the head of the college, wanted to see me appointed because it seemed amusingly idiosyncratic. His upper-class, Bloomsburyish hostility to the establishment intersected for a surreal moment with my own 'Pope John Marxism', as he approvingly called it. Wadham was then – probably still is – a progressive, mildly left college. Most of the fellows voted Labour, which was pretty unique in an Oxbridge college.

To my surprise, I later heard that Cecil too was very much in favour of me. I can't imagine why. He did, admittedly, seem to doze off for some of the interview, so perhaps that explains it. Maybe he thought I was a Tory Anglican, or mistook me for Roger Scruton. Isaiah Berlin apparently later remarked that Cecil 'was of course much downcast by Eagleton's later development'. And somebody told me at the time that the formidable Helen Gardner, who ruled the roost in the English faculty then, had said to Bowra, 'Maurice, you must be bonkers to take Eagleton!' But the Oxford system is such that the college can take who they like and the university has to put up with them. That was one of my first recognitions that the faculty was not at all happy about my appointment.

Exiles and Émigrés: Studies in Modern Literature [1970], a monograph on modernism and expatriatism, was published shortly after your move to Oxford. Its thesis is that, because of their partial, parochial attachments, the indigenous English writers of the early twentieth century were incapable of totalizing society, a task that was consequently left to foreigners like Conrad, Eliot and Joyce. Retrospectively, how do you situate this book in relation to your intellectual development?

I think *Exiles and Émigrés* was a transitional work. It was still very Cambridge in its close reading and detailed criticism, but it was also trying to find some way of breaking beyond that. I don't think it does it very adequately. I think it's an under-theorized book, a literary-critical work with a hinterland of more general concepts that don't really come sufficiently to the fore. It was a tentative foray into theory, but it didn't quite make it. Looking back on the book now, it seems to me very much the kind of book that a socialist of the time might write if he didn't have much access to theory. It was the furthest you could push that criticism without the theory. It was comprised of the critical techniques of Cambridge but with a different politics attached to them, as indeed was Williams's very early work.

It had very little general effect, actually, but it didn't do me any harm. It was a book I published as soon as I got to Oxford, a place that was pretty notorious, at least in those days, for having a patrician scepticism about the whole rather vulgar idea of publishing. It's one of three or four books I've written that really don't figure very much in the general consciousness. Nor does it figure all that much in my own.

Were you semi-consciously writing yourself out of the Slant *moment in this book? Apart from the chapter on Graham Greene, there isn't much theology in* Exiles and Émigrés.

No, there isn't. Interestingly, though, the seed of that book was actually the essay on Greene which had appeared in *Slant*. So there was a hidden connection between *Slant* and that book: the bridge was Greene. I think that theology and criticism seemed to me rigorously separate at the time. I didn't see any way of bringing theology into criticism. And at that time I was much less interested in it anyway.

If it is in part a product of Cambridge literary criticism, it can also be read as a coded critique of Oxbridge culture more broadly. Interestingly, it contains a discussion of Brideshead Revisited, *in which your rather nuanced critique of the 'upper-class novel', as you call it, can also be interpreted as a displaced attack on Oxford as a social and intellectual institution. You state for instance: 'Because all is possible to this privileged social class and to the literary form which mirrors it, nothing is especially valuable; because no conventional definition is more than improvised, momentary, experimental, no event or identity can be given the fixed limits of substantial meaning.' Everything is brilliant, as you point out, because nothing is constrained by social reality. This seems to echo your attitude to Redpath; and to anticipate your criticisms of John Bayley.*

There I go again about the value of constitutive limits . . . Bowra was a close friend of quite a few of the people I was discussing in that book – certainly Evelyn Waugh and Virginia Woolf – so there may have been some kind of semi-conscious connection. But it was the first book I published in Oxford, as you've pointed out, and I'd only arrived the term before, so I hadn't had a lot of time to develop a critique of Oxford in particular. Nevertheless, it is perhaps interesting that the first book I produced there has this chapter on the 'upper-class novel', which indirectly perhaps is a critique of Oxford or Oxbridge culture.

You've mentioned Woolf. Although the book was from one perspective a coded attack on the class culture of Oxford, you nonetheless reproduce some of its other characteristic prejudices. Most strikingly, you relegate Woolf, and female writers more generally, to a relatively marginal role. You effectively exclude Woolf, who you discuss in relation to the 'upper-class novel', from the high modernist canon. Woolf was of course a vehement critic of the patriarchal culture of Oxbridge. Can you say why you ignored her status as an experimental outsider, albeit an ambivalent, contradictory one?

I had no clue that I was doing that. I was shamelessly innocent. No doubt in 1970 I should have been more alert than I was to those issues, because although most of the major feminist work was still to happen it was certainly incipient. But that didn't enter into my critical purview at all. Later, in *The English Novel: An Introduction* [2005], I quote a blistering political statement by Woolf that I describe as more radical than any other statement by an English novelist. So I tried to make belated amends, even though I continue to think that a good deal of (especially US) feminist commentary on Woolf outrageously ignores or plays down some of her more odious social attitudes. An Irish feminist critic, however, described the later chapter on Woolf, which is for the most part highly positive, as 'spectacularly negative'. Politics quite often lies in the eye of the beholder.

As you've implied, there is an imprecision and tentativeness about the application of theoretical ideas in this book. For example, in the chapter on Orwell and the 'lower-middle-class novel' you talk about the importance of recognizing that particular genres of the novel seem intimately related to particular areas of social reality. This is obviously an attempt to supersede a vulgar sociological reductionism, but the spatial metaphor that you use – 'areas of social reality' – is a very vague one.

Yes. I didn't really know how to push it further. It was influenced by Perry Anderson's 'white emigration' thesis in 'Components of the National Culture' [1968]. On the one hand there was this enormously exciting, ambitious argument of Anderson's about exile and on the other hand there was the text. I didn't know quite how to put it together.

Another of the theoretical concepts that you reach for is 'totalization', which is obviously derived from Lukács, though you don't mention him by name. You define 'totalization' in this context as 'a cohering standpoint, framework or symbolism by which a writer can surpass the immediate prejudices of his own partial experience to achieve a complete, impersonal, and "objective" version of reality in the image of nineteenth-century realism.' This makes me think that what the book lacks, in theoretical terms, is an encounter with Lukács's reflections on reification in History and Class Consciousness *[1923] – although this book wasn't translated into English until 1971.* Exiles and Émigrés *is evidently indebted to* The Historical Novel *[1937], but that relationship only takes it so far.*

It lacks Lukács's more political concepts. I'd encountered Lukács's *Historical Novel*, as I've said, at one of Raymond's seminars on the novel in Cambridge. And in *Exiles and Émigrés* I was half-consciously thinking through its legacy. I was beginning to teach the Marxist seminar at the time, and we used some Lukács there, so he was a shadowy presence.

There are of course different epistemologies in Lukács at different points. In his discussion of realism you can see a reflectionist or correspondence epistemology at work; but that isn't adequate to the complexities of *History and Class Consciousness*, where a much more active, interventionist notion of consciousness is at stake, one that can't be accommodated in the reflectionist model. There is an unevenness or difference in Lukács in that respect.

And is the concept of the totality you use in Exiles and Émigrés *derived from theological thinking too?*

Solely in the sense that a predilection for system is a Catholic impulse. I think that what *Exiles and Émigrés* lacks, among a lot of other things, is the idea of the truth as one-sided. Because I was dealing with partial standpoints that were clearly open to left-wing criticism, I didn't really see that the truth is one-sided –

which I think does indeed have a theological resonance. In other words, I didn't see that a partisan stance of a particular kind – not necessarily Waugh's or Orwell's – could actually illuminate the truth more sharply than the rather idealist notion of totality that I was looking for.

From a dialectical perspective, as you've often insisted, totality and partisanship aren't opposites, since society is most effectively totalized by those who have a partial, sectional interest in systemically transforming it.

Yes. Once you begin to see the totality as itself constituted by contradiction and conflict, then the picture obviously changes. I was aware at the time of the dangers of liberal dispassionateness, of the view from nowhere, but I wasn't sufficiently alert to the idea of truth and engagement being internally related.

Let's turn to the concept of exile that you deploy in this book, which is a highly suggestive one. Fredric Jameson has referred admiringly to 'the position of Terry Eagleton's stimulating Exiles and Émigrés *that all the most important modern writers of what we think of as the English canon are in fact social marginals of various kinds, when not outright foreigners.' But it's a fairly attenuated notion too. At one point, for example, you affirm that 'Conrad the expatriate, Waugh the upper-class observer, Orwell the social critic, Greene the Catholic metaphysician: all are in various ways exiles within a society.' On the basis of this claim it's almost impossible to think of a 'modern writer' who isn't an exile of some kind.*

Exactly. All those who see yourselves as insiders, put up your hands . . . It's far too capacious a concept of exile; it's not politically and historically specified. I also wasn't aware at all in writing this book – such is the self-blindness of authors – how far the question of exile applied to my own situation. Clearly I felt an outsider in

Oxbridge, and that must have been one of the major impulses behind writing it, and yet that didn't enter into it at all. I can almost never see the life-situations that help to shape my work except in retrospect. That is my own personal Owl of Minerva.

It's what Ernst Bloch called the 'darkness of the lived moment' . . . I suppose I'd argue that this sense of being an outsider does in fact enter into the writing. Like Williams's book The English Novel from Dickens to Lawrence *[1970], which appeared in the same year as yours,* Exiles and Émigrés *ends with a chapter on Lawrence, a working-class exile within bourgeois or upper-class institutions. Significantly, you congratulate Lawrence for his foreigner's eye and capacity for estranging institutions.*

Yes, that's true; and Williams speaks of Lawrence as the working-class boy who never came home. I don't remember any deep sense of identification with Lawrence, although given his prominence in the Cambridge I'd just left it does seem surprising that I didn't have some sense of affinity with him. There were certainly people in Cambridge at the time who felt that Lawrence just put everybody else in the shade, that there was really no point in reading pallid authors like Jane Austen once you'd been subjected to the burning intensity of Lawrence. I suppose I never really fell for that Leavisian cult of Lawrence entirely. On the other hand, Lawrence clearly did speak to me – as to Raymond – in this personal kind of way. I always appreciated Raymond's essay on Lawrence in *Culture and Society* as a political corrective to Leavis, although it too is silent about the more rebarbative and negative aspects of Lawrence, which is in line with the general trend of that book. I suppose the Lawrence that one was invited to identify with in Cambridge was not an exile so much as an alternative centre, artistically, philosophically. He represented the idea of spontaneous, creative life, and embodied a world vision that the Leavisites saw as spiritually central. Yet that's odd in a way, because there's nothing in the least liberal about Lawrence, as opposed to radical. He just isn't at home with the likes of Eliot, James and Forster. He's a most un-English species of extremism, and a full-blooded metaphysician to boot. His true coordinates are all continental. The Leavisites didn't see this; and neither, I think, did Williams.

Perhaps it's only because there were so few canonical modernists from a working-class background that it seems tempting to ascribe an autobiographical impulse to you and Williams in addressing Lawrence.

That's right. The class thing didn't matter much to Leavis. For the Leavisites – apart from a defence of Lawrence's lower-middle-class Methodistic background as a culture in itself – the class issue dropped out. That might also have made it more difficult for me to see any connection with my own situation. In fact, much of the Leavisian ideology is explicable in terms of his petit-bourgeois provincial roots, as I would argue later.

There is an interesting chapter on George Orwell in Exiles and Émigrés *in which you diagnose the problem of the 'lower-middle-class novel', as you call it, as 'the dilemma of a class marooned between orthodox decencies and deprivation, unable either to fully accept or fully reject the social system, and so critical of both the common life and of its possible alternatives.'*

What I think can be got from Orwell is that, with all the limitations of liberal moralism and amateurism, and an Olympian touch at times too, he nevertheless refused to abandon the wider field of social criticism. After all, it is in Orwell's work that what is conventionally called cultural studies begins to germinate. Like the Leavises, he is one of the sources of that, and one can very often suppress one's ancestors. There are, I think, a lot of other good reasons for being critical of Orwell. It is interesting that Williams, who knew Orwell personally – in fact, he told me that he lost on a train the very last piece Orwell ever wrote! – shifted from a very sympathetic position in *Culture and Society* to a much more hostile one in his small book, *Orwell*. But what that perhaps doesn't say is what kind of a critic Orwell was, increasingly bereft of a public sphere but nevertheless trying to keep that idea warm by holding to a discourse which was really very capacious but which also had the limits of such capaciousness, the rather too grandly generalizing crossings from field to field. I think that Williams's own work can be seen in that tradition – Orwell was, after all, one of the last characters in the 'Culture and Society' lineage. But also, as in Williams's quite astringent critique of Orwell's over-generalizing, it is a work which has learned from Orwell's mistakes.

I want to come back finally to the concept of exile – partly because subsequently it was of such importance in Edward Said's criticism and then became a central term in the lexicon of postcolonial theory. In The World, the Text and the Critic *[1983], a book explicitly indebted to Williams, Said discusses Erich Auerbach and the conditions in which* Mimesis *[1953] was produced. He asks, 'How did exile become converted from a challenge or a risk, or even from an active impingement on his European selfhood, into a positive mission, whose success would be a cultural act of great importance?' I think* Exiles and Émigrés *had already articulated an answer to that question. 'The great literary achievements of the war years,' you write there, 'the art which most intimately caught and evaluated the characteristic experience of the age, was made possible by the existence within English society of alien components.' According to your argument, the rootless, marginal position of the modernists rendered them peculiarly sensitive to the contradictions of a disintegrating society that was nonetheless not their own.*

I can't remember my response to Said's book, but in general I felt that Said was romanticizing exile in ways that I never really wanted to. I was always impressed by Raymond's distinction between the vagrant and the exile: the vagrant is somebody who is quite content to be marginal as long as he can keep dodging the system, whereas the exile wants the system to change so that he can come home. I always felt that was the correct emphasis, and I never really sympathized much with Said's occasional idealizing of the unhoused intellect, with its rather suspect, etymologically inaccurate implication that the rootless is always the radical. Anderson's thesis – that these white immigrants were originally rootless but put down conservative roots precisely because of that – is in a sense exactly the opposite. I think I was too strongly under the influence of Raymond's stress on community, and on the dangers of the romantic dissident who in a sense parasitically lives off the very system that he is bugging, to believe that exile was always a creative position. And later on I tend to stress the pains or pangs of exile more than the pleasures, or at least to try to look at both sides of it. All this, incidentally, is considerably more subtle and nuanced than the simple-minded postmodern affirmation of 'marginality', which I've always been critical of. Some margins ought to remain just that. Neo-Nazism for example.

Reading

Anderson, Perry, 'Components of the National Culture', in *English Questions* (London: Verso, 1992), pp. 48–104.

Aquinas, St. Thomas, *Summa Theologiae, Prima Pars, Vol 3: Knowing and Naming God*, ed. Herbert McCabe (Oxford: Blackfriars, 1964).

Eagleton, Terry, *Shakespeare and Society: Critical Studies in Shakespearean Drama* (London: Chatto and Windus, 1967).

Eagleton, Terry, *The Body as Language: Outline of a 'New Left' Theology* (London: Sheed & Ward, 1970).

Eagleton, Terry, *Exiles and Émigrés: Studies in Modern Literature* (New York: Shocken Books, 1970).

Eagleton, Terry, 'Lawrence', in Ian Gregor and Walter Stein, eds., *The Prose for God: Religious and Anti-Religious Aspects of Imaginative Literature* (London: Sheed & Ward, 1973), pp. 86–100.

Eagleton, Terry, *Criticism and Ideology: A Study in Marxist Literary Theory* (London: New Left Books, 1976).

Eagleton, Terry, 'The Poetry of E. P. Thompson', *Literature and History* 5:2 (1979), pp. 139–45.

Eagleton, Terry, 'Criticism and Ideology: Andrew Milner interviews Terry Eagleton', *Thesis Eleven* 12 (1985), pp. 130–44.

Eagleton, Terry, 'Radical Roots' (review of E. P. Thompson, *Witness Against the Beast: William Blake and the Moral Law*), *New Statesman and Society*, 26 November 1993, pp. 39–40.

Eagleton, Terry, 'The Flight to the Real', in *Cultural Politics at the Fin de Siècle*, eds. Sally Ledger and Scott McCracken (Cambridge: Cambridge University Press, 1995), pp. 11–21.

'Interview with Terry Eagleton,' in *Lukács after Communism: Interviews with Contemporary Intellectuals*, ed. Eva L. Corredor (Durham: Duke University Press, 1997), pp. 127–50.

Eagleton, Terry, 'A Conversation with Terry Eagleton' (with José Manuel Barbeito Varela), *Atlantis: Revista de la Asociación Española de Estudios Anglo-Norteamericanos* 23:2 (December 2001), pp. 169–85.

Eagleton, Terry, 'Romantic Poets', in *Figures of Dissent: Critical Essays on Fish, Spivak, Žižek and Others* (London: Verso, 2003), pp. 37–41.

Eagleton, Terry, *The English Novel: An Introduction* (Oxford: Blackwell, 2005).

Eagleton, Terry, *Criticism and Ideology: A Study in Marxist Literary Theory*, new edition (London: Verso, 2006).

Jameson, Fredric, 'Modernism and Imperialism', in *Nationalism, Colonialism, and Literature*, ed. Seamus Deane (Minneapolis: University of Minnesota Press, 1990), pp. 43–66.

Mulhern, Francis, *The Moment of 'Scrutiny'* (London: New Left Books, 1979).

Redpath, Theodore, *Tolstoy* (London: Bowes and Bowes, 1960).

Rowbotham, Sheila, *Edward Carpenter: A Life of Liberty and Love* (London: Verso, 2008).

Said, Edward, *The World, The Text and the Critic* (London: Faber & Faber, 1984).

Thompson, E. P., *The Poverty of Theory* (London: Merlin Press, 1995).

Williams, Raymond, *Culture and Society 1780–1950* (London: Chatto & Windus, 1958).

Williams, Raymond, *Orwell* (London: Fontana, 1970).

Williams, Raymond, ed., *May Day Manifesto 1968* (Harmondsworth: Penguin, 1968).

CHAPTER FOUR

Politics/Aesthetics

In Oxford in the early 1970s you led a long-running, indeed legendary series of Marxist seminars at Wadham. Could you describe this class? What form or forms did it assume?

I launched it more or less instantly after arriving at Wadham in 1969. Initially, the seminars centred on specifically Marxist criticism; we read and introduced people to all kinds of Marxist critics. Later on, they changed their character and effectively became literary theory classes. Finally, they were taken over by the students, who founded a radical pressure group in the English Faculty called Oxford English Limited, and I just dropped in occasionally. The classes ran throughout the eighties and right up to the time that I left Oxford.

The classes started in my college room with a small group of people, mostly postgraduates of mine, and then gravitated to the Wadham lecture room. It quite quickly became a forum for intellectual and political waifs and strays, exiles and émigrés, in Oxford. They ranged from miners from Ruskin College to young left-wing intellectuals. There were also several members of the IMG and the IS. The audience was a very mobile one, and a lot of people passing through Oxford came to them, so it was difficult to run a consistent programme. The seminars were intensive cultural forums. Over the years they assumed a variety of experimental pedagogical forms. Sometimes I would address them, but often the participants would decide the topic for the next time and would give papers. It was very democratically run. We also frequently invited visiting speakers – people like Stuart Hall and John Goode, though I don't think Raymond ever addressed us. One of the good things about it was that it never had an institutionalized setting. It was very informal. We were engaged in a process of collective learning.

What about the intellectual content of the classes?

Its history followed wider political history. At first, as I say, it was almost exclusively a Marxist affair. Then, increasingly, other bodies of theory came in, particularly post-structuralism and feminism, and there were consequently debates and conflicts between these positions. The class was absolutely rooted in its political moment. These were the years of the excitement of Althusser, of *Screen* and of early post-structuralism. Chris Norris, who was our man on the phone to Paris as it were, would relay the latest Barthes, and gradually these ideas would circulate. Somebody would hunt out Derrida's work, which would be little more than a rumour, and give a paper on him. We would struggle through the early Julia Kristeva. It was all conducted at a formidably high intellectual level – too high in the sense of being too self-consciously rigorous, too humourless. But I still remember undergraduates of mine – not postgraduates – whose ability to dissect the third volume of *Capital* was quite startling. The classes acted as a hostel for battered leftists – for people who weren't getting on in the Oxford system; for people who were passing through Oxford as visiting lecturers or researchers and wanted something different; and for public-school types who had been trained to believe that they should have the best and who had the uneasy feeling that John Bayley was not the absolute acme of European civilization.

How did the faculty react to the emergence of this oppositional centre of intellectual and political debate?

I think there was quite a lot of informal faculty displeasure. There was a fair amount of grunting in the background. In a sense, we were making the students unteachable on Oxford's terms. But, because of the university's belief that it could tolerate or absorb anything, they didn't actually make a move against it. For a long time the seminars weren't on the lecture list. Indeed, I deliberately kept them off the list, and ran them in addition to my duties at the university, because we didn't want to formalize them. The faculty did however ultimately attempt to co-opt them to show that they weren't afraid of them. So they ended up on the lecture list, but that suited me in so far as it advertized them.

All of this was exhilarating, but it was a lot to carry and I felt burdened by it. There was considerable hostility to me personally, particularly in those first years at Oxford. There were people that I'd never met or spoken to who would literally cross the street to avoid me. I'd never provoked these people personally, but they thought I was misleading the youth. I was extremely isolated, and I had a hard time of it, partly because I'm not particularly thick-skinned, partly because it was so palpably unjust. They couldn't tolerate one radical in a faculty of 120 people ...

So what role did Oxford English Limited perform in the development of the class?

The class transformed itself into Oxford English Limited in the 1980s, and in this shape it became the base for a campaigning group which, however modest its political profile in the great scheme of things, did work on an extraordinary number of levels – all the way from brazenly providing translations of *Beowulf* for students who didn't want to waste their time doing it, to advising people who were trapped with some intolerable tutor. Sometimes we would leaflet lecturers, handing out critiques of anti-left lecturers. One of our more mischievous projects was to inform prospective English students about the university so as to give them a profile of the English teaching in the colleges – a very useful thing to do of course. Once the English faculty caught wind of this they went to the proctors and disinterred some old regulation about bringing the University into disrepute, which they then brandished over our heads. We consulted a lawyer to find out whether they could get us for this and the issue petered out.

So the class didn't just die a death around 1979, say, when the political shades began to come down. It found a practical role for itself, and that really did worry the University in some respects. According to certain members of the Oxford English faculty, Oxford English Limited was my private bid for power. The fact that I finally left the university largely because I didn't want the power that went with the administrative duties of a professor is somewhat ironic in that regard. But there was a certain paranoid view that this group was Eagleton's instrument. I hadn't even created it. People like Ken Hirschkop and Robin Gable, who were effectively Williamsites, had founded it. And although I was initially central to it I took more of a back seat as the eighties wore on.

What were you personally working on between 1970 and 1975? You didn't publish any books in that time, so on the face of it you appear to have been uncharacteristically unproductive – perhaps partly because of the demands and responsibilities of running the class.

I think it was the usual business of starting a family and getting established and so on. Then my first marriage ended in divorce in 1976. I did write various essays in that period. But this hiatus may have had some significance, because I didn't know exactly what to write or how to write. There's a sense in which *Exiles and Émigrés* [1970] – though I'm exaggerating this – was written for the sake of writing a book. I wrote it because of my desire to write, but it wasn't the book that I wanted to write. I knew I didn't want to write conventional criticism – and I felt slightly negative about *Exiles and Émigrés* because I thought that that was what it was – but I didn't know how else to do things at that point. I was fumbling in the dark towards certain ideas, certain theories. The book on the Brontës, *Myths of Power* [1975], is exemplary in this regard, because there I use the word 'Marxist' in the subtitle. Even in 1974 or 1975 that was a fairly provocative thing to do. In fact, I remember a Marxist critic – John Goode – saying, 'Do you really mean to use the word?' I said, 'Yes, why not?' By that point I had enough behind me in terms of the Oxford situation to feel confident about making my mark. But in the Brontës book I'm still taking canonical authors as central, even if I wheel up far more heavy-duty theory than previously.

Criticism and Ideology *[1976] was presumably the turning point . . .*

Criticism and Ideology was the moment when things really gelled. That was the book waiting to be written – though not necessarily by me. I had a strong sense that somebody was going to write this book. There were several possible authors; it just happened by some statistical law that I authored it. It was the kind of book that was both necessary and possible. By 1976 it was possible to write that book, which hadn't been the case at the time of *Exiles and Émigrés* and still wasn't at the time of the book on the Brontës. So if *Criticism and Ideology* is a work of the 'break', in Althusserian parlance, the other books are hanging about in some kind of antechamber.

There are obviously parallels here with Williams, in that at a certain point he discovered a new way of writing. If you examine the difference between *Drama from Ibsen to Eliot* [1968] and *Drama from Ibsen to Brecht* [1987] you can see that he's writing in quite a different way. He has broken with the Cambridge emphasis on close reading – perhaps in his case rather too much – and has found his own voice. There are early books of his, like *Drama from Ibsen to Eliot*, where, as with *Exiles and Émigrés*, you can hear that voice off-stage, so to speak, but he can't see a way of bringing it on. I think his concern in the drama books with the break from realism to whatever lies beyond realism is allegorical of that. He's looking for a way of bringing onstage what can't be dramatized centrally in realist or naturalistic drama. When he says that in drama there's a break towards expressionism, he's partly talking about himself.

Were the other things that you were doing in the early 1970s, like reviewing, a more or less conscious attempt to find a voice or subject?

It's possible that the strangely disparate things that I was doing might have had some secret coherence. I was running the Marxist classes at Oxford and feeling towards some correlative of that in terms of my writing. *Slant* had folded, but I still had connections with *New Blackfriars*. Then there were the strange poetry reviews that I did for *Stand* for years. I think I was Jon Silkin's longest-standing reviewer, partly because he was so adept at alienating the rest of his contributors. I heard of people who changed their addresses and phone numbers and wore shades because he was such an intimidating, draconian presence – though that's actually what helped him almost single-handedly to keep the magazine going. I valued doing these reviews because it wasn't like anything else I did. It was close analysis of poetry. Later, people often said, 'Look, what you were doing there wasn't the same kind of thing that you were talking about theoretically' – and that was true. I was schizophrenic. I didn't know how to bring these things together. This reviewing was almost the hardest thing I've ever done: I valued it, but I dreaded it.

These reviews weren't five-finger exercises at all, then?

Not in the least; not like reviewing sometimes is for me now. I was proud of doing it. I liked the politics of the journal, I liked the idea of collaborating with a group, and I liked writing to a certain line, in a loose sense; but I found the actual reviewing really difficult.

So can How to Read a Poem *[2007], your recent introductory book on poetry, be read as an attempt to resolve that 'schizophrenia', that conflict?*

Yes; I think that in the meantime I realized there were theories of poetry as well, which I probably wasn't much aware of at that time. But I was still in this kind of antechamber, if you like, where I was doing different things without quite knowing how to bring them together – whereas *How to Read a Poem* does that more fluently.

Did you yourself write any more poetry at that stage?

No, I think I'd pretty well stopped by the time I left Cambridge. When I came to Oxford I started writing songs. The project continued, but in a different style. I realized I could write songs, and it wasn't as sweated a labour as writing poetry. It was quite easy, and it was great fun. I used to be involved in this Irish music session every week in Oxford throughout the 1970s. It was run by an Irish builder, but I was one of the people in on the ground floor. I valued it greatly because it was a way of living in the town even though I worked in the university. It moved from pub to pub, partly because it ran into some trouble in the worst days of the IRA campaign in Britain. After the Birmingham bombings, for example, the cops would sometimes turn up, and there were Irish friends of mine who didn't dare open their mouths in public because of their accents. But it survived that. There were occasions when we'd hire a pub and they'd put the prices up when they realized we were Irish. But that was great fun, and for me it was an alternative centre to the university. I wrote songs and sang them at these sessions.

Can you recall any of the songs you wrote?

I remember one song I wrote in the early seventies, as the Watergate affair was unfolding, to which I added verses as events became more dire. I can still sing it. There's also a 'Ballad of Marxist Criticism', which never did well in the charts, never got covered by Britney Spears, for reasons that escape me. I've always felt a strange reluctance to have my songs committed to print, though – I like them to remain in the oral tradition. I also wrote a song about a ridiculous airport that they built out in County Mayo. The builder who started the session took it to Ireland and bribed some DJ to play it, and when a documentary was made about the airport they used it in the soundtrack, so we had our fifteen minutes of fame. But it was a wonderful experience, and for me there were obvious strains of nostalgia. It was home from home. I knew a lot of the songs anyway from my childhood, so I'd write satirical and political songs to familiar Irish tunes.

Were there Marxists amongst the republicans?

They were leftists, certainly. One or two of them had the Oxford Irish vote in their pockets, so the prospective Labour candidate for East Oxford would always make sure that he was accompanied by these guys in visiting certain parts of the city. There was quite a lot of politics going on. This was the time that I joined the International Socialists, so I was working around the car factory, and there was certainly an overlap between those two worlds. The people who attended the classes at Wadham would also often repair to these sessions. This was for me the golden age, and it could in a sense only have happened because of the political context of the time. My postgraduates and I, and some others, would go to the King's Arms regularly and sit at the same table every time, and we later discovered that it was known as 'Trots' Corner'. The King's Arms was both a leftist and a gay pub in this period. It was an interesting time to be in Oxford.

Is this what you mean when you refer – as you have done in the past – to 'the socialist culture of the 1970s'? In the new Introduction to Criticism and Ideology *you characterize the period that succeeded this decade in terms of the loss of a certain socialist common sense . . .*

There was an ambient socialist culture. Although there were a lot of people around who were convinced and active socialists, there were at the same time a lot of people who weren't but who were nevertheless steeped in that atmosphere, influenced by that climate. So it didn't seem at all bizarre or esoteric to examine Marxist ideas. They had a general currency, and a currency beyond academia as well. It was a minority socialist culture, to be sure, but it really was a culture. It was not confined to ideas.

In 1974 you edited the New Wessex edition of Thomas Hardy's final novel, Jude the Obscure, *which is of course a profoundly pessimistic account of a working-class intellectual's tragic exclusion from Oxford as a place of learning. Was that at some level also an engagement with the class politics of Oxford?*

It was, although I don't remember thinking that at the time. It was a case of the publisher saying, 'Oh, we'll give *Jude* to the Marxist critic.' I remember Frank Kermode reviewing some of the volumes, and in rather patronizing tones saying something like, 'Of course, *Jude* lends itself to Eagleton's approach, but nothing else does . . .'

And did you review academic books extensively at this time?

I published a few critical articles here and there, in *Essays in Criticism* and *Critical Quarterly*, and I did a bit of reviewing. I even reviewed in the *Review of English Studies*, and aspired to write the odd note or query for *Notes and Queries*. (A friend of mine claims to be the only person in history to have got two articles on the same page of a journal – i.e. two notes in *Notes and Queries*, if not a note and a query.) Yes, I was doing all that, but there weren't a lot of professional pressures on me to publish, as there would be for somebody now. I had a job for life, and the fact that I had a doctorate was neither here nor there as far as Oxford was concerned. Indeed, in a sense it was regarded as somewhat *petit-bourgeois* to call oneself 'Dr'. An academic fellowship is the ruin of many a great intellect. I saw that as time wore on. The more books I published, the more hostile Oxford seemed to grow.

You were writing fairly regularly at this time for New Blackfriars, *a Dominican journal to which you still contribute. Could you describe your involvement in it?*

Blackfriars, the Dominican house in Oxford, was an important centre of radical theology – it still is to some extent. There was no official hook-up between *New Blackfriars* and *Slant*, but there was a lot of overlap personally and intellectually. After *Slant* folded I carried on those connections around *New Blackfriars* and around Blackfriars itself. For example, when Bloody Sunday happened in 1972, Herbert McCabe put on a Mass for the dead at which he recited the names of people who had been murdered. Blackfriars became tarred with the brush of terrorism as a result – either out of simple ignorance or malice, people claimed that when monks rattled cans after a meeting they were collecting for the IRA. At one point I was poetry editor of *New Blackfriars*. The poetry editor of such a journal is like the doorman at the Ritz – his job is not to let people in but to keep them out. So I spent my time rejecting, say, Mother Mary Joseph's sonnet about St Francis.

I'd like to ask you in more detail about the theoretical reading you were doing in the early 1970s, and specifically about Althusser. For Marx *[1965] appeared in an English translation in 1969,* Reading Capital *[1968] in 1970. The earliest reference to Althussser that I've found in your work is in an essay called 'Myth and History in Recent Poetry', from 1972: 'History, as Louis Althusser has reminded us, is a complex rather than a monistic reality: we should talk of* histories, *and of the conflicting unities they form.'*

I remember coming across a volume of *Reading Capital* in the library of Jesus College, Cambridge, of all places. I don't know who put it there. We focused on a predominately Hegelian form of Marxism when we started off the sessions in Oxford. Then some time in the early 1970s we started reading Althusser. The Marxist seminars were not in any strict sense Althusserian, but they were within that ambience.

Did you feel a sense of intellectual excitement on reading him?

I wouldn't say 'excitement' was exactly the right word, but there certainly was an invigorating sense that here was a series of concepts being cut that one could really work with, or deploy, in all sorts of areas: psychoanalysis, literature, culture and so on. I didn't ever see myself as a card-carrying Althusserian, so I was in fact slightly surprised suddenly to read about myself as one. I always had some reservations about most of Althusser's central concepts. Although it might be hard to read *Criticism and Ideology* and believe it, I never bought them wholesale. I attempted to draw up a balance sheet of the gains and losses of Althusserianism in the preface to *Against the Grain* in the mid-1980s, though nobody seemed to notice that. There I argued that the benefit of Althusser's central theoretical concepts was that they corrected the distortions of other traditions of Marxist thought, but these alternative formulations themselves turned out to be distortive in their emphasis. Althusser's anti-empiricism, for example, served as an important corrective at the time to positivistic forms of Marxism, but at the cost of lapsing into a neo-Kantianism that pushed the 'real' to a vanishing point beyond discourse. His anti-historicism, and the highly differentiated theory of temporality that he opposed to it, was also extremely useful, but its effect was to collapse historical narratives into localized 'conjunctures'. Perhaps most influentially, his concept of ideology, which decisively overturned previous, mechanistic theories of ideology, nonetheless threatened to expand its meaning so much as to be politically ineffectual.

Did reading Althusser reorganize your relationship to socialist humanism? In For Marx *he critiques socialist humanism as an ideological concept rather than a scientific one, and argues that it offers the 'feeling' of the theory that humanist Marxists lack.*

Althusser's anti-humanism helpfully displaced the subject fetishized by existentialist and phenomenological currents of Marxism, but it fell prey to a structuralism that fatally under-emphasized the importance of class struggle. And even in the mid-1970s I thought that different forms, different meanings, of humanism could be too quickly conflated. I was an anti-humanist at that time in the sense of not being subject-centred or phenomenological in analysis, but I always thought that the moral tradition of humanism, which I'd inherited from Williams, was important. I thought people were getting their wires crossed too easily.

What did Williams think of Althusser? In the introduction to Marxism and Literature *[1977], he briefly refers to Althusser, alongside Goldmann and the later Sartre, when he evokes the excitement he felt in the late 1960s and early 1970s at 'contact with more new Marxist work'.*

My guess is that Raymond had actually read very little of Althusser. He had a slightly mixed response: he liked the study of whole structures or systems, and even said a few kind things about structuralism in that regard; but it was from a very wary distance. Similarly, I always felt that Fredric Jameson didn't fully understand what it was all about – although he talks more about Althusser of course – perhaps because he was so firmly rooted in the Western Marxist tradition, a Hegelian Marxist tradition. For me, the fact that Althusser was an ex-papist was important, though I never thought so at the time. My Catholic predilections for clarity, system, totality, rigour were all being caught up in a different form.

In an essay on Jameson from 1982 you point out that the famous slogan of The Political Unconscious *[1982] – 'Always historicize!' – isn't a specifically Marxist injunction, and you criticize him for failing to understand the ideological character of historicism, which implicitly posits a linear, homogenous concept of the historical process. Is that what you have in mind?*

There were various meanings of historicism hanging around and they were frequently conflated. I think that Fred, in keeping a lot of daylight between himself and Althusser, was probably rejecting an idea of historicism that wasn't Althusser's, which he somehow interpreted as a rejection of history as such. But I also think it's a grave mistake to imagine that historicizing is *ipso facto* a radical move.

Incidentally, can you recall the impact of Jameson's Marxism and Form, *which appeared in 1971?*

It was very important to me. One of the people who passed through the Marxist classes was James Atlas, a very bright man who became a journalist on the *New Yorker* and who now runs a publishing firm in New York. He said, 'Have you seen this book?' and gave me *Marxism and Form*. It was the first time I'd heard Jameson's name. (In fact, I still have that book. When I wrote a piece for Atlas recently I rang him in New York and said, 'Oh, by the way, do you want your Jameson book back? The fine must be mounting up.' He said, 'It's okay, I've read it.') The book was extraordinarily illuminating. I didn't quite know what was going on because I didn't know where this man was coming from. If somebody had told me that he was really a Central European called

Emile Gluckstein who had adopted the name Fredric Jameson under pressure from his publishers, it would have made more sense to me. I knew Jameson was at San Diego, but I was surprised by this late Frankfurt School connection. Later, he wrote a reader's report for *Marxism and Literary Criticism*, and then in 1976 I taught alongside him in San Diego for a semester.

I'd like to come back to that visit to the States. In the meantime, can I ask what it was about Marxism and Form *that seemed so illuminating?*

The beauty of the style. Here was a Marxist who could write, and this literary quality was indissociable from a scintillating intelligence. For me, as somebody who had only encountered Lukács a few years earlier, it was an introduction to thinkers I knew hardly anything about – Adorno and Benjamin and so on. All of that then fed into our Marxist classes, and we did a lot of intensive work on Benjamin in particular. Perry Anderson's *Considerations on Western Marxism* [1976], which was very helpful in putting this tradition in historical perspective, came out some time after. Materials were pouring in and there were all kinds of things that one could use. Jameson was an important part of that.

The debates about aesthetics among Western Marxists of the 1930s and 1940s were first appearing in translation in New Left Review *in the early and mid-1970s. These documents – by Lukács, Brecht, Bloch, Benjamin and Adorno – were later collected as* Aesthetics and Politics *[1977].*

I thought that was a superb collection. I still do. It was wonderfully timely and it revived for the present some utterly central issues and debates. It was beautifully edited and introduced, and was the product of a genuinely collective effort. In the years when I was in IS I got very interested in those sorts of debates, in Bolshevik cultural policy and the culture of the Weimar period. In fact, one of my roles in IS was to fill in the dimension of cultural politics. This involved doing a slightly different thing to what I was doing in the classes, so I was glad that these issues – which I had discussed in a confined space, as it were, to straight-down-the-line intellectual Marxists – suddenly opened up to a wider audience through the Verso book.

The one figure from the Western Marxist tradition that almost never crops up in your work – I'd be interested to know if he was discussed in the classes – is Ernst Bloch. On occasion you've seemed to echo him. In Ideology *[1991], for instance, you argue at one point that the present is non-identical: 'there is that within it which points beyond it, as indeed the shape of every historical present is shaped by its anticipation of a possible future.' In light of Bloch's reputation as the 'theologian of the revolution', as Jameson called him, appropriating Bloch's description of Thomas Müntzer, I'd expect him to be an important point of reference for you.*

I have read a little Bloch, and I have thought about him, but I've never felt confident in writing on him. Bloch was largely an absence in the Marxist seminars – though a prominent member of that seminar, Robin Gable, who was one of the founder members of Oxford English Limited, wrote a fine thesis on him. Bloch was the missing figure, to be sure – and a theological Marxist to boot, which ought to have inspired me to read him more attentively.

Could you say something, too, about the impact of The Country and the City *[1973]? Williams thanks you in its acknowledgements.*

I lived with that book in a way, because we talked about it a lot when he was deeply embroiled in the project. He found it curiously hard to finish. The issues touched him so nearly that I think it felt like the hardest thing he'd come to write. The book was quite monumental.

Among other things, it was a caveat against assuming too brashly that the English or British tradition had nothing to offer.

This is the first of Williams's books in which Marxism shapes the terms of debate; but it's noticeable that at no point does it mention Marx. Interestingly, a collection of essays called The Country and the City Revisited *appeared in 1999, stating that its intention was to connect Williams's analysis of urban and rural spaces with what it called 'current critical concerns'. It too contained no reference to Marx. Of course, in contrast to the book that it emulates, Marxism doesn't inform this collection at all. Do you think, though, that one consequence of Williams's celebration of the British tradition was a certain theoretical insularity?*

Yes. The least convincing section of that book is the one on the city, because it projects an interest in urban cosmopolitan experience that Williams might notionally have had but that wasn't a vital aspect of his personal life at all. I think the book is part of his whole attempt to work out a relationship with Marxism in that period. I believe that after I'd left Cambridge, he argued for a course called 'Marxism and Literature' in the English Faculty. I don't know if it was successful at that point in the early seventies. He was trying to define his position over, against, or in relationship to Marxism. On the whole, though, he just pursued his own projects, ploughed his own furrow – in a period when arguments and conflicts were raging. He was to a certain extent rather distant from those debates. I doubt, for example, that he ever read much Derrida or Foucault – for one thing, he wouldn't have been greatly sympathetic to that level of philosophical abstraction. He preferred someone like Bourdieu; and when the two of them met, what else would a Welshman and a Frenchman have in common to talk about but rugby?

Did you relate to others of Williams's generation – people like David Craig and Arnold Kettle – in the Marxist classes?

We'd looked at the British Marxist tradition of the 1930s a fair bit, but the contemporary current of 'CP Leavisism', as I used to call it, was not at all sympathetic or hospitable to what we were doing. Kettle, who was of course the first English professor at the Open University, wrote a rather hostile little piece on *Criticism and Ideology* in which he attacked it for its abstract jargon. Craig was much the same.

In the *Slant* days we had dialogues with the CP. I always thought they were dialoguing with us because they had little else to do. We rapidly found that we were far to the left of them, and there was really very little common ground. I spoke at one or two CP literary-type meetings, and I sensed an unholy alliance between a Leavisite sensuous particularism, which was deeply anti-theoretical, and a brand of CP vulgar Marxism, equally suspicious of airy-fairy ideas.

I'd like to move on to Myths of Power, *the 'Marxist Study of the Brontës' that you published in 1975. How do you situate that book today?*

I see *Myths of Power* very much as a transitional work in which I'm trying to find a way both to theorize and to keep one foot in the practical criticism camp. It was the most theoretically ambitious book that I'd written, in spite of its focus on canonical authors, and I felt that I'd achieved something theoretically. But it nonetheless failed to some extent to practice the sort of theory I set out the following year in *Criticism and Ideology*, where the literary text is the *production* of an ideological contradiction rather than simply a reflection of it. It risked a certain idealism, because it unintentionally suppressed the materiality of the text, its specific productive strategies and devices.

The most striking theoretical influence on this book is Lucien Goldmann, and specifically the idea of 'categorical structures' as a

*means of mediating between literary form and the social formation –
though you are in general fairly critical of his 'genetic structuralism'.
Goldmann gave a couple of lectures in Cambridge in 1970, didn't he?*

He did, but I missed them and I never met him. He died that same
year. Raymond liked him very much personally, and I heard about
them through him.

*In his memorial tribute, based on a lecture that he delivered in 1971,
Williams intimated that Goldmann enabled him to break free from
'a sense of certain absolute restrictions in English thought, restrictions
which seemed to link very closely with certain restrictions and deadlocks
in the larger society'. Did this resonate with you?*

Like many other Marxists working in literature at that time, I was
deeply impressed by Goldmann's work from my first encounter with
it. I was however from the outset a little suspicious of Goldmann's
homologies because of a new awareness of the contradictions
and perplexities between ideologies and class fractions. I was also
very much attracted by the Brechtian and Machereyan assault upon
organicism, and Goldmann could be read as a kind of left organicist.
In retrospect, I thought that the Althusserians' anti-humanism was
productive, but I nonetheless felt that this anti-humanism must
confront the problem of the subject. It had to confront the problem
of the subject given that we couldn't go back to essentially Hegelian
or homogenizing notions of the subject. That meant at once an
indebtedness to Marxist structuralism and a critical opposition to
it. For although there is of course a subject in Althusser, it is a
bleak and depressed and rather drooping subject, an attenuated
and subjected subject. Subsequently, I wanted less to rethink the
subject than to rethink the agent, to rethink the agent in a context
where unworkable ideas of agency, the agent as a transcendental
source, had been properly discredited.

So what role did Althusser play in Myths of Power? *In the introduction to the second edition you refer to its 'Althusserian background', and that background is immediately manifest in your use of the term 'overdetermination' to describe the Brontës' historical situation; but apart from that Althusser doesn't appear to be a potent presence in the book. He certainly doesn't displace Goldmann.*

No. The book is out of line, interestingly, with what I was generally thinking at the time in theoretical terms. Goldmann was never at the centre of my interest, and I did feel that Althusser had in many ways surpassed Goldmann. But it seemed to me that this particular theory could cast light on these particular texts, and it was to that extent still a text-centred book.

One of the impressions that I had from rereading Myths of Power, *incidentally, is that in one sense it's the banal, sociologizing appropriation of Marxist methodological techniques by liberal humanist critics that actually provoked it. I'm thinking of the references to Donald Davie and Graham Hough. Can you say something about the neutralization, or sociologization, of Marxism at this time?*

There was a current of that, though a fairly thin one. There were people in the early 1970s who called themselves sociologists of literature, and some of the people who later hung around the conferences on the 'sociology of literature' at Essex University in the late 1970s were similar. They were acceptable to the critical establishment. I suppose that in the Marxist class we had been doing some thinking about how to establish our differences from people like Malcolm Bradbury, who were writing books on the sociology of modern literature and so on. That work was of course very depoliticized, and it forced us to work out our differences from it. I think the Brontë book partly came out of that background.

Why did you decide to produce a study of the Brontës, to go back to the book's basic premise?

The seed of the book was an article I'd written for *Critical Quarterly* about power in Charlotte Brontë. *Myths of Power* was an extension of that article. At that stage I still didn't know what to write about. That lasted until *Marxism and Literary Criticism* [1976]. Bred as I was in the Cambridge way, I still felt that I had to write about authors. The Brontës interested me, of course, but I knew I didn't want to write about them in the conventional critical way.

Did they seem especially appropriate territory for a battle over critical methodologies in Oxford in the mid-seventies? More or less biographical studies of the Brontës by Winifred Gérin and Tom Winnifrith had appeared in the early seventies.

I don't think the book was a deliberate attempt to intervene in debates about interpreting the canon. We happened to take the Brontës' novels as exemplary texts in the Marxist class at one point, and people had done good work on *Wuthering Heights*. The idea of 'myths' was important because these were the latter days of Lévi-Strauss and structuralism, and we'd become interested in the question of history and myth. But I suppose there was also some continuity with the theme of exile, of the insider-outsider, that I'd explored in *Exiles and Émigrés*. That seemed to condense so many contradictions.

I wonder whether, if you'd written the book on the Brontës a couple of years after you did, you'd have replaced the concept of myth with some concept of ideology. In Exiles and Émigrés, *myth had functioned as the means by which modernists like Eliot and Yeats attempted to achieve a totalization of society in the absence of viable realist paradigms for representing it. I can see that it's still useful in the context of the Brontës, not least because of the biographical myth of the sisters themselves, the*

transposition of their contradictory historical situation into a universal,
supra-historical realm; but you seem to be reaching beyond it even as
you exploit it in that book.

There was no pressing need to combat mythological criticism at
the time, since it wasn't much in the air, so it wasn't for that reason.
I suppose I was beginning to explore the ambivalence of myth
as both ideology and utopia, and I found a way of doing that in
relation to the Brontës that seemed to be theoretically illuminating.
I certainly never felt I had to go toe-to-toe with Northrop Frye.
He was out of favour anyway. He once referred to me, when I
was briefly at Linacre College, as 'that loon from Linacre'. He also
wrote that what distinguished himself from other influential critics
was that he was a genius. Myth criticism doesn't seem to be too
good for the soul.

What about the 'imagination'? You remarked in the introduction to the
second edition of Myths of Power *that the book was 'too ready to take*
on board such essentially Romantic concepts as "the imagination"'.

I became a little sceptical of the idea of the imagination, exactly
because nobody ever seems to criticize it. It's one of those concepts,
like 'community' or 'compassion', which everyone reveres, and
this inspires the perverse side of me to question it. The creative
imagination, with the Romantics, is among other things a politically
transformative force; but a few decades later it came more or less
to substitute itself for that political change. There's an idealism,
philosophically, about the concept of the imagination, which in
different historical circumstances can go either left or right. In the
eighteenth century, it's certainly deeply tied up with a progressive
humanitarianism. I discuss this decentring of the egoistic self of
possessive individualism, which allows one to project oneself
empathetically into another's situation and experience emotional
solidarity with them, in the section on the Imaginary in *Trouble*
with Strangers. The imagination is all along an ethical category, and

represents one of the points where the ethical and the aesthetic blur and merge together.

Literature comes to be important partly because it allows us vicarious textual access to the lives of others, cut off as we are from them in actuality by the divisions and fragmentations of modernity. You can find out what it feels like to be Argentinean by reading certain novels, since you're never going to have enough money or leisure to find out by going there in person. The richness of the imagination, then, may paradoxically conceal a certain lack or poverty. It's very often a form of psychic compensation. The same goes for the Romantic idea that the imagination is the power by which one understands others' situation from the inside. It represents no position in itself. It is just the endless capacity to enter into and appropriate the positions of others, transcending them in the very act of possessing them – what Keats calls 'negative capability'. For all its undoubted value, I think this concept is historically tied up with the emergence of colonialism. The colonizer has no position or identity in himself – his position and identity lie simply in the act of entering into all other peoples' identities, indeed knowing them better than they know themselves. So this most selfless, generous-spirited of all aesthetic notions also perhaps carries with it the traces of a certain submerged history of violence.

At the same time, we should recognize that the imagination, as well as being a somewhat sublime idea, is also an integral part of everyday life – not, as the Romantics sometimes thought, something necessarily opposed to it. The simplest social interaction involves imagination. When I lift a cup to my lips, I do so because my imagination can foresee – drawing on previous experience – what the result will be. When I hear the sound of a diesel engine, the imagination tells me that the bus I'm waiting for is just about to arrive. Without such imagination, which really means making that which is absent present, we couldn't operate for a single day. There's this phenomenological sense of the imagination, which Merleau-Ponty among others explored, which is part of our *Lebenswelt* and not merely a specialized aesthetic category.

The most glaring omission of Myths of Power *is the issue of gender, and that's something for which you were subsequently attacked. As the Marxist-Feminist Literature Collective commented in the late 1970s: '[Eagleton's] treatment of Jane Eyre herself as an asexual representative of the upwardly-mobile bourgeoisie leads to a reductionist reading of the text. It neglects gender as a determinant by subsuming gender under class.'*

I was sternly rapped over the knuckles at the time for forgetting that the Brontës were women. Indeed, when Macmillan republished the book there was talk of it going into a series called 'Language, Discourse, Society'; but even though I thought I had made grovelling amends for this unfortunate omission in my new introduction, the editor of the series refused to include it. They brought out a new edition anyway but didn't put it in the series. I can't say I was suicidal about the fact.

There is however a sentence in the first edition in which you underline the fact that they were 'socially insecure women – members of a cruelly oppressed group whose victimized condition reflected a more widespread exploitation'. Presumably that was an emphasis that you didn't feel you could extend at the time.

No, I couldn't benefit from the work subsequently done on the Brontës by feminist critics like Sandra Gilbert and Susan Gubar; but I ought to have been more responsive to feminist views of them even so. At the same time, a lot of good feminist work on the Brontës, especially in the States, almost completely ignored the crucial class situation. So the exclusions weren't unilateral.

At the end of the introduction to the first edition of Myths of Power, *you state that 'the aim of historical criticism is not to add specialist footnotes to literature; like any authentic criticism, its intention is to possess the work more deeply.' I wondered what you think of that formulation in retrospect. What did you mean by 'possessing the work more deeply', for example?*

There's certainly a Leavisian resonance to that sentence, isn't there? In spite of that, though, I think I'd still defend the formulation. There were various positions in those years that the cultural left won, to put it crudely, and where we managed to make it hard for our opponents to argue certain cases. One was the issue of eternally fixed value; we won the battle to talk about the grounds and conditions of value, of valuation. We also won with the idea that history is inscribed in the work, so that in a genuine sense you aren't reading the words on the page unless you are reading them in a historical context. It was no longer a case of pitting the words on the page against some historical or sociological argument. The title of Jameson's *Marxism and Form* makes the point. From a very early point in the Marxist class I remember insisting on that emphasis on the historicity of form and the need to take form utterly seriously. That was partly because I believed in its importance, and partly strategic, because I saw how quickly we could be outflanked by the case that we were no more than reductive sociologizers.

You've subsequently argued that theory shouldn't have to justify itself simply in terms of its ability to do close reading better than practical criticism. It's a justification in itself, because it throws up various more or less closely related questions that are worth pursuing on their own terms or in relation to history. Does this notion of 'possessing the work more deeply' evince a residual embarrassment about using a theoretical language?

There are two points here. I did on the one hand want to assert the relative autonomy of theory. People sometimes used to say things like, 'It's almost as though the theory is more interesting than the text ...' My response was, 'Well, in the case of Freud versus Charles Kingsley's *Water Babies*, it is. So what!' Foucault is a lot more fascinating than A. E. Housman. Theory shouldn't only justify itself as a superior form of criticism. But when it does analyse a text, it can nevertheless possess it more fully.

In 'Ideology and Literary Form', which appeared in New Left Review *in 1975, an article that tests the thesis of* Criticism and Ideology, *the Leavisian traces in your thought disappear. This piece, your most important theoretical statement up to that point, elicited an interesting response from Francis Mulhern. He criticized it for its sociologism (ironically perhaps, in light of what you've been saying about the sociology of literature); and he complained that you seem to assume that class is the only material determinant of consciousness, and so ignore national and cultural form as much as you ignore sexuality and biology. He also argued that you fail to grasp that the ideology of the text is internal to its form. In effect, then, he positioned himself on the side of formalism and you on the side of historicism.*

Both positions became too extreme. I remember being very impressed by Francis's response, though it did indeed strike me as too formalistic. Incidentally, Francis was an editor at New Left Books when *Criticism and Ideology* was submitted for publication. He liked the project, but he was fairly acerbic in his criticisms. He was very confident and extremely bright and judicious, in his canny, circumspect Ulster way. And indeed his criticisms of my book were apposite for the most part; but they were rather severe, in the manner of earnest young male intellectuals. I was just the same myself.

Pierre Macherey's Theory of Literary Production *[1966], which informs both* Myths of Power *and, more deeply,* Criticism and Ideology, *didn't appear in English translation until 1978. It is obviously of decisive importance for your theoretical development. When did you first encounter it?*

I read it in French some time after the move to Oxford. Then I wrote an article on Macherey for the *Minnesota Review* in 1975, when he

was still little-known in Britain. That was quite a useful piece
for disseminating his ideas. Macherey himself came to one of the
'Sociology and Literature' conferences at Essex. He was wearing a
suit that was so many sizes too big for him that we wondered whether
the real Macherey had been hijacked on the way from Calais, to be
replaced by some dwarfish impersonator. I remember attempting in
very poor French to give him some idea of how influential his book
had been. He wryly responded, 'Well, I'm a philosopher, I don't
really understand the success of this book at all.' He very much
played it down. I think of all of the various books that were coming
in it influenced me very deeply. I remember Perry Anderson, who'd
read it quite soon after it came out, being somewhat amused by
this. I don't think Perry thought all that much of it, and I got the
impression that he wondered why I did. In fact, it's a good question.
I think there are all kinds of things wrong with it – a few of which I
mentioned in my article on him – but I thought it was a profoundly
original work. For a while it was a key text for us.

I think I found the Althusserian notion of symptomatic reading
particularly valuable at this time. It seems to me that Macherey's
work was an excellent piece of deconstruction, but it wasn't taken
up by the deconstructionists, no doubt because he was talking
not just about presence but about property. Macherey was a
communist, a known ally of Althusser, and therefore in many ways
less fashionable and acceptable than other actors, like Derrida,
whose *Of Grammatology* [1966] appeared in the same year as *A
Theory of Literary Production*.

*Thinking about your subsequent work, it seems to me that one of the things
that might have been attractive to you is the way in which Macherey's
book combines Freud and Marx, though without committing itself to
Freudo-Marxism. It is interested in Freud as a reader of texts and of
the codes and processes by which they are constituted.*

Macherey doesn't mention Freud much, does he? Yet he's certainly
there throughout the book as a subtext. Yes, I thought that the idea

of the unconscious of the text was extremely powerful. I think one can productively speak of the unconscious of the text as long as one is alive to the perils of anthropomorphizing the work in this way. I don't think the unconscious subtext is that of the author. That isn't to say that authors don't have unconscious as well as conscious intentions. Intentionality for Freud is by no means always conscious. The text has an unconscious because, like any piece of language or any human subject, it is by virtue of its performative statements inevitably caught up in a network of significations that exceeds and sometimes subverts that performance, and which it can't fully control. And this unconscious is not just some more-than-text that is beyond the work's control; it's a lack of control, a way in which the text evades itself and is non-identical with itself, which is inscribed within the text itself and without which it would be able to say nothing at all.

I also remember being profoundly struck – though perhaps this was naivety – by Macherey's emphasis on the constitutive disunity of the text. It seemed to me – not that he makes this point explicitly – that from Aristotle to I. A. Richards unity is a crucial postulate. It's astonishing how long-lived and consistent the dogma of the unity of the work is, how long it goes unchallenged. Although Macherey doesn't refer to it, an entire history of avant-gardism stood behind him in this respect. He was putting a detonator under a sacred tenet of criticism – the idea that everything has to hang together, that there mustn't be a hair out of place. Literary fetishism, really.

There's a certain constitutive disunity to A Theory of Literary Production *too, isn't there? The English translation of the book's title is of course misleading, because in French its title is* Pour une théorie de la production littéraire. *In English it's reified in the form of an apparently completed, self-contained theory of literary production. In fact, the book has a rather provisional, piecemeal structure because it consists of a series of fragmentary essays to which Macherey added the appendix containing Lenin's articles on Tolstoy. Did its formal composition interest you?*

Yes, precisely because it consisted of these tentative little conceptual forays. The first section is called 'Some Elementary Concepts', and he just works through a series of ideas. I was attracted by the terseness and the unpretentiousness of that. Formally speaking, it wasn't a bloated thesis. But it contained an argument that I thought was quietly subversive. It was a massive assault on some of the most sacred of literary-critical cows.

Reading

Althusser, Louis, 'Marxism and Humanism', in *For Marx*, trans. Ben Brewster (London: Verso, 1990), pp. 219–47.

Bloch, Ernst, et al., *Aesthetics and Politics*, trans. Ronald Taylor et al. (London: New Left Books, 1977).

Eagleton, Terry, 'Myth and History in Recent Poetry', in *British Poetry since 1960: A Critical Survey*, eds. Michael Schmidt and Grevel Lindop (Oxford: Carcanet, 1972), pp. 233–9.

Eagleton, Terry, 'Class, Power and Charlotte Brontë', *Critical Quarterly* 14:3 (1972), pp. 225–35.

Eagleton, Terry, *Myths of Power: A Marxist Study of the Brontës* (London: Macmillan, 1975).

Eagleton, Terry, 'Ideology and Literary Form', *New Left Review* 1:90 (1975), pp. 81–109.

Eagleton, Terry, 'Reply to Francis Mulhern', *New Left Review* 1:92 (1975), pp. 107–8.

Eagleton, Terry, '*Aesthetics and Politics*', *New Left Review* 1:107 (1978), pp. 21–34.

Eagleton, Terry, 'Interview: Terry Eagleton' (with James H. Kavanagh and Thomas E. Lewis), *Diacritics* 12:1 (1982), pp. 53–64.

Eagleton, Terry, 'Pierre Macherey and Marxist Literary Theory', *Philosophy* 14 (1982), pp. 145–55 (repr. in *Against the Grain*, pp. 1–8).

Eagleton, Terry, 'Fredric Jameson: The Politics of Style', *Diacritics* 12:3 (1982), pp. 14–22 (repr. in *Against the Grain*, pp. 65–78).

Eagleton, Terry, 'Criticism and Ideology: Andrew Milner Interviews Terry Eagleton', in *Thesis Eleven* 12 (1985), pp. 130–44.

Eagleton, Terry, *Against the Grain: Essays 1975–1985* (London: Verso, 1986).

Eagleton, Terry, 'Two Approaches to the Sociology of Literature', *Critical Inquiry* 14:3 (1988), pp. 469–76.

Eagleton, Terry, 'The Ballad of Marxist Criticism', in *The Eagleton Reader*, ed. Stephen Regan (Oxford: Blackwell, 1998), p. 400.

Eagleton, Terry, *Myths of Power: A Marxist Study of the Brontës*, anniversary edition (Basingstoke: Palgrave Macmillan, 2005).

Eagleton, Terry, *How to Read a Poem* (Oxford: Blackwell, 2007).

Eagleton, Terry, 'Must We Always Historicize?' *Foreign Literature Studies* 30:6 (2008), pp. 9–14.

Gérin, Winifred, *Emily Brontë* (Oxford: Clarendon, 1971).

Kettle, Arnold, 'Literature and Ideology', *Red Letter* 1 (1976), pp. 3–5.

Maclean, Gerald, Donna Landry, Joseph P. Ward, eds., *The Country and the City Revisited: England and the Politics of Culture, 1550–1850* (Cambridge: Cambridge University Press, 1999).

Mulhern, Francis, '"Ideology and Literary Form" – A Comment', *New Left Review* 1:91 (1975), pp. 80–7.

Williams, Raymond, *Marxism and Literature* (Oxford: Oxford University Press, 1977).

Williams, Raymond, 'Literature and Sociology: In Memory of Lucien Goldmann', in *Problems in Materialism and Culture: Selected Essays* (London: Verso, 1980), pp. 11–30.

Winnifrith, Tom, *The Brontës and their Background* (London: Macmillan, 1973).

CHAPTER FIVE

Criticism/Ideology

So you taught alongside Fredric Jameson as a visiting professor at the University of California, San Diego, in 1976. How did that come about?

It wasn't Jameson's idea. A colleague of Jameson who'd come across me invited me and I went over there for ten weeks or so. Universities never know what to do with visiting professors – it's a David Lodge-like anomaly – so they locked me in this little apartment overlooking the Pacific and left me there. Finally someone came back to visit me and found I was still alive. I taught thirty-odd postgraduates who had come to work with Jameson in a whole range of areas. One of them was his wife, Susan Willis. I had regular classes with these students and also some individual sessions with them. I taught an undergraduate class too. That was the first time I'd met Jameson, and we got to know each other pretty well. We shared a great deal politically and intellectually, but were temperamentally very different.

Did you come across theoretical material in this context that you hadn't encountered before?

It was probably my first proper introduction to the work of Bakhtin, who'd been no more than a name to me before. I also met Herbert Marcuse, who was still based at San Diego, although he had retired. I remember him saying to me, 'Who is important in Britain today?' And I said, 'Well, Raymond Williams is doing some very interesting work with affinities to your own.' 'Williams? Williams?' he responded. 'No, no I don't think I know this name.' In a mildly historic moment, I stood over Marcuse while he laboriously wrote down *Culture and Society* and various other titles. I think that Raymond, for his part, was pretty conscious of Marcuse's work.

In the same year you published two important books, Marxism and Literary Criticism *and* Criticism and Ideology. *This established a distinctive pattern, of publishing an introductory book and a more specialized theoretical one almost simultaneously. Did you set out deliberately to be double-handed in your approach to the ideas that you were thinking through?*

No, it wasn't conscious, but you're right that it started there. *Marxism and Literary Criticism* was initially commissioned by Methuen for the 'Critical Idiom' series, which was attempting to expand beyond metaphor and the semicolon and similar topics that it had effectively exhausted. What I was actually getting together at the time was the material for *Criticism and Ideology*, so it was a spin-off from that. But I suppose this did become a conscious pattern later on, in the sense that I discovered I enjoyed popularizing and thought I was quite good at it. *Marxism and Literary Criticism* was the first example of that. From then on I've tended to alternate more difficult and more popular work. I wish Homi Bhabha would do the same . . .

Criticism and Ideology *was the equivalent of what Fredric Jameson has called his 'laboratory experiments'; and like a laboratory experiment it was shaped by a collective intellectual effort, in the form of the Marxist classes. Could you start by saying something about what you refer to in the preface as the 'whole hinterland of cooperative effort, not to speak of a whole political culture' that informed the book's composition.*

There was an enormous amount of input in that book from all kinds of people, and particularly from those who attended the Marxist classes. The book talks a bit about the 'death of the author', and it is almost an example of that in itself, in the sense that a whole set of forces and processes converged in it. Of all the books I've written I see that one as most purely a product of its moment. I had an intense desire to resolve certain problems at this time. Often in those sessions in Oxford we were pretty much shooting in the dark. As an example, let's take the schematic relation between ideology and history, or ideology and the text. So many variants of that were circulating, so many different models, that there was a lot of creative confusion. I remember sitting in a cottage in Galway discussing the question with Francis Barker, who was central to the debate but who sadly died in 1999. He was in the IMG at the time, and so represented another point of contact between militant politics and what was happening intellectually. We used to argue for hours about the different models of literary production, reproduction, transmission. They were rather arcane epistemological issues – I think we vastly overestimated the importance of epistemology in that period – but they became a vehicle for other more practical debates. I felt that we had to get some clarity on these issues. They were becoming very clouded, and of course they were often inherently intractable questions. That was the project of *Criticism and Ideology*.

Were others interested in the question of aesthetic value, which was distinctly unfashionable on the left at this time? You discuss it in some detail and, inspired perhaps by Brecht, insist on retaining a transitive conception of value.

I was more out on a limb there. There was a rather prudish, puritanical disavowal of the value question at this time. Some people who were quite active in the class thought that the whole project was completely irrelevant and even slightly suspect. Ann Wordsworth, for example, thought that an attention to value was a grave humanistic lapse. But at the same time I always resisted the right-wing suggestion that value had been ditched altogether. I don't think it had been; it's simply that a lot of people didn't know what to do with it. I'd always thought it was important, and indeed thought it was an élitist position to deny the importance of value. I now think that the attempt to address that problem in the book is pretty inadequate. Everyone evaluates all the time, and I don't just mean in artistic matters.

Today I'd probably want to be more conjunctural about value than I was in *Criticism and Ideology*. I'd want to say that when we analyse the question of value we are analysing the ideological and psychoanalytic questions of consumption. I'd want however to add – in order to qualify what may be an excessive conjuncturalism – that one of the factors that may well be dominant in that is the moment of production. It is because the text is produced as such that it speaks to certain people in a certain situation, however dispersed the two moments may be historically. In *Criticism and Ideology* I was trying very inadequately to cling to both of those poles, and, while making value transitive, to avoid the increasingly fashionable position that thinks it can wholly disregard the question of production when looking at the value question.

Did it surprise you that Criticism and Ideology *was read by many simply as a transposition of Althusserian categories into literature?*

Yes and no. 'No' in the sense that that's clearly part of what's going on in it; it accounts for a lot of it. 'Yes' in the sense that, as I said before, I certainly didn't see it as a doctrinaire piece of Althusserianism. And I still felt sufficiently influenced by other sources, though maybe that didn't come through. Williams was simply one example. There was also a growing interest in post-structuralism, though that's rather stiffly dealt with in the book itself. I think that it was too quickly labelled as Althusserian. While there is no single major concept of Althusser's that I would not have serious reservations about, and did not have serious reservations about even when writing *Criticism and Ideology*, as a style or frame of thinking Althusserianism was nonetheless valuable then, and not least in its reaction against Hegelian Marxist criticism.

I would highlight a couple of areas of Althusserianism that I found on the one hand productive in combating various Hegelian Marxist theories, but on the other hand related to Stalinism. One is the clear theoreticism of Althusser's early insistence on the effective autonomy of theoretical practice. In so far as that is trying to bend the stick against a historicist notion of theory, whereby any theory would be no more than the self-consciousness of the revolutionary class, it is a necessary insistence on the specificity of theoretical production. At the same time, it raises grievous epistemological problems. For example, Althusser ominously draws many of his models of theoretical practice from mathematics; and there is almost no concern with the problem of evidence in the relation between theory and practice. Although I felt uneasy about that at the time of *Criticism and Ideology*, I subsequently felt the need to relate that much more firmly to a very specific history of Althusser's fight within the PCF [Parti Communiste Français] – as a kind of closet left Maoist sympathizer attempting to establish a theoretical position within the PCF primarily by establishing the autonomy of theory, by appealing to Marx and Engels and Lenin in ways he could use against a certain practice in the PCF.

The other point is that in the writing of *Criticism and Ideology* I was much too uncritical of the expansionist definition of ideology in Althusser, which I also think is related to Stalinism. If ideology becomes effectively coterminous with reality, as the early Nicos Poulantzas wrote, then it's deprived of any political cutting-edge as a concept. It has been removed from the terrain of class struggle and becomes primarily an epistemological category, one that is synonymous with culture or lived experience. That relates to the suppression of the class struggle in Althusser, which I find also mars the essay on ISAs [Ideological State Apparatuses]. There is an apparently inexorable subjecting of the subject to what look like suspiciously monolithic or superego-like ISAs – which seems a drastic simplification of the real, contradictory process of interpellation found in any particular social formation. I think Althusser misunderstands Lacan's categories of Imaginary and Symbolic here. Althusser's notion of the subject being subjected through interpellation looks very much like the censoring moment of the superego, what in Lacan's system would figure as the birth of the subject. But in fact Althusser is talking about the imaginary; he's talking about the ego, which is obviously for Lacan the tip of the iceberg of the subject. So there are definite confusions in Althusser's appropriation of Lacan.

Criticism and Ideology *seems to me not the last monument to structuralist Marxism, as it's sometimes assumed it is, so much as one of the first interventions in a period in which Marxism has to take the measure of post-structuralism. There's even a prescient reference to 'post-modernist literature' at one point. To what extent were you conscious of the gravitational pull of post-structuralism?*

That's an interesting question. Although most of what I say about post-structuralism in the book is somewhat negative, I was actually becoming more aware of it and also more interested in it. In Oxford, we were trying to build a certain materialist case, to stake out a certain terrain; but there were alternatives, particularly the journal *Screen*, which was very Cambridge in its rigour and austerity and its coterie nature (in some ways one could draw parallels between *Screen* and *Scrutiny*). Of course, Stephen Heath and others were far more open to post-structuralism, to Barthes and Kristeva, than we were, but we were certainly aware of them and were trying to deal with them. The difference was that we were trying to relate to them as self-conscious Marxists. *Screen* tended to append Marxism somewhat lamely, almost as a pious afterthought. So there was an important political difference there.

Were you incipiently aware of the emergence of post-Marxism, then, in the form perhaps of post-structuralism?

Yes, absolutely. There was an important phase in the class from the late seventies and in the eighties when Barry Hindess and Paul Hirst were extraordinarily popular and influential, and in a way that one felt must correspond to a certain historical moment. That obviously interested people in this Oxford setting, particularly people like Ann Wordsworth. Neither Hindess nor Hirst actually spoke at the class, but various people like Tony Bennett who were effectively post-Marxists did. I was certainly following their work with great interest, particularly noting the way that people moved from high Althusserianism to post-Althusserianism and then out of Marxism altogether, as Hirst did. This seemed a kind of law. They were deconstructing themselves out of a case, with very specific political effects. It was really all about the end of the left's brief era of flourishing.

Could you reconstruct the sense in which you were using the terms 'science' and 'scientific criticism' in Criticism and Ideology? *These are not terms that you interrogate particularly closely in the book, perhaps because you felt confident enough not to have to defend them pre-emptively against the inevitable liberal misunderstandings of them.*

The terms 'science' and 'scientificity' were of course very much in currency in leftist circles at the time, particularly cultural or literary ones, and I think that my own failure to unpack them reflected a general failure to do so. They were too easily taken for granted. I remember classes in which there was some discussion of what was meant by 'science', and of the relation of that to theory and to ideology. I think we needed to do a lot more work on it than we actually did. For example, in spite of the problematical notion of the word 'science', we never really discriminated sufficiently between what might be described as a science of the text, or those aspects of the literary text that might in some sense be said to be amenable to a science of ideologies or a science of forms, and the more discursive or rhetorical aspects of a text that couldn't be reduced in that way. But in a sense that whole vogue was over before we'd even worked out the questions, let alone the answers.

What role do you think the scientific categories that you devised for a Marxist criticism in Criticism and Ideology *played in your subsequent work? Not perhaps as great as one might have expected . . .*

No, I think they were so bound up with that moment that when that moment passed their relevance seemed to fade. Perhaps it shouldn't have done. I suppose one could imagine a possible trajectory where I'd followed up on the categories I'd devised in *Criticism and Ideology* and actually produced works of materialist criticism drawing upon them. I didn't do that and I'm not quite sure why I didn't. The next project was the Benjamin book, which was on a different tack. I was less and less interested in writing about individual authors, though the Richardson book and the one on Shakespeare were exceptions to that. I could nonetheless see how the categories for a materialist criticism constructed in *Criticism and Ideology* might have been taken up – either by myself or somebody else – and worked through. Norman Feltes, who'd attended the classes, wrote a book called *Modes of Production of Victorian Novels* [1986], and that was deeply indebted to my book. And I came across the odd concept from the book from time to time, but not perhaps as much as I might have wished. There were a lot of positive responses to the book but little sense of taking it forward, though it was actually the kind of project that could have been. In a strange way, some of my concepts pointed forward towards Williams's concept of cultural materialism – not that he deliberately took up those concepts. There were parallel developments that never really intersected.

Tell me about Norman Feltes, whose work I've always admired.

He was an American who had fought as a Marine in Korea, but gave up his American citizenship over Vietnam and became a Canadian. He taught in the southern States during the civil rights movement and went on civil rights marches, but since he was six foot eight inches tall he was strongly advised to get out of the place quick, before he was killed, which he did. He lectured at York University in Toronto and then came to Oxford on a sabbatical year. He too had a Catholic background. He came to the Marxist class and, in a typical Norman gesture, tore up the lecture notes he had been using and announced that he had to start again! It wasn't so much me that he'd discovered as Althusser, and that then fed into his Victorian work. He ultimately retired from York University because he was very dissatisfied with academic work. In his final years, just before he died, he went and worked in a homeless project in Toronto. He was a close friend and comrade at Oxford at the time.

One criticism that has often been made about Criticism and Ideology *– it's one that you've accepted pretty readily – is that in spite of its discussion of value it neglected to theorize the consumption of the literary text. To me that seems understandable, because at this time literary criticism in its institutionalized form was still residually a part of that patrician tradition defined by 'taste'. In Althusser's dismissive phrase, it was a form of gastronomy. Commenting on Cremonini, Althusser had emphatically announced that 'we have to abandon the categories of the aesthetics of consumption'.*

How fitting in this context that my Cambridge tutor became a wine merchant . . . On the one hand, I think that quite a lot of what I said in the book about literary production stands, despite the absence of a real reception theory. I became interested in reception theory rather later, although much of it was cast in a philosophically idealist mode. On the other hand, I did sometimes ask myself the question – rather idly – 'How different would the thesis of the chapter on the science of the text look if one were to introduce the readerly dimension?' That was a project that I never followed through: the development of a materialist reception theory.

It might be interesting to see reception theory, like all other recent literary practices, as having its roots back in the 1960s. I played with this idea in a piece I wrote called 'The Revolt of the Reader' [1982]. Readers demanded participation, just as within that climate demands for democratic participation of various kinds were clearly very strong. It would be interesting to trace the development of reception theory in the various institutional changes, demands and programmes that are characteristic of the 1960s. At the same time, one has to say that much standard reception theory has been criticized for positing a reader who is very often merely a function of contemporary reading formations, and not a function of the whole political system as well. We are never simply in the first place readers. Nor can we put the rest of our existence magically into suspension when we approach a text. There is a danger of a kind of left academicism there, which would seem to presume that the classroom is the only place in which meanings are constructed. That obviously has to be challenged. The other problem in relation to the work of left reception theories is the emphasis on consumption, which can sometimes lead to a kind of carnival of consumerism or a fetishism of the immediate reading conjuncture. This can be just as narrowly dehistoricized in its own way as the more standard forms of bourgeois criticism. We are always more than the current reading conjuncture.

Did you see Criticism and Ideology *as exclusively concerned with the literary text, or did you see it more broadly as a work of Marxist aesthetics? I imagine that once again this question relates to the focus of the Marxist classes.*

The seminars were mostly literary-based because most of the people were literary, but there was certainly an interest from the beginning in a more general Marxist aesthetics. We were reading

people like Ernst Fischer and Herbert Marcuse. I was certainly
interested in aesthetics more generally. And although the book is
very literary-centred, I hoped that this duality was reflected in the
book, and that it could serve as a contribution to a wider theme
– which I then more consciously explored in *The Ideology of the
Aesthetic* [1990]. Even at that point I resisted the attempt to ditch
the concept of the aesthetic associated with the discourse analysts.
That was partly because I could see that the Russian Formalists and
the semioticians had done such interesting things with it. It was
partly because I thought that the anti-aestheticians were making
a mistake in reducing aesthetics to the question of beauty or value
or both – which is indeed what they were doing. They simplified
an extraordinarily complex issue into a couple of items and then
wrote them off in a rather lordly way. In fact, as Jameson said in
his blurb for *The Ideology of the Aesthetic*, aesthetics is a concept
that we needed to turn back to in order to make sense of it again in
a new context.

You don't actually discuss culture much in Criticism and Ideology.
*At one point, interestingly, you refer to an 'ideology of the aesthetic',
which you include in the category of 'aesthetic ideology', and you
define it as 'a signification of the function, meaning and value of
the aesthetic itself within a particular social formation, which is in
turn part of an "ideology of culture" included within GI [general
ideology]'. Might this idea of a 'cultural ideology' have been a
helpful mediating concept?*

It might have been. I've had some interesting discussions since
then with students on the differences between culture and ideology.
I don't know why culture is missing as a category there. It's
possible that I saw it as too tied up with Williams's work. Maybe
I was trying to break with that. It wasn't a fashionable concept
in that Althusserian world. Culture as a concept comes back with
postmodernism, after its long sojourn with anthropology.

Can I ask you about Williams's response to Criticism and Ideology*? Interviewed in the journal* Red Shift *in 1977, Williams conceded that he'd accept much of your account of him; but he also said, 'What I want to ask is who Eagleton is . . .'*

'. . .Where is he coming from?'

Exactly. He continued: 'The basic fault of the kind of formalist Marxism which Eagleton is now in is that it assumes that by an act of intellectual abstraction you can place yourself above the lived contradictions both of the society and of any individual you choose to analyse, and that you yourself are not in question.'

I remember reading that, actually, almost by chance. But he'd written to me before that piece appeared to say what he says there. He agreed with quite a lot of my critique of him. Rather frustratingly, he said, 'I'm sure you know what I agree with' — I didn't, actually. I suppose the increasing distance that Raymond took from his own early work, *Culture and Society* and so on, might have been part of that. As for his comments on me, I think they reveal a typical suspicion of abstraction.

What about his substantive criticism that you'd situated yourself at a point of transcendence?

I think he was correct, but I resisted it at the time because I was still too affected by the idea of theory as unhistorical, and also too wary of the alternative to that being an excessive relativism. It wasn't long before I came to understand that 'Who is Terry Eagleton?' was quite a good question. It's one I often ask myself. I suppose I thought – and probably still do think – that Raymond was bending the stick too far the other way. He was apparently suggesting that one couldn't distance these contradictions analytically, or that it wasn't politically necessary to do so. His response to the book is rather like his response to modernism, isn't it? In *The Politics of Modernism* [1989] he finds this arm's-length attitude bracing but also cold. My point had of course been that he was on the contrary too ready to endorse the 'lived', which is the term he uses there.

The irony underlined by Raymond's comment is that, as I've said, more than any of my other works *Criticism and Ideology* was indeed a historical product. It was a historical product that for historical reasons put too much emphasis on the ahistoricity of theory. No doubt that was partly to do with a certain sense of ebullience on the part of the left, a sense that it had the resources, the conceptual vigour, to analyse as if from nowhere. So I'd agree with Raymond's comment now, in the sense that I'm very much aware of how historically rooted the book was. If that's what 'Who is Terry Eagleton?' means, then that would be the answer. If it means 'Theory has to be a reflex of lived experience', then I'm tempted to reply with Foucault: 'What does it matter who is writing? What does it matter where I'm coming from?' What mattered about Williams's own arguments was how valid they were. This isn't entirely irrelevant to his personal background. But it isn't reducible to it either.

There are some ways in which Criticism and Ideology *seems continuous with Williams's thought rather than discontinuous with it. I'm thinking for example of his definition from the early 1970s of what constitutes 'the specific literary phenomenon': 'the dramatization of a process, the making of a fiction, in which the constituting elements, of real social life and beliefs, were simultaneously actualized and in an important way differently experienced, the difference residing in the imaginative act, the imaginative method, the specific and genuinely unprecedented imaginative organization.' In its talk of experience, 'real social life', etc., this sentence is obviously infused with Williams's distinctive critical temperament. Perhaps it also contains traces of Goldmann's slightly suspect distinction between 'actual consciousness' and 'possible consciousness'. In its emphasis on the 'dramatization' of ideological relations, though, it also seems fairly close to your argument in* Criticism and Ideology *about the 'production' of ideology.*

It is. Raymond later wrote an article in *New Left Review* that discriminates between those apparently radical theories that he thought fitted the orthodox paradigm, and those that interestingly challenge it. There are forms of formalism and semiotics that he thinks are perfectly compatible with the dominant critical model, and then there's his notion of cultural materialism, which challenges it. I suppose he felt that *Criticism and Ideology* fell too much into that first category – that in spite of the high jinks it got up to conceptually, it left the received idea of the text in place. Incidentally, 'text' was a word he wouldn't use; he preferred 'work'. There wasn't enough emphasis on labour for him in *Criticism and Ideology*. I do talk about the production of the work, but for him it was probably too intellectualized. Raymond was becoming more and more interested in the social history of dramatic form or fiction. That's a long way from my own book.

The theatre is an important metaphor for discussing the 'production of ideology' in your book. Could you say something about the theoretical role that the idea of dramatization played in the chapter called 'Towards a Science of the Text'? Was drama emerging as a particular interest?

I think there was a certain hinterland to that concept in *Criticism and Ideology*, which as it stands remains a strictly abstract or, you might say, metaphorical one. I had always been interested in theatre, and was acting in an amateur way when I was eighteen. I think I'd been thinking about the idea of the text as a production some time before I formulated it in *Criticism and Ideology*. But somehow the Althusserian framework enabled me to crystallize it.

Can I ask you about the style of Criticism and Ideology*? You've been relatively critical of its puritanical high-mindedness. Others, like E. P. Thompson, strenuously objected to its use of acronyms. The book is informed by an intense intellectual excitement, but at times it fails to transmit that at the level of the sentence itself.*

It does. It was an exciting and fulfilling project to work on because I did feel I was doing something quite important. I felt I was making a fairly coherent statement and drawing together things that were in the air. On the other hand, if you contrast the style of that book and the style of the book on Benjamin a few years later, the difference is clear.

Having said that, stylistically speaking it's actually a much more heterogeneous book than it's often taken to be. The polemical critique of Williams is pretty compelling, for example. So there's a contradiction in some of the responses to Criticism and Ideology, *which complain both that it's too abstract and that it's too polemical.*

That's true. The critique of Williams is the most polemical of the chapters, and that caught up something different in me that the others didn't.

Anthony Barnett rebutted the critique of Williams in New Left Review. *Did his defence of Williams reflect broader divisions on the left, do you think?*

Yes, probably. Barnett stood on what might be politely called the more moderate edge of the left at the time. I believe that since then he may have fallen off it altogether. In other words, Barnett's essay has to be taken in the context of his own growing hostility to the revolutionary left, of which he became almost a professional critic. I remember Barnett speaking about Williams at a memorial conference for him, and telling somebody later that he had set out to rescue him from the Trotskyists. Then Tariq Ali stood up and said, 'What I remember of Raymond is that he was a comrade.' That's not a note that Barnett would have struck. So in that sense there were political conflicts at stake here. I've said already that I would still defend most of what I said about Williams, but I think the tone was wrong. It should have been more comradely and more respectful.

Barnett says at one point that 'the art of polemic is something that most of us on the left have still to learn.' In a sense you're making the same point as him. Polemics are something that you subsequently addressed quite directly in your work. You deliberately developed a polemical rhetoric.

I did, although I don't know about 'deliberately'; it also came naturally to me. It's a mode in which I feel at home, as I've said before. In a sense I think there's too little of it in this area. I've always pointed to Jameson's failure to polemicize, although I admire him enormously in other ways. Polemic and satire are ways of breaking with a certain academic style that a lot of American cultural leftists seem not to challenge or even be aware of. On the other hand, I'm sometimes told that my work is abrasive even when I wasn't aware of this when writing it.

Chapter 4 of Criticism *and* Ideology *consists of short sections on canonical authors in which you systematically critique the ideology of organicism from its emergence in the late eighteenth century. This emphasis, however, provoked the criticism that the book is excessively canonical in its approach to literature.*

I wouldn't really want to counter that criticism. It's certainly a limitation of that book, but it's a limitation of my work in general. One reason for that canonicity was that the book emerged so much out of my teaching, and of course at Oxford that was largely focused on canonical authors. I've not written on film or television, for example, whereas Williams did. Williams also worked on Welsh literature, although I too finally strayed beyond the English canon by writing about Ireland and Irish culture. In fact, canonically speaking, my work on Irish literature roams around a great deal more than my work on English literature. Perhaps the distinctions between high and low, or high and popular, are not so clear in Ireland.

In the section on George Eliot in Chapter 4 you write that 'the phrase "George Eliot" signifies nothing more than the insertion of certain specific ideological determinations [. . .] into a hegemonic ideological formation'. It's a striking formulation, and one that upset some of the book's critics. You don't refer to the relevant articles, but presumably you'd read Barthes and Foucault on the author . . .

I think I had. Certainly the idea of 'the death of the author' was much in the air. To use a phrase of Derrida's that I only came across later, I wanted to 'dislodge rather than liquidate' the subject – although there's a fair amount of liquidation of a rather brutal kind going on in that particular sentence. In general I wanted to retain the concept of authorship, though. I remember one of my students saying to me, 'Do you really need the category of Authorial Ideology? Isn't that itself reducible to some combination of Aesthetic and General Ideologies?' I was reluctant to let that go. While being generally anti-humanistic as far as the author went, I'd always held that there are occasions when knowing that two texts were written by the same author might cast interesting light on them. It seems a very commonsensical point of view, but it's one that was much criticized at the time. Not all theories of authorship need to be Great Man theories.

George Eliot is in a sense a cunning choice of author in this context, since as a pseudonymous name it is already a rhetorical stratagem – an 'author function' in Foucauldian terms. There are lots of examples you could have taken from the canon – D. H. Lawrence for instance – such that the same claim might have sounded, at least superficially, more extreme.

There is an interesting inconsistency within *Criticism and Ideology* on that score, because while in that section of the book the author is dispersed into wider ideological formations, in an earlier section the concept of Authorial Ideology is retained. I think that the concept of agency interests me more from the standpoint of revolutionary politics than from the standpoint of analysing literary texts. You mustn't throw out the political agent along with the humanist subject. Shortly after this book I became more attuned to cultural practice and production, more engaged with questions of enjoyment, questions of pleasure. But I don't think that contradicts what I was doing in *Criticism and Ideology*, which was a different kind of textual analysis.

A further criticism of Chapter 4, one that a couple of critics raised at the time, is that your analysis of authors like Eliot and Lawrence is fatally limited to ideologies, and that there's little attempt to come to terms with the economic and political complexities of the period. On the one hand, then, you were accused of not doing enough practical criticism; and on the other hand you were accused of not thinking about politics and economics enough.

Which for a Marxist critic doesn't leave very much, does it? Yet a third criticism – which has I think a lot of justice – is that in being too influenced by a certain version of the Althusserian concept of ideology, I wasn't looking at what might be potentially progressive or radical about those texts. The book operates far too much with a hermeneutic of suspicion rather than with a hermeneutic of redemption. That's a sign of the excessively negative, tight-lipped, begrudging people we were. Ironically, I was at the time intensely interested in the social and economic history of the nineteenth century, which had been my original academic patch. I taught it a lot, and I always try to teach it in that historical way. But it's true that this gets lost in that highly compressed format.

And the point about practical criticism? You'd originally planned to include a chapter on Conrad's The Secret Agent, *I understand, but then decided to place it in the* Sociological Review *instead.*

That article was so to speak stolen from a huge pile of notes I'd made for my teaching. And in my teaching I did indeed go through those canonical texts, *The Mill on the Floss* or *Lord Jim* or whatever it might be. I think I was simply afraid that I might lose sight of the wood for the trees if I included too much of that in the book. I was trying to track this ideology of organicism, and I didn't want it to become a literary-critical essay – perhaps in too sharp a reaction to my previous literary-critical focus.

At this point, I'd like to go back to the companion piece to Criticism and Ideology, Marxism and Literary Criticism. *You've mentioned that Fredric Jameson was one of the readers commissioned to referee it. The other one was Edward Said, wasn't it?*

Yes, the first contact I had with Edward was when he wrote to congratulate me on that little book. I then met him in 1978, the year he published *Orientalism*, when I spoke at a seminar he was running in Columbia (I was on my way home from Yale, where Fred had invited me to speak). I dedicated *The Idea of Culture* [2000] to him a few years before he died and he responded with a typically warm-hearted letter of thanks – that was the last contact we had.

What's your assessment of Said in retrospect?

I think it's vital to appreciate that Said wasn't primarily a theorist. One might say that he was more important than that. In fact, he ended up quite hostile to so-called theory. His trajectory was really from Auerbach to Foucault and back to Auerbach. His great fellow US radical, Noam Chomsky, is equally scornful of theory. Theory is partly, though only partly, the problem to which it offers a solution, as Karl Kraus remarked about psychoanalysis. Said was intellectually speaking a quite old-fashioned humanist who was forced by the exigencies of his personal history into kinds of intellectual work that challenged the tradition in which he was bred. Perhaps he would have liked simply to listen to opera, rather than write about

Palestine. His aim, like that of every radical, was to get to the point politically where writing about oppression is no longer necessary because oppression has been overcome. Then we can all get on with enjoying Schumann and writing about colour imagery in the early D. H. Lawrence. When we can do that with a good conscience it will be a sign that we've succeeded. The quicker we can dispense with radical politics the better. Beware of any political radical who hasn't grasped that simple fact. But radical politics are like social class and nationhood: to get rid of them you first have to have them. And you mustn't give them up prematurely.

This wariness of theory makes Said's work a lot more interesting than that of a theorist who has been, so to speak, born and bred to the trade – the New Historicists for example. It meant that he assailed Western culture from a standpoint that was steeped in that culture, which had a deep affection for it, and that kind of critique is always harder for a governing power to ward off than a merely external one. He had absolutely no patience with what one might call theoreticism. Given his urgent political situation, it simply wouldn't have been possible for him. So there is a sense in which to lump Said together with, say, Roland Barthes or Harold Bloom, or even with Jameson, is to commit a category mistake. If he was interested in Foucault early on, it was partly because Foucault was a political activist like himself, who viewed ideas pragmatically rather than abstractly.

Said and I once crossed swords in a session in London when he spoke up against theory and I claimed rather glibly that this itself was a theoretical position. He dismissed this case, a move which at the time I thought was wrong, but which I now suspect to be right, because it involves an illicit word-play on the term 'theory'. On the other hand, Said's nervousness of theory had its limitations. He steered well clear of Marxism, for example. Was he even a socialist? It's significant that we don't really know – or at least I don't. All I can say is that if he wasn't he ought to have been. There was a whole dimension of leftist politics that seemed closed to him, no doubt partly because of his well-heeled background.

Could you say something about the audience you were writing for in
Marxism and Literary Criticism?

That's a hard question. The strange thing was that such an arcane
kind of discourse was nevertheless engaging more people than one
might expect. So a book that in different historical circumstances
might have been a somewhat academic tome, did get through
because of the times. It also found some readers because of the
formidably high quality of debate at the time. Without adopting a
deteriorationist view of history, I think this diminished somewhat
over the eighties, particularly with the onset of certain postmodernist
ideas that were almost programmatically unrigorous. Of course,
Marxism and Literary Criticism is a highly conceptual book, and it's
not until the book on Walter Benjamin that I really start thinking
about issues of political culture. Ironically, it's just as the political
climate is darkening, between 1976 and 1981, that I start turning to
Brecht and Weimar and Bakhtin.

*In the preface to the book you predict that Marxism will soon be
'comfortably wedged between Freudian and mythological approaches to
literature, as yet one more stimulating academic "approach", one more
well-tilled field of inquiry for students to tramp'. In a sense, that proved
to be prophetic. I'm thinking of books like Michael Ryan's* Literary
Theory: A Practical Introduction *[1999], where Marxism functions
simply as a method one might pick up and sample as if shopping in
some conceptual supermarket. I wonder if you could comment on the
co-optation of Marxism in the years that succeeded this.*

On the one hand, I was always acutely conscious, going back to what
we were saying about the sociology of literature, of the danger of
co-optation – sometimes perhaps too sensitive to it. The possibility
of co-optation was built into the whole enterprise from the outset,
partly because it was possible to shuck off the politics and isolate
it as a cultural approach. In a way that is what happened, certainly
in the States. On the other hand, I was always looking for new

forms, new languages, in which to articulate problems. So I didn't think the answer to co-optation was simply to dig your heels in. In other words, although I was never a liberal pluralist, in the sense of trying to accommodate all of these approaches, I always believed, at least from the Benjamin book onwards, in trying to be open to other approaches. So it was a precarious balancing act. There were people — maybe Jameson was one of them — who talked rather too confidently about Marxism as a master narrative that effortlessly scooped up everything else, and at precisely the time when Marxists and feminists, for example, were involved in deep conflicts and debates. I think this was far too bland a position to take. But it was hard to know how to resist the bland appropriation without falling into the opposite error. I don't know if I ever got that straight.

Can I come back to the question of historicism in relation to Marxism and Literary Criticism? *You tackle the problem of past and present there in a discussion of Marx's notoriously thin comments in the* Grundrisse *on the 'eternal charm' of Greek art. You then cite Brecht's celebration of a dialectical delight in the historical past, which he proposes should be prised open and jammed up against the present, as opposed to folded into some smooth historical narrative.*

All of that is an implicit riposte to an increasingly fashionable 'presentism', which was very much associated with post-Althusserianism and discourse theory, and later with aspects of new historicism. I had various stabs, including the one you mention, at trying to formulate that relation. I suppose you could say that I was anti-historicist in that I wanted to avoid a historical relativism, but historicist in the sense of appealing to historical context. Truths are historical in the sense of historically bred, but not in the sense that what is true is true only in its own time.

One of the reasons I ask is because in the issue of New Left Review *in which you published 'Ideology and Literary Form' there is an article*

*by Henri Lefebvre on precisely that – the relation of the present and
the past. He rejects the Lukácsian notion that the past is the prehistory
of the present, and in devising the category of the 'possible' comes to
a much more dialectical position on the relationship between past and
present. Do you remember that article?*

I don't remember reading it or indeed being particularly conscious
of Lefebvre's work in general. But it was certainly a recurrent issue
at the time. There were a lot of out-and-out presentists, who as far
as historical knowledge went were complete sceptics. For a while
that masqueraded as a radical position. I certainly saw the need
to combat that attitude. Such 'presentism', in which the needs of
the present become the index of the truth of the past, is really a
form of temporal imperialism. It forgets Brecht's insistence on
the difference and strangeness of the past; or, indeed, Benjamin's
vision of the past as incomplete, awaiting its full realization at the
hands of the present. This thrusts past and present into relation,
but not in an imperializing way.

What about Trotsky? Literature and Revolution *plays quite an
important role in* Marxism and Literary Criticism. *Presumably he
helped you to relate your theoretical labours to your political activism?*

That was one of the bridges. Trotsky was one of the few bridges
between the political scene in Oxford and the cultural left scene
more generally. When I was in IS, one of my tasks was to make
people aware of the cultural dimension of Trotsky, which they
knew about only vaguely. I was impressed by Trotsky's work on
culture, and indeed the whole Bolshevik cultural experiment, and
tried to bring that into what was otherwise in danger of being a too
theoreticist atmosphere.

What do you think Trotsky meant when he talked in Literature and
Revolution *about the importance of judging the work of art in the first*

*place by its own law, the law of art? It's an important formulation —
one that you refer to in the book — but a highly ambiguous one too.*

Yes; it's a Kantian phrase in fact. I remember Raymond writing
in *Culture and Society* that in one sense art for art's sake is no
more than a demand for attention; in other words, that when
you're looking at art you're looking at art. It's refreshingly banal,
or instructively banal. I wondered whether Trotsky meant that
to look at the work in itself is in fact to look at it historically. It
rejects a false dichotomy. On the other hand, in the context of the
rampant vulgar Marxism or sociologism that was prevalent then,
the battle for the autonomy of the work of art obviously has more
importance. It presumably prefigures his later interest in surrealism
and avant-gardism in general. He had learnt from the Formalists
that art relates itself to reality only by being a specific, irreducible
configuration of elements.

*Incidentally, Adorno is a notable absence in this book. You mention
him briefly at the end of* Marxism and Literary Criticism, *but don't
discuss him alongside interlocutors of his like Benjamin. Did he figure
in the seminar discussions at Wadham?*

Yes, he did; it was *Aesthetic Theory* that was lacking, because it
didn't appear in English until the mid-eighties and my German
isn't up to the original. But some of the other work had been
translated, and there was a keen interest in the Frankfurt School
in the Oxford classes. So I'm surprised that, arising as it did out of
that, the book doesn't have more Adorno in it.

S .S. Prawer was teaching at Oxford at this time, and his Karl Marx
and World Literature, *which also came out in 1976, was reviewed
alongside* Marxism and Literary Criticism *in a couple of places. Did
you communicate with him at all?*

I knew him a little. The book was awarded the Deutscher Prize, and I remember Perry Anderson ringing me up and rather nervously asking whether I knew anything about Prawer's politics. Presumably they were reluctant to award the prize to a fascist. I could reassure them on that score. He was an Eastern European émigré, the brother of the novelist Ruth Prawer Jhabvala. He kept his distance from the Marxist criticism sessions, but I met him a few times. Shortly after I arrived in Oxford the class put on a day's conference called 'Literature and Revolution', and Prawer came to that. He turned up and sat at the back, looking interested. So from a certain rather detached viewpoint I think he was intrigued by what was going on. He had an air of cosmopolitanism about him that was clearly non-Oxfordian. On the other hand, he sat loose to our politics, if not to our aesthetics.

René Wellek, who was one of the critics to consider Marxism and Literary Criticism *alongside Prawer's book, wrote a fairly positive review of it, but complained in a slightly bemused tone that 'Mr Eagleton accepts uncritically even the most Utopian features of Marxism.' Was that typical of the liberal-humanist response to the book?*

Yes, I think it was. Even so, his response was probably more positive than I'd expected. The book was on the whole better received than most of my earlier stuff, perhaps partly because much of it is expository, albeit in partisan mode.

I wanted to ask what you thought of Marxism and Literature *(1977), the elaborate notations of Williams's probing but slightly laborious engagement with Marxism at this time. It too was frequently reviewed alongside your books from the previous year.*

I was quite surprised by the fact that he produced it at all, given his rather ambiguous relationship to Marxism. At times I felt he kept this relationship deliberately non-committal. The book staked a position far more boldly than I would have expected. I'm not sure that I learnt an enormous amount from it, but I was very cheered by the fact that he'd done it. In an embattled situation, the very existence of the book was a kind of gesture.

What about his critical reflections on the metaphor of base and superstructure, where he emphasized that the cultural forms that maintain capitalism are material rather than merely ideological productions? Were they at all helpful to you?

Raymond and I always disagreed over that, and I wrote an essay on that very aspect of his work. I always felt that he had misconceived it in experiential terms. It was certainly one of his sticking points with Marxism; that's to say, however hospitable his work became to Marxism, he preserved the suspicion that it was not taking culture with full seriousness but was relegating it to secondary status. I think the argument between him and me, or him and others, was effectively one over what was meant by secondary status. You can regard culture as material without regarding it as primary. To claim it's not culture we live by isn't necessarily to denigrate or disembody it.

So do you think that 'cultural materialism' is ultimately a displacement of Marxism?

It's a notion that is compatible with Marxism, as he says, but it all depends on what it means. If it means extending materialism to culture then it's surely compatible with or even identical to Marxism, because Marxists do that anyway. In which case, the question arises as to why he needs a special category. That's why the category is so ambiguous: it resists a Marxist position at the same time as it mimes one. I was always a little sceptical about how much was gained by that category. It's a compromise formation, in the Freudian sense.

*It was in 1978 that you published a critique of John Bayley – your
predecessor as the Warton Professor of English at Oxford – in* New
Left Review. *Originally I think it had been scheduled to form part of a
longer series of critiques of liberal humanism. Could you say something
about why that project never came to fruition?*

Why should one suddenly turn and savage John Bayley, of all
people? The article was left looking strangely high and dry
because the rest of the series never materialized. It made sense
as one of a series of critiques of eminent critics, I suppose, but it
didn't make too much sense on its own. I remember Bayley saying
that he thought parts of my article were extremely well done, and
that although he hadn't read this man Macherey he obviously
should do. I can't say it came as a stunning surprise to me that he
hadn't read Macherey, any more than if he'd said he didn't read
Playboy. I'd concluded the article by referring to Bayley's obituary
of F. R. Leavis, in which he had commented on his 'marvellous
taste', adding that one might as well congratulate Gramsci on his
common sense. Bayley said, 'I suppose one could congratulate
Gramsci on his common sense'! It was water off a critic's back.

*You've already briefly alluded to the Essex conferences on the sociology
of literature, which you participated in from the late seventies. In 1976
a fairly ecumenical collection of academics presented papers there,
including Jay Bernstein, Gillian Beer and Raymond Williams. Did
these conferences actually centre on the idea of a sociology of literature?*

No, not at all, so my guess is they called it that to get it past some
bureaucrat. They were extraordinarily rich and fertile meetings. I
sometimes rather cynically tell students that academic conferences
are basically anthropological rituals, celebrations of solidarity, but
this was quite different. These events were packed with people
from all over the place, from different academic disciplines, and
produced some work and debate of extraordinarily high quality.
In fact, they represented a cultural left that had now more or less

seized the commanding heights of critical production, a striking new development. I sometimes ask myself where all these people went. Because almost exactly thirty years ago there were lots of people involved in literature and culture who would have called themselves either Marxists or fellow travellers. If Marxism was true then, why isn't it true now? Did they all succumb to political disenchantment?

Representatives of the Marxist-Feminist Literature Collective were also there. Did you have a dialogue with them?

Not as a group, but I knew almost all the people in the group. Some of them, including Maud Ellmann, had attended the Wadham classes from time to time. The Marxist-feminist debates became increasingly important. Nobody could ignore them. I think I would say that they were a major challenge – though sometimes it was a confirmation, of course – to the position that we were trying to develop. This challenge had to be taken into account at all costs.

There seems to have been an interesting shift from the 1976 conference to the 1981 conference. The title of the latter was 'Literature and Power in the Seventeenth Century', which clearly signalled a Foucauldian emphasis. Were you conscious of that shift at the time?

Yes, very much so. In the Wadham class at this period there were growing conflicts between what you might roughly call the Foucauldians and the Marxists. Essex itself – not just the conferences but the literary department in the university – became more and more Foucauldian in emphasis at this time. I think the effects of this were actually disastrous. There was at that time a particular kind of student – quite a few of them were at Essex – whose political brains, often fine organs in themselves, had been addled by a loose and disjointed form of Foucauldian relativism.

This resulted in a catastrophic epistemological scepticism. For example, they made palpably unreal assertions about the supposed non-existence of the state. I myself felt that it was necessary to have at least two readings of Foucault. The first should be for his deep value for a Marxism that had in some of its developments become so concerned with general theories that it had not had a real theory of conjuncture. The second, simultaneous one should be a reading of Foucault's works as consistently and quietly anti-Marxist.

This Foucauldian shift marked the point at which a certain kind of intellectual rigour – not an oppressive rigour but an abrasive one – was beginning to disintegrate. Politically speaking, we're talking about the shift to Thatcher and Reagan at the end of the seventies and the beginning of the eighties. Those Foucauldian strains included the discourse theory of post-Marxists, though of course at a much higher level of intellectual competence. Ernesto Laclau, who was himself at Essex, became a very robust force indeed. There was certainly something real to be challenged here, something which had come out of Marxism but which was now one of its most unrelenting critics. 'Discourse' was now running riot. A particularly good example of this, for me, came when a young Australian radical (discourse had taken over the Antipodes) sent me an essay of his which began, 'For the purposes of this article, I shall refer to human practices as "discourses".' Why? I thought. Isn't this rather like saying, 'For the purposes of this article, I shall refer to Brazilians as "umbrellas"'?

Reading

Althusser, Louis, *Lenin and Philosophy and Other Essays*, trans. Ben Brewster (London: New Left Books, 1971).

Barnett, Anthony, 'Raymond Williams and Marxism: A Rejoinder to Terry Eagleton', *New Left Review* 1:99 (1976), pp. 47–64.

Eagleton, Terry, *Criticism and Ideology: A Study in Marxist Literary Theory* (London: New Left Books, 1976).

Eagleton, Terry, 'Form, Ideology, and *The Secret Agent*', *Sociological Review*, Monograph 26 (1978), pp. 55–63 (reprinted in *Against the Grain: Essays 1975–1985*, London: Verso, 1986, pp. 23–32).

Eagleton, Terry, 'Liberality and Order: The Criticism of John Bayley', *New Left Review* 1:110 (1978), pp. 29–40 (reprinted in *Against the Grain*, pp. 33–47).

Eagleton, Terry, 'Tennyson: Politics and Sexuality in *The Princess* and *In Memoriam*', in *1848: The Sociology of Literature*, ed. Francis Barker et al. (Colchester: Essex University Press, 1978), pp. 97–106.

Eagleton, Terry, 'Psychoanalysis, the Kabbala and the Seventeenth Century', in *1642: Literature and Power in the Seventeenth Century*, ed. Francis Barker et al. (Colchester: Essex University Press, 1981), pp. 201–6.

Eagleton, Terry, 'Interview: Terry Eagleton' (with James H. Kavanagh and Thomas E. Lewis), *Diacritics* 12:1 (1982), pp. 53–64.

Eagleton, Terry, and Peter Fuller, 'The Question of Value: A Discussion', *New Left Review* 1:142 (1983), pp. 76–90.

Eagleton, Terry, 'Criticism and Ideology: Andrew Milner Interviews Terry Eagleton', *Thesis Eleven* 12 (1985), pp. 130–44.

Eagleton, Terry, 'Marxism and the Past', *Salmagundi* 68–69 (1985–6), pp. 271–90.

Eagleton, Terry, 'The Revolt of the Reader', *New Literary History* 13:3 (1982), pp. 449–52 (repr. in *Against the Grain*, pp. 181–4).

Eagleton, Terry, 'Interview with Terry Eagleton' (with Andrew Martin and Patrice Petro), *Social Text* 13/14 (1986), pp. 83–99.

Eagleton, Terry, 'Base and Superstructure in Raymond Williams', in *Raymond Williams: Critical Perspectives*, ed. Terry Eagleton (Cambridge: Polity, 1989), pp. 164–75.

Eagleton, Terry, 'Norman Feltes', *English Studies in Canada* 28:3 (2002), pp. 473–7.

Eagleton, Terry, 'Edward Said, Cultural Politics, and Critical Theory (An Interview),' *Alif: Journal of Comparative Poetics* (January 2005). (http://www.thefreelibrary.com/_/print/PrintArticle.aspx?id=135888177)

Eagleton, Terry, *Trouble with Strangers: A Study of Ethics* (Oxford: Blackwell, 2008).

Feltes, N. N., *Modes of Production of Victorian Novels* (Chicago: University of Chicago Press, 1986).

Higgins, John, *Raymond Williams: Literature, Marxism and Cultural Materialism* (London: Routledge, 1999).

Jameson, Fredric, *Jameson on Jameson: Conversations on Cultural Marxism*, ed. Ian Buchanan (Durham: Duke University Press, 2007).

Lefebvre, Henri, 'What is the Historical Past?' *New Left Review* 1:90 (1975), pp. 27–34.

Ryan, Michael, *Literary Theory: A Practical Introduction* (Oxford: Blackwell, 1999).

Trotsky, Leon, *Literature and Revolution* (London: Redwords, 1991).

Wellek, René, review of *Criticism and Ideology*, *Slavic Review* 36:3 (1977), p. 531.

Williams, Raymond, *Culture and Society 1780–1950* (London: Chatto & Windus, 1958).

Williams, Raymond, 'Base and Superstructure in Marxist Cultural Theory', *New Left Review* 1:82 (1973), pp. 3–16.

Williams, Raymond, 'Literature and Sociology: In Memory of Lucien Goldmann', in *Problems of Materialism in Culture: Selected Essays* (London: Verso, 1980), pp. 11–30.

Williams, Raymond, 'Marxism, Structuralism and Literary Analysis', *New Left Review* 1:129 (1981), pp. 51–66.

CHAPTER SIX

Marxism/Feminism

In the early 1980s you became a member of the Workers' Socialist League [WSL].[1] How did this come about?

This was a time when Alan Thornett and some other seasoned militants were very active in Oxford around the Cowley car factory, and I joined WSL because I very deliberately wanted to provide some bridge between what was going on in the town and what was going on in the Marxist classes. That was difficult, of course, because the guys who were working around the car factory weren't interested in Gramsci's views on Balzac or whatever. But one of the strengths of that organization, or the current of Trotskyism that it came out of, was that it wasn't averse to culture. It allowed me to put on sessions about cultural figures. It didn't give it great priority, but it wasn't philistine about it either.

Was the WSL more accommodating than the International Socialists in this respect?

Yes, because most of the Oxford branch of IS were in fact middle-class students, some of them thinly masquerading as militant workers, and it is often people like that, ironically, who tend to be especially workerist, especially hostile to intellectual work. Although IS at that point had

---

1   Workers' Socialist League: British Trotskyist group formed in 1975 by Alan Thornett and others after their explusion from the Workers' Revolutionary Party.

some fine intellectuals at a national level – Nigel Harris, Mike Kidron, Alasdair Macintyre, Alex Callinicos – it didn't seem ever to know what to do with that at local level. An academic like myself was an embarrassment rather than an opportunity. To be fair to the kind of much harder-line Trotskyism that the WSL represented, it didn't have that problem. If you could do something useful it was quite prepared to accept it.

And one of the useful roles you performed, I understand, was to edit Thornett's book From Militancy to Marxism *[1987].*

It was one of my modest roles. They gave me this huge pile of typescript containing newspaper cuttings about Thornett and the workers' struggle around Cowley, and I had to make some sense of it and put it in publishable form. I can't pretend I enjoyed doing it, but I do remember reflecting that it was somehow exemplary of what an intellectual might practically do. They also published a pamphlet of mine called *Makers of Modern Marxism*, which was made up of sessions I'd done in order to introduce workers to Western Marxist figures that they either knew nothing about or were highly suspicious of. I wanted to bring the ideas of Althusser, Benjamin, Gramsci, Sartre and others to the attention of Trotskyist militants, and to do that not in some simple oppositional sense but inviting them to think through central doctrines of Trotskyism in the light of these unfamiliar concepts. The pamphlet on Western Marxism was an attempt to try to put that tradition before a very different theoretical orthodoxy, and to see what could be accepted, what qualified, what rejected. So although in one sense the Althusser-Trotsky couple seems incongruous, it was also an attempted mediation, and the political ambiguity of theoretical concepts was one thing that seemed to ratify that mediation. Having said that, I remember one pugnacious comrade saying to me, when I proposed talking about Althusser, 'Should you give us an account of him or should we just smash him?' So it was a perilous balance.

Were you active during the miners' strike in 1984?

I was moderately active, although I was no longer in the Workers' Socialist League at that point. Oxford had the largest miners' support group in the country, and Thornett and quite a lot of people from both town and gown were involved in it. There were at least a couple of very big meetings in Oxford Town Hall, and we picketed Didcot Power Station, where there was a massive police presence but little violence. It was interesting from a tutor's point of view as well, because you were seeing a generation of students who had the best political will in the world but no memory of anything politically significant or progressive. Then they suddenly saw things coming alive and pitched in, politics materializing as real possibilities. Some of the left-wing women students had unfortunately to run the gauntlet of miners' sexism, but they nevertheless stuck it out. It was an interesting time, in that you saw the transformation it wrought in people who were looking for change but had despaired of it ever happening.

Did you become a point of political focus for students?

I did to some extent, in that there was quite a lot of activity around Wadham, involving especially the English students, who were usually the college leftists, though not just the English students. I suppose that I acted as a kind of funnel, channelling some of them into the wider movement.

Do you think that students in the humanities experienced difficulties in reconciling the theoretical interests that were so fashionable at this time, which were largely post-Marxist, with the commitments that the political situation demanded? What was the relationship, to put it simplistically, between post-structuralism and student politics?

I think the political situation separated the armchair theorists from the militants, and to my pleasant surprise, as I say, a lot of students did pitch in. The support group for the miners was enormous, and its meetings were always at least a hundred strong. A lot of them were students, and I remember being struck at the time by how non-theoreticist they were, how willing they were to plunge into politics. They didn't know their way around that kind of world but you could see them visibly picking it up.

Did your colleagues at the university have a problem with your political activism at this time?

One of them came across me selling socialist newspapers on the street and reacted as though I was wearing a clown's outfit. He simply looked quickly away, as you would from some indecent exposure. Then the WSL in Oxford was persecuted by a couple of journalists from the *Daily Mail*. They turned up on our doorsteps and proceeded, in an admirably systematic and on the whole accurate way, to take us apart. They finally produced a two-page spread in the newspaper that included a section on the class traitors in the group – people who had betrayed their class, like the local doctor and myself. We had been to help out on a picket line somewhere near Reading and there had been various people taking photographs of us, some of whom were clearly undercover employees of the *Daily Mail*, so our photograph appeared too. I finally took flight to St. Ives, which seemed to offer a refuge.

Like D. H. Lawrence, then, you fled to Cornwall as an internal exile?

Exactly! It wasn't for very long, but I remember I was writing the poem that ends the Benjamin book at the time. I was in a certain schizoid position, I think, because I don't imagine that any of the comrades in WSL would either have read the book or, if they had read it, approved of it. I was trying to bring the political and the theoretical together, but in some respects the book and my activism were bizarrely separate. In a way, the political and theoretical interests came together in the material on the affinities between Benjamin and Trotsky in the final chapter of the book. It was fairly original at that time to make any kind of parallel between Benjamin and Trotsky.

Let's move on to the Benjamin book, Walter Benjamin, Or, Towards a Revolutionary Criticism *[1981] – in my opinion probably your most important book. In the preface you write that the shift in your work from* Criticism and Ideology *to* Walter Benjamin *can be explained partly by 'a general mutation in the capitalist system' and partly by what you call your 'own individual evolution'.*

The general mutation was of course signalled by the emergence of Thatcherism. I remember one fairly sympathetic left-wing critic giving me a terrible review for this book, and when I later raised the matter with him personally he said that he was so crestfallen at the fact that Thatcherism was by then completely embedded that he just didn't see the relevance of the book. He felt that it didn't offer a way out. It certainly wasn't a book of its political moment in the way that *Criticism and Ideology* [1976] had been. A lot had changed drastically between those two publications with the advent of the Reagan and Thatcher regimes, and although there was only five years between them this man's comment demonstrated the extraordinary swiftness with which the climate had changed. He was right in a sense that the Benjamin book wasn't addressing that particular moment, and that it already looked slightly anachronistic. I'm not sure exactly what the book was doing. It did in a sense behave as though nothing had happened, but then that might be a good thing as well as a bad one. In spite of a severe downturn in that period, a book that brashly uses the word 'revolutionary' in its subtitle suddenly appears on the scene . . .

In terms of their respective political tone, one might almost expect the books to have been produced in a different order, Criticism and Ideology *appearing in the mid-seventies, on the final crest of the political euphoria of the late sixties, and* Walter Benjamin *in the early eighties, at a far less politically auspicious moment in which there is a sense that theoretical positions need to be consolidated.*

That's true, they do seem to have appeared in a peculiar order. I suppose the Benjamin book was trying to reach back to that particular moment of Brecht and Weimar, when there was an increasingly ominous political climate. The book was conscious of a need to politicize criticism. Perhaps *Criticism and Ideology* had to some degree taken that for granted; but from now on, in the face of new pressures, there was the need to summon the resources of the avant-garde. In the Wadham class, rather than looking at Goldmann and Lukács and Sartre, we were increasingly turning back to the revolutionary avant-garde, both Bolshevik and later. A lot of that teaching fed into the book in an indirect way.

What about your 'individual evolution'?

The major development was that I had learnt in the interim to bring my critical or theoretical and creative writing closer together. I'd written a play about Brecht, *Brecht and Company*, which was a great experience, and I knew that I could write effectively in that form.

Could you tell me about Brecht and Company? *It was staged at the 1979 Edinburgh Fringe, wasn't it? In spite of that, it hasn't been published, though you mischievously quote from it in* How to Read a Poem *[2007].*

Brecht and Company wasn't the first play I'd written but it was the first one to be staged. It was produced for the Fringe by a group called the New Oxford Theatre Group, which was made up of both amateurs and professionals. I attended most of the rehearsals in Edinburgh, and the run of the play, and it was very exciting. I've sometimes talked about theatre as the artist's or the humanist's equivalent of the scientist's laboratory, because it's collective, experimental, practical, provisional and open-ended – and I liked that. In form the play was probably a little too avant-garde even for the Edinburgh Fringe. In content it was rather too left-wing for the likes of Michael Billington, who nonetheless gave us a mildly favourable review.

It was very finely directed by a postgraduate student of mine called Justin Gregson, a Marxist who went on to become a professional theatre director. He was anxious to get a London production of the play, so we duly touted the script around various metropolitan theatres. Somewhat to my surprise, Charles Marowitz, who was running the Open Space Theatre, said that he would take it. Then he said, 'So who are you going to get to play Brecht?' and reeled off a list of names of Stratford-type actors. It was clear that no theatre would produce it unless they'd got a household name, so it didn't get a London production after all. Its first and last production was pompously described as the Edinburgh world premiere. There were a lot of firsts-and-lasts on the Edinburgh Fringe.

Why did you choose to write about Brecht creatively?

I was intensely interested in what Brecht did and what he thought and felt, but I had no sense of rapport with him as a character. So the seed of the play wasn't an interest in Brecht as a personal figure but in the possibilities he opened up. It stages different disjointed scenes, crossing theatre with political history and mixing political ballads with parodies of Shakespeare.

Some material in Brecht and Company *seems to overlap almost directly with material in the book on Benjamin, especially in relation to your argument that for Marxism history is ironic in form. So in the former: 'Hitler a housepainter yesterday, chancellor tomorrow. And the day after? Maybe Hitler down a sewer and the Soviets in Berlin. Everything can be stood on its head'; and in the latter: 'Hitler as housepainter yesterday and chancellor today is thus a sign of the comic, because that resistible rise foreshadows the unstable process whereby he may be dead in a bunker tomorrow.' Were you deliberately trying to bridge the gap between the critical and the creative?*

Yes; at that point there was quite a lot of experimentation with genre going on. The play itself is montage-like, and I suppose the Benjamin book was equally experimental. There were certainly crossovers in my mind between the critical work and the dramatic work. This was the point at which I began to discover that both kinds of writing felt the same to me. Both were equally fulfilling forms in which to write. There was no difference experientially.

The Benjamin book had a deliberately broken-backed structure, and that was very much part of that formal experiment. I didn't even want chapter headings or a contents page, and I had a small disagreement with New Left Books about it. I remember Perry Anderson writing me a long letter, admiring the book very much, to my immense gratification, but saying that it certainly was not in line with his own 'staider notions of composition'! I like it more than the books of mine that most people like, though I don't think it is by any means the most important book I've written – *Literary Theory* [1983] is probably the most important book I've written in terms of impact. The books of mine that have been taken up most are not on the whole the books I have a secret liking for. For example, I have a secret liking for the little Shakespeare book, *William Shakespeare* [1986], which is not generally much referred to.

Returning to the comment in the preface to the Benjamin book about your individual evolution, you also note that 'this shift in direction was in turn obscurely related to certain deep-seated changes in my own

personal and political life since the writing of Criticism and Ideology.'
Could you decode this?

I suppose the point about my personal mutation was a reference
to coming under the influence of feminism in that period, mainly
through Toril Moi. I've always thought that the influence of
feminism on my work was not primarily a matter of substance –
apart perhaps from *The Rape of Clarissa* [1982], which was on the
whole shot down by feminists for treading on their toes – but of
form and style. The Benjamin book is probably the first book in
which, in however minor a way, humour begins to creep in. In that
sense it was a bit of a breakthrough.

I'd intended to ask you about humour in this context. When I reread
it, I expected to find its tone more comic than I did – not least because
in one chapter you use Freud to demonstrate how jokes, like works
of literature, flaunt form. The book's remarkable sense of polemical
urgency is I think its most striking stylistic characteristic. There isn't
actually much humour, in spite of the fact that it's flamboyantly
conscious of its own frequently daring rhetorical strategies. And I can
only find one joke, a footnote in which, in heavily sarcastic tones, you
explicate the word 'girning'.

That's right. It's a book that's ready to begin to joke, but it doesn't
actually joke much. It sort of warms up for the main comic act.

There is however a magnificently cocky provocation at one point: you
list the major Marxist aestheticians of the century to date, and include
yourself among them!

Yes! I got a furious letter, probably written in a moment of
drunken rage, from someone who quoted that sentence and just
added, in capital letters, 'All I want to know is, how do you have
the fucking nerve?' I wrote back to him and said, 'Well, I did it

partly to antagonize people like you.' I also said, 'Why shouldn't one include one's own name?' and I talked about the proper name as the sign of a body of work. Occasionally I gave that chapter as a lecture, and the joke always worked in that context because I could add a slight ironic pause before 'Eagleton'. But I realize how offensive it must have looked to some people on the page – certainly to this guy.

Aside from this enraged correspondent, did you have a different audience in mind for the book?

I'm not sure I did. I wrote it very much as a Verso book, if you like, an intellectual left book, but at the same time it mobilized resources – like Bakhtin and to some extent Adorno – that challenged a too intellectual sort of socialism. Perhaps it was to some extent an implicit critique of *Criticism and Ideology* in this respect. It was also very much *using* Benjamin. It wasn't really a study of Benjamin so much as an attempt to use him as a peg on which to hang various topics. I was able now to be more diverse. It is one of the more versatile books that I've written, and for that reason, though also perhaps for others, the Benjamin people didn't like it at all. They hardly reviewed it. It was a case of the circus clown running off with the suitcase – having laboured for years over the minutiae of *The Arcades Project*, they were slightly scandalized by this newcomer nipping off with their work.

The book doesn't offer much biographical information about Benjamin. Did you feel that you didn't have to take on the responsibility of providing an introduction to him because at this time he was suddenly beginning to be reclaimed by anglophone scholars?

Yes. As I state at the beginning of the book, he opens up in so many different directions. This fitted with a new climate of pluralism, and with my growing interest in other, non-Marxist or post-structuralist methods, including Bakhtin. Again, this was part of an attempt to muster as many instruments as one could in a bad time. The book has a certain – not euphoria exactly – a certain positive, affirmative quality, both in the way it's written and in its breaking up of the book form. But that oddly doesn't sit at all well with the bleak political situation. The downturns have their advantages as well as the upturns. You're less sectarian, less severe, less jealously discriminating. All that has dangers, but you're less willing to look gift horses in the mouth. Benjamin's own style, especially his montage technique, opened me up to ways of talking that, politically speaking, might not look very promising on the surface. And I'd learnt from Brecht – both through writing *Brecht and Company* and from a more general engagement with him at that time – of the attractiveness of dismantling. That got into the book fairly consciously. But I don't think it was only Benjamin and Brecht. I wrote the book at the moment before pluralism became completely modish, before a liberal, multi-culturalist ideology appropriated it. There seemed to be a need to pull in more resources without worrying too much about how they sat together.

You talk in the Benjamin book about the madness and violence of deconstruction. Did there seem to be a dialogue at the time between the avant-gardist tradition and what Derrida and other post-structuralists were doing?

I felt there were some affinities. I'm fairly critical of Derrida in that book, and was so generally at that time. I thought that the avant-garde represented a more obviously politicized form of pluralism, or politicized form of deconstruction. In some of its characteristic motifs, the avant-garde had anticipated Derrida – as indeed had Bakhtin – but in a more historical or political context. In fact, I remember once asking Derrida in Oxford whether he could see any connections between Bakhtin and his own work. He was very cagey about it and said, 'Maybe . . .' I suppose he said 'maybe' rather a lot. Perhaps he was wondering why I asked. I was deeply interested in Bakhtin and the avant-garde, and I wanted to find out what he felt; but despite having written very positively on Benjamin, he was distinctly guarded about it.

When did you first meet Derrida?

I met him first in Cambridge, where he was giving some lectures, some time in the early eighties. Then somebody from the *Oxford Literary Review* invited him to give a seminar in Oxford. What struck me on that occasion, however, speaking of caginess, was that he was rather reluctant to be drawn into ultra-deconstructionist positions by some of his more zealous Oxford acolytes. In a typical way perhaps, he did not want to proceed too quickly. Somebody would ask him a question that was clearly hostile to the idea of the dialectical, and Derrida would say that he had nothing against dialectics, it was just that there was that which was not dialectizable – something like that. He seemed to me quite cautious and canny in spirit and approach. He tended to shift from the hedonistic position to the sober one, depending on the direction of the fire. When his disciples were waxing lyrical he tended to put the brakes on, but he could take them off himself, at times, with a certain irresponsibility.

The last time I met Derrida was when he came to Dublin to give some lecture. I'd heard in the meantime that he was somewhat agitated both by my review of *Specters of Marx* and also, of all things, the game I'd played with his name in the epigraph to one of the chapters of the Benjamin book – a deliciously ironic situation. He didn't seem to like floating the signifier when it came to his own name. Perhaps he thought it wasn't proper . . . Because we had only met infrequently and because he had visibly aged by the time I encountered him in Dublin, I could see that he didn't remember who I was. We had a lively conversation, but as soon as I'd gone he apparently asked, 'Who was that very nice man?' Then, when he was told, he said, 'Oh! He has played with my name!' So that was the last I saw of Monsieur Derrida. Or Monsieur Dare-I-Die . . .

You must have been writing the book on Benjamin at almost exactly the time of the so-called MacCabe affair in Cambridge, when the English Faculty, shockingly, denied tenure to Colin MacCabe, who was closely identified with the reception of post-structuralism in Britain.

Yes, I knew Colin quite well and found his book on Joyce very eye-opening. I was dismayed when I heard rumours that people on certain appointment committees in Cambridge were reading bits of it out to each other in a satirical tone. I obviously sympathized with him politically and theoretically, but also because in a way I'd been in a similar situation in Cambridge, though not nearly so well trumpeted. Some years before, when Colin was an undergraduate and I was a young fellow, I was in a similar situation in that it was clear that, because I was a Williamsite, they weren't going to give me a job. This is why I left in the end. I had a couple of interviews with the faculty in Cambridge for assistant lectureships but got turned down. So that was one reason why I identified with Colin's situation. Beyond that, it was one of the first blasts in the theory battle. Frank Kermode and Raymond Williams made unlikely common cause in defending Colin. At that point Kermode was still influenced by having sat in on Barthes' seminars, and in his coolly detached, English way he was interested in theory. That was of course a phenomenon of the time – people like David Lodge were similar. But in almost all of those cases their true liberal, empiricist colours ultimately showed.

I remember Oxford English Limited inviting Colin over at the time, and he gave a lecture in the Faculty on Milton. Hundreds came because of his notoriety. I showed him a cartoon from *Private Eye* in which a middle-aged working-class couple is having breakfast over the newspaper and the woman is saying to the man, 'Have they caught the Cambridge structuralist yet?' There'd been an infamous Cambridge rapist a year or so before . . .

It was in the Benjamin book that you first used Lacanian theory, the resources of which you've often returned to, most recently, and most extensively, in Trouble with Strangers *[2008].*

Lacanianism also entered into the Wadham classes, where there was quite an emphasis at one point on psychoanalysis. We'd looked at Reich and the Marxist psychoanalytic tradition, and at the Frankfurt School too. I remember trying to read Reich in the Bodleian and finding a strange symbol against him in the catalogue. I asked a librarian if this meant it was confined to Duke Humfrey's Library, and was told instead that it was classified as pornography. So I had to read it chained to the desk; that is, the book had to be chained to the desk, not me.

Increasingly, Lacan was a name to be conjured with, although there was very little available until the English selection of *Écrits* appeared in 1977. He was always a nagging influence on me, but he lay dormant for some time. I remember a surreal occasion when the psychiatrist Anthony Storr, who was a fellow at Wadham, stopped me in the quad and said, with a rather panic-stricken air, that he'd been asked by the *Observer* to review this strange thing by this man Lacan. It was the translation of *Écrits* and he had three days to the deadline. He said that he'd read a few paragraphs and had seriously wondered whether Lacan suffered from word disorder. I said, 'It's more interesting than that . . .' 'All right!' he said, 'Tell me one interesting thing he says!' So I said, 'Well, among other things he says, "I am not where I think and I think where I am not".' And he said, 'My God, that's true!' He was a practising psychiatrist and that absolutely struck home. At the time, though, Lacan was a signifier for Parisian gobbledegook, as this incident illustrates. But he was slowly being taken up – although not by the Oxford post-structuralists, it should be said, who were turning against psychoanalysis because it wasn't linguistically reducible.

On reflection, I suppose I'm slightly surprised that in *Trouble with Strangers* I should have used Lacan so full-bloodedly. It's not unlike the case of Althusser and *Criticism and Ideology*, in that both books make me out to be more of a supporter than I am. At the time I wrote *Criticism and Ideology*, as I've said, there probably wasn't a single position of Althusser's I didn't have serious reservations about, and much the same would go for Lacan. But I found that his thinking on the Imaginary, the Symbolic and the Real, in particular, provided a useful framework for thinking about ethics. And, I hope, a reasonably original one.

In the discussion of Milton in the opening chapter of the Benjamin book, which exploits another opportunity to critique Leavisism, you use Of Grammatology *[1966] to explore the phonocentrism of Puritanism. Were you implicitly identifying Catholicism, in contrast to Puritanism, with the kind of artifice and semiotic density that Benjamin identifies in his treatment of allegory and the baroque in* The Origin of German Tragic Drama *[1928]?*

That only occurred to me a lot later, but I think it is there. It's a very anti-Protestant kind of book in that way. Although the idea of semantic materialism was somewhat overworked at the time, somewhat voguish, it did appeal to me deeply, and I suspect that Catholicism was one reason for that. I suppose, incidentally, that the other reason I was interested in Benjamin, though it doesn't come out so strongly in the book, was theology. It was perhaps a way of raising some of those deep issues but not in explicitly theological terms.

In The Magic Mountain, *a novel about which you've written in both* Sweet Violence *[2003] and* Trouble with Strangers, *Thomas Mann points out that Judaism has much more in common with Catholicism than with Protestantism, because of what he calls its 'secular and materialistic leanings', its 'socialism'. Incidentally, were you aware that in the early 1980s Jameson was working on broadly similar problems to the ones you were exploring? There are interesting parallels between the Benjamin book and* The Political Unconscious, *both of which were published in 1981. In lots of ways they're quite different of course; for example, Jameson treats allegory as a hermeneutic rather than an aesthetic or a semiotic. But both books attempt to come to terms with the impact of post-structuralism, creatively accommodating it but*

refuting the idealism of post-structuralism in the name of historical
materialism. For both books, Marxism is in effect the untranscendable
horizon of critique.

No, I wasn't aware of these connections. One of my more negative
feelings about Jameson's work was that he was at once too
pluralistic, to the point of succumbing to the danger of eclecticism,
and too insistent on the master narrative, on the subsumption
of other narratives to the point of not giving due weight to the
various elements to be subsumed. Certainly the feminists thought
that about him at the time. The other thought I had about Jameson
at the time of writing, as I think I've said, was that he never really
engaged with Althusser – for better or worse. Althusser passed
him by because of the deeply Hegelian cast of Jameson's Marxism.
He writes about him a little in *The Prison-House of Language* [1975]
and elsewhere, but at a time when there were intense theoretical
rivalries between Althusserians and others he seemed to sit quite
loose to that whole debate. But no, I wasn't aware of *The Political
Unconscious* until later.

One of the most arresting differences between these books – and it
might surprise those who have criticized you for your attachment to the
canon – is that Jameson derives his literary examples from the realist
tradition, in Lukácsian fashion, and you derive yours mainly from the
modernist and avant-gardist one, in Benjaminian fashion.

That's true. Jameson has always had far wider range than I could
aspire to. As Colin MacCabe has said, there's nothing in the
humanities that is alien to him. But he has never really been a
public intellectual in the States. That's a striking thing about him.
Some of his less creditable colleagues at Duke, like Stanley Fish,
have been public intellectuals to some extent. Obviously there are
extremely limited opportunities for activities like that in the States,
but I nonetheless think it's an interesting reflection on his work
that he doesn't appear to see the need to popularize his ideas. He

conceptualizes popular culture at a pretty high level. The Benjamin book was in a certain sense making an attempt to break free from the usual academic ground. Jameson seems more content with that.

You talk at one point in the Benjamin book about the extent to which Marxism is itself a narrative, and finally reject that model as too simplistic, too evolutionist. Perhaps that's relevant to what you're saying about Jameson's attachment to narratives. I wonder a bit more broadly whether, in the aftermath of the postmodernist attempt to discredit Marxism and other grand narratives, you would shift your position and say that, in certain respects that are politically enabling, it does constitute a narrative.

I think I would want to qualify that. I was too much under the then fashionable influence of anti-teleology, so to speak, with which Jameson never had a problem. In my reflections on the affinities between Benjamin and Trotsky at the end of the book, I'm looking for a mode of historical narration that has something of the non-linear quality that both of them ascribe to it while continuing to believe in the possibility of progress.

So is the idea of tradition – which you've often defended against the leftist assumption that it is an inherently conservative notion – one that you'd substitute for the idea of narrative?

I think so. If one is to say that one of the reasons for preserving tradition is because it contains precious resources for the present and the future, then one is speaking of a developmental narrative, but in so far as that means a genuine engagement with the past rather than seeing the past as ancient history, then it's not a naively evolutionary narrative. For both Benjamin and Trotsky it involves torsions, compressions, recurrences, telescopings and so on. In Benjamin, specifically, the concept of tradition has a resonance of the tradition of the dispossessed, of enslaved ancestors. So you're looking at two different kinds of historical model. What wasn't seen enough at the time was that the debate between historicism and anti-historicism squeezes out too many different options. There are different ways of narrating and historicizing, some of which are more evolutionary than others. And 'evolutionary' of course doesn't necessarily mean teleological anyway.

From a Marxist point of view the concept of tradition is certainly immensely important. Perhaps this is more than stating the obvious. There was, in the great explosion of radical thought and practice in the 1960s, a valuable scepticism about the very idea of tradition. And a kind of eternal 'nowness' later found resonances in postmodernism, which fetishized the present conjuncture, and for which everything rests on the current roll of the dice. Williams said long ago in *Culture and Society* that a society that can live only by contemporary resources is poor indeed. It's a structural effect of late capitalist societies that they must repress history, because they must suppress alternative forms of history. Also their history tends to be the history of the same, tends to be the eternal return of the commodity in whatever fashionably varied guise it comes back. So the first point would simply be to underline the vital nature of the concept of tradition for Marxists. 'We Marxists,' Trotsky once said, 'have always lived in tradition.' This of course is not to signal the uncritical or subservient relations to tradition which one finds, characteristically in conservative thinking. Benjamin's distinction between history, meaning I suppose ruling-class history, and tradition, or an alternative set of histories, was very important to me because it made some sense of what I think is a problem within the British left. In the seventies and eighties there was a lot of working-class, labour and feminist history, which largely stemmed from the History Workshop movement. One of the criticisms made of that movement was that one can fall into the trap of seeing socialist or radical tradition simply as a ready-formed alternative, in the sense of some suppressed but unbroken continuity that 'ghosts' official history. Benjamin's thinking about tradition, about the resources of the oppressed, is a way of breaking with that model. His tradition is much less an alternative ghostly history, which could be blocked out whole and entire; it is rather a set of crises within history itself, a set of points of confrontation, of rupture or conflict, where you can glimpse the outline of an alternative world. His tradition is the assemblage of those moments, which are always reassembled and reconstructed according to the demands of the present conjuncture.

It's a question, according to Benjamin, of constantly wresting this kind of tradition from the conformism that threatens to overpower it ... Moving on to another matter, it's in the Benjamin book that you first refunctioned the idea of rhetoric. You argue persuasively that rhetoric provides an ancient and potentially radical paradigm for criticism, because it provides a method for 'analysing the material effects of particular uses of language in particular social circumstances'. In effect, you were attempting to radicalize the discourse theory dominant at this time by exploiting the resources of a long history of attempts to theorize the articulations of discourse and power. You then revived this attempt in the conclusion to Literary Theory: An Introduction *[1983]. When did the idea of rhetoric come to you as a solution to the problem of how both to use and critique discourse theory, if I can put it like that?*

This was a bit of a bolt from the blue. That section of the Benjamin book attracted enthusiastic responses from all kinds of people, mainly in the States, who had studied and thought about rhetoric for decades. I didn't have any history of working in that tradition, but it suddenly occurred to me that the idea of rhetoric might weave together a number of different strands. Having said that, it's a bit of a free-floating topic in my writing. I don't really pick it up again, after *Literary Theory*, except in a lecture I've been giving since then, in which I point out that rhetoric meant, and still means, both the detailed study of tropes and figures and more broadly the public or political institutional dimension of criticism. It seems to me that most of the high points of critical achievement have been moments where both of those things are brought together, so that to read the words on the page is already to do more than that. Part of the crisis of contemporary criticism is that both of those traditional functions – which have interpenetrated from time to time to produce major bodies of criticism like the Romantics or the Cambridge School – are for different reasons now in trouble. On the one hand we've lost the habits of close textual analysis, and on the other the role of the critic is tied up with the fate of the public sphere or the role of the intellectual in general.

I do also try to make the point in this lecture that the role of the intellectual has always shifted around historically, from the theologian in the Middle Ages, through the figures of the Enlightenment, to the natural scientist in the nineteenth century. It's probably not until the early twentieth century that the buck stops with literary types. At that point, for reasons connected with the growing importance of culture, the culture industry, national identity and so on, the literary critic, who had previously scribbled away harmlessly in his little corner, is suddenly shot to prominence – from Auerbach and Bakhtin through Empson and Richards to Said. Literature is, in this context, the field that has to assume a more general significance, partly because adjacent fields, like philosophy or political theory or sociology, which might have assumed this role more obviously, have become either empiricist or positivist or behaviourist. This is not unlike Perry Anderson's thesis in 'Components of the National Culture' [1968]. So this chapter of the Benjamin book was an attempt to see the critic as, ideally, bringing together these two meanings of rhetoric, the close analysis and the public discourse.

And this can only happen in the least instrumentalized of discourses . . .

Yes, exactly. Both the dwindling of the public sphere and the commodification of language and experience, which makes sensitive verbal analysis more and more difficult, less and less familiar to people, are conspiring to break down this role.

Looking ahead, do you see a book like How to Read a Poem, *which offers lessons in close reading, as a contribution to the same project?*

That's probably one aspect of it. Blackwell more or less forced me to add a final, rather lame chapter about poetry and society, which I didn't want to do. Certainly, my general argument there is that it's not theory that has acted as an obstacle to close reading but the commodification of experience itself. The Leavisites perceived the importance of this early on, and realized that it both endangered the role of the critic and made it more necessary, if in an idealist form from their standpoint.

I mention How to Read a Poem *in this context because it assumes a pedagogic role in relation to language, and the discussion of rhetoric has potentially important pedagogic implications. Perhaps you address some of these implications, if rather elliptically, in* The Function of Criticism *[1984]. But in the Benjamin book, which is supremely self-reflexive, one of the few political problems that you don't discuss with sufficient self-consciousness is the role of the leftist teacher in higher education. You set out the practice of the 'socialist cultural worker', but without quite admitting the no doubt regrettable fact that he or she is often located in an academic institution.*

I probably haven't done enough of that. I'm now quite often asked to speak publicly about education, but it's not something that I've gone in for enough. On the whole I've been more interested in the role of the public intellectual than I have in the role of the teacher in specifically academic institutions. I've also spent a lifetime trying to sit loose to these institutions. That's partly a temperamental matter, though, and I wouldn't claim any great political significance there.

I also wanted to ask you about comedy in relation to the Benjamin book – not simply jokes but comedy. In the penultimate chapter you state that, so far as you know, there has never been a Marxist theory of comedy, before making some intriguing openings into this field. Since that time you've developed a Marxist theory of tragedy, in Sweet Violence *[2003]; but there is still no Marxist theory of comedy. Is that something you'd ever consider constructing?*

That's intriguing. I have been interested in writing more on comedy, but I haven't specifically thought of it in terms of a Marxist theory of comedy. I suppose part of the problem is that, although I was fascinated by Brecht in this period, and found so much that resonated for me in his work, I'm not as temperamentally upbeat or affirmative as him. In that sense I'm more of a Beckettian than a Brechtian. That may simply be a sign of the times, but I think it's also a matter of personality.

Although Brecht makes a point of starting from the bad new days rather than the good old ones . . .

That's true; and Brecht is by no means just a load of laughs. Bakhtin might be the character that should be tackled more centrally, although to what extent he's a Marxist is clearly a different matter. I suppose the Benjamin book sees that in Bakhtin there are some of the roots of a materialist theory of comedy, especially in relation to the body. And I've always been interested in a kind of *comédie noire* – partly Beckett, partly Wilde, partly a general Irish debunkery. *Saint Oscar*, my play about Wilde, which is effectively tragicomic, is an instance of this. The English reviewers found the mixture of tragedy and comedy hard to cope with. There was no problem at all in Ireland: they didn't object to the mixing of genres, to having knockabout songs in the same play as the fall of the tragic protagonist. But the English critics who came over from London to see it – who were all very proud of themselves for arriving in Belfast unhelmeted and unshot, bearing a rather smug air of survival – didn't seem to understand that at all. It was no problem whatsoever for the Irish. I suppose a kind of tragicomedy is traditional in Ireland.

I suspect that you assimilate Bakhtin slightly too easily to Marxism in the book on Benjamin; at least, you don't address the problem of his relation to Marxism directly. You do use him very productively, though, to construct a kind of somatic politics, and in that sense it reads like a pre-emptive strike against the postmodernist obsession with bodies that you've criticized on a number of occasions.

Yes. I suppose my grouse about that was always that the bodies in question were too selective. Bakhtin at least opens the way for a wider conception of it there.

In one of the reviews of Walter Benjamin, *David Forgacs argued that it exhibits too much revolutionary romanticism. He also argued that the role you ascribe to Benjamin himself allowed you to embrace him 'as an* alter ego *living the same spiritual crisis in an analogous historical conjuncture (the thirties, the eighties), but also to spurn him for his retrograde elements like his mysticism, his idealism, his mandarinism'. It seems to me that the book is careful not to spurn those elements, indeed to demonstrate that they can't simply be conjured away by a materialist criticism. What though do you think of this idea that he acted as an* alter ego?

That's interesting. He's right to some extent about the parallel moments. We weren't of course facing anything as desperate as fascism in the eighties, but there was a need nonetheless to mobilize resources. But I've never seen Benjamin as an *alter ego* at all; nor Brecht for that matter. I might be downbeat but I'm not melancholic.

Your next book was The Rape of Clarissa, *a study of 'Writing, Sexuality and Class Struggle in Samuel Richardson' that appeared in 1982. It's a book that is profoundly influenced by feminism, and in particular perhaps by your relationship with Toril Moi.*

Toril wasn't a direct influence, and although she read the book I don't remember her collaborating with me on it. Neither did I consciously see it as a feminist book. I was therefore rather surprised when some feminist critics took it up as though it was a self-consciously feminist work. Both Toril and I took it for granted that feminism moved within a broader left or socialist context – in her case partly because she came from Norway, hence from a continental European rather than Anglo-Saxon tradition. Our thought was compatible in that respect, so we could escape a lot of tedious spadework and discuss things together. She shared my views about the limits of what in those days would have been called 'bourgeois feminism', and the bourgeois post-feminism around the place these days. So there was a political as well as intellectual affinity between us. I was genuinely interested in Richardson as a writer, but I also thought he was an almost ridiculously paradigmatic figure for thinking through relations between class, art and sexuality.

The most prominent feminist to criticize The Rape of Clarissa *was Elaine Showalter, who wrote a piece in which she attacked you under the subtitle 'Terry Eagleton and the Rape of Feminist Theory'. She depicted you as a 'Marxist McHeath' who had written a book that was 'meant to have the dash and daring of a highwayman's attack'; and argued that, 'energetic and entertaining though it be, Eagleton's phallic feminism seems like another raid on the resources of the feminine in order to modernize male dominance.' You then responded to her in the self-consciously ironical form of an autobiographical account of your experiences as a working-class socialist at Cambridge who resented the presence of upper-middle-class leftists. After reflecting on the lasting political commitment of many of these people, at a time when a number of working-class socialists were selling out, you concluded: 'I still think that we were wrong to have been so self-righteous.'*

She seemed to find that utterly irrelevant, and accused me of the old patriarchal trick of changing the topic of debate. She didn't understand that it was about class, perhaps partly because she is an American. I thought she displayed an extraordinary, overweening confidence in what counted as a continuation of the argument and what didn't. That was one of my earliest experiences – I was to see so much of it later – of the way in which, by some inexorably perverse logic, American academics translate issues of general political substance into squabbles over academic patches.

One of the more provocative suggestions you make in this book is that Richardson's works can be productively thought of less as novels than as fictional 'kits', meaning 'great unwieldy containers crammed with spare parts and agreeable extras'. Here you are blurring the older meaning of 'kit', still current in the eighteenth century, of a container or vessel, and the newer one, used from the nineteenth century, of an 'outfit of tools'. The 'kit' is thus a kind of primitive hypertext. Where did this idea come from? Brecht, perhaps, and Lévi-Strauss?

It's possible that the idea of bricolage was at the back of my mind. The techniques of 'epic' theatre certainly were. What interested me was that a lot of what the post-structuralists or deconstructionists were saying seemed applicable to Richardson and his techniques, though at the same time he was entirely hostile to their epistemological assumptions. Here was a stout, puritanical, *petit-bourgeois* Protestant talking about matters that seemed to pre-empt a lot of the discussions that were going on in our own time – about identity, the self, narrative. Richardson is brilliantly alert to the *jouissance* of writing, but at the same time he is almost the last person to lend himself to an ideology of *jouissance*. Indeed, that ideology is condemned in the figure of Lovelace. It was this incongruity that interested me. Attempts by the post-structuralist camp to appropriate Richardson *tout court* failed miserably because there was too much they couldn't take account of. And yet anybody reading him for his substance had to take on board some of his techniques and his ideas.

The idea of Clarissa *as a 'kit' is in part effective — not least in implicit opposition to the post-structuralists — because of its emphasis on the materiality of the text. But there is no systematic discussion of the material processes of production and consumption in this book. Richardson himself was of course a professional printer and publisher as well as a writer, and this bears paradoxically on his attempt to develop what you describe as his 'anti-writing', a writing that 'strives to abolish the materiality of the sign'.*

Yes, that's another way in which he is wondrously, almost absurdly paradigmatic. He was somebody who earned his living from the materiality of the word, but also from the fact that printing plugged him into an entire network. This book is probably the closest I've come in my work to developing something like Williams's cultural materialism. If I'd had that concept at my disposal at the time, I think I could have done more with Richardson.

Critics have in the past complained that you don't write enough about consumption, but you do talk about Richardson's relationship with his female friends and readers, and the relation of this to what you call the 'feminization of discourse'.

I don't think that anywhere else in my work has there been such a convenient congruity of the analysis of the text and the analysis of its material situation — he was the figure in which this could come together so neatly.

There's a terrific discussion of Clarissa's death in the book, which you characterize as a kind of liturgical act that's shot through with political meaning. You effectively present her as a martyr and a tragic scapegoat, and in that respect this book is aligned with your work both from the sixties and from the last decade. Were you also influenced by contemporary political events? I'm thinking in particular of the death of Bobby Sands in 1981, the year before The Rape of Clarissa *appeared.*

I think so, although that doesn't come through explicitly. I was conscious that there were aspects of hunger-striking that the English didn't necessarily understand. For example, I was aware because of my Irish background both that it was an ancient, highly traditional form of protest and that, far more than a generalized desire to do away with oneself, it constituted a specific refusal, a refusal of something from a particular somebody. In medieval Ireland someone who had a grudge against a landlord might go and sit on his doorstep and starve. I was interested in the political uses of the body. I suppose I did see Clarissa as an early precursor of this. Maud Ellmann then picked that up, interestingly, in her book *The Hunger Artists* [1993].

To what extent do you think your theological background still informed your thought at this stage, explicitly or implicitly? At one point in The Rape of Clarissa *you criticize Williams for failing to understand that, for Richardson, an adequate social solution to the historical conditions that he depicts had to include the religious dimension. You point out that Williams is incapable of relating Richardson's political insight to his representation of Clarissa's religious faith, and go on to argue that any 'adequate social response' at this time needs to be as 'absolute and all-encompassing' as Clarissa's God.*

The point is that for Richardson what might later be articulated in political terms has to be articulated in religious ones – that's his kind of other-worldliness or trans-worldliness. The early eighties was probably the time when I was furthest from theology. But that would be one example of a point in my work at which you can still hear it dimly in the background. It never entirely went away, but I didn't really know what to do with it at this time. More recently, I've been greatly helped by the fact that people like Žižek and Badiou and Agamben have spoken up so boldly about it, quite often from an explicitly atheistic perspective – in contrast to Benjamin's image of the wizened dwarf who has to remain silent. I wasn't being coy about it, it had simply moved a long way from my thoughts – although even in *Criticism and Ideology*, which one might think of as extremely remote from my early theological upbringing, one can detect its presence. I remember somebody disagreeing with my attempt to find some materialist basis for morality – perhaps when I talk about the development of powers and capacities in one of the later chapters – and thinking at the time that it was morality that was the point of opposition. There was a certain gung-ho Althusserianism which assumed that you could dispense with morality altogether, and I remember thinking at the time, although again I was pretty far from theology, that it was because of my theological background that I didn't want to let go of it.

As far as Clarissa goes, I return to her in more explicit theological terms in *Trouble with Strangers*, where she becomes one of several examples of the ethics of the Real. Theologically speaking, she's a martyr, as well as a version of the sacrificial victim or *pharmakos*. It's from this that her dangerous, deathly power derives.

Reading

Anderson, Perry, 'Components of the National Culture', in *English Questions* (London: Verso, 1992), pp. 48–104.

Benjamin, Walter, *The Origin of German Tragic Drama*, trans. John Osborne (London: Verso, 1998).

Clifford, John, and John Schilb, 'A Perspective on Eagleton's Revival of Rhetoric', *Rhetoric Review* 6:1 (1987), pp. 22–31.

Derrida, Jacques, *Of Grammatology*, corrected edition, trans. Gayatri Chakravorty Spivak (Baltimore: Johns Hopkins University Press, 1998).

Eagleton, Terry, 'Marxism and Deconstruction', *Contemporary Literature* 22:4 (1981), pp. 477–88.

Eagleton, Terry, *Walter Benjamin; or, Towards a Revolutionary Criticism* (London: Verso, 1981).

Eagleton, Terry, *The Rape of Clarissa: Writing, Sexuality and Class Struggle in Samuel Richardson* (Oxford: Blackwell, 1982).

Eagleton, Terry, *Literary Theory: An Introduction* (Oxford: Blackwell, 1983).

Eagleton, Terry, *The Function of Criticism: From the* Spectator *to Post-Structuralism* (London: Verso, 1984).

Eagleton, Terry, 'Criticism and Ideology: Andrew Milner interviews Terry Eagleton', *Thesis Eleven* 12 (1985), pp. 130–44.

Eagleton, Terry, 'Ideology and Scholarship', in *Historical Studies and Literary Criticism*, ed. Jerome J. McGann (Madison: University of Wisconsin Press, 1985), pp. 114–25.

Eagleton, Terry, 'The Subject of Literature', *Cultural Critique* 2 (1985–1986), pp. 95–104.

Eagleton, Terry, 'Interview with Terry Eagleton' (with Andrew Martin and Patrice Petro), *Social Text* 13/14 (Winter/Spring 1986), pp. 83–99.

Eagleton, Terry, 'Response', in *Men in Feminism*, eds. Alice Jardine and Paul Smith (London: Methuen, 1987), pp. 133–5.

Eagleton, Terry, *How to Read a Poem* (Oxford: Blackwell, 2007).

Eagleton, Terry, 'Comrades and Colons', *Antipode* 40:3 (2008), pp. 351–6.

Ellmann, Maud, *The Hunger Artists: Starving, Writing, and Imprisonment* (Harvard: Harvard University Press, 1993).

Forgacs, David, review of *Walter Benjamin*, *Poetics Today* 4:1 (1983), pp. 183–6.

Jameson, Fredric, *The Political Unconscious: Narrative as a Socially Symbolic Act* (Ithaca, N.Y.: Cornell University Press, 1981).

MacCabe, Colin, *James Joyce and the Revolution of the Word* (London: Macmillan, 1978).

Roberts, Julian, *Walter Benjamin* (London: Macmillan, 1982).

Showalter, Elaine, 'Critical Cross-Dressing: Male Feminists and the Woman of the Year', in *Men in Feminism*, eds. Alice Jardine and Paul Smith (London: Methuen, 1987), pp. 116–27.

Showalter, Elaine, 'Elaine Showalter Replies', in *Men in Feminism*, eds. Alice Jardine and Paul Smith (London: Methuen, 1987), p. 136.

Smith, James, *Terry Eagleton: A Critical Introduction* (Cambridge: Polity, 2008).

Thornett, Alan, *From Militancy to Marxism: A Personal and Political Account of Organizing Car Workers* (London: Left View, 1987).

Williams, Raymond, *Culture and Society* (London: Chatto & Windus, 1958).

Wolin, Richard, *Walter Benjamin: An Aesthetic of Redemption* (New York: Columbia University Press, 1982).

CHAPTER SEVEN

Theory/Practice

Literary Theory: An Introduction, *first published in 1983 and currently in its third edition, is the book for which you are still, no doubt, most famous. It has apparently sold almost a million copies. Did you expect it to be as successful as it became?*

No, I was absolutely astonished. I didn't say to myself, 'There's a market for the popularization of Theory.' Like *Criticism and Ideology*, though at a very different level, *Literary Theory* was the kind of book about which one might say – this wouldn't be exactly accurate – that it was waiting to be written. Somebody was going to write this book. It too emerged from the Wadham class. There was so much in the air, and so many ideas knocking around, that they had to be drawn together. The success of the book, I think, is largely accounted for by the fact that it was taken on as a textbook by so many American classes – that's what keeps a critical book ticking over. So what's peculiar about it is its perennial quality.

I wrote it because I thought there wasn't a simple, comprehensive introduction to all the new sorts of theories that had been proliferating over the previous decade or so. There wasn't a popular introduction to the subject at the time, so there was a lot of mystification about it. People feared that it was as esoteric as nuclear physics and that they'd never be able to understand it, and that played into the hands of orthodox critics who had a vested interest in people not having access to that kind of work. I felt that theory was important because it raised uncomfortable questions about what we habitually do. Theory tends to arise at points where our habitual assumptions and practices for one reason or another are breaking down. It is simply a way of trying to step back from that and say, 'What actually is going on? What are we doing and what is its relevance?' I saw theory less as something esoteric, less as a matter of specialist methods, than as a way of raising general questions about our habitual practices. I think those questions are really political questions, in the sense that they're asking how those practices relate to a wider structure of power.

Literary Theory notoriously presented itself as an obituary for the concept of 'literature', which it demonstrated was finally an ideological category, a historical sedimentation of competing institutional definitions, rather than an essence. The book's slogan in this respect was Barthes' statement that 'literature is what gets taught'. This outraged your more conservative colleagues. Could you comment on your attitude to this aspect of the book?

I would still want to defend the claim that literature has no ontological unity. However, I'd also make two qualifications to my argument in *Literary Theory*. First, I was trying to show that literature has no essence; but this is in fact true of many phenomena, and there's nothing very unusual or distinctive about literature in this respect. How, as Wittgenstein asks, do you define 'game'? And the fact that there's no essence, whether of 'game' or 'literature', doesn't necessarily mean that there are no significant interrelations between the various objects people group under these headings. Wittgenstein's idea of 'family resemblances' is precisely about grasping the connections of objects, but in a non-essentialist way. There are, I think, family resemblances between the various pieces of writing we call 'literature', but there is still no essence – though in *The Illusions of Postmodernism* and elsewhere I have of course defended the more radical aspects of essentialism against its postmodern critics. Heretically, I think that some essentialism can be progressive.

I think we need to shift from the idea of literature to the idea of writing. This doesn't involve abandoning value judgments, which are utterly inescapable, or abandoning Balzac and Tolstoy, it simply means redefining the field. A great deal of important writing after 1800 – historiography, philosophy – wasn't actually called 'literature'. Even so, though literature may have no ontological coherence, that doesn't mean that it can't have great practical and institutional power. Some critics of my book were right to point out that I rather too swiftly swept this aside. Literature might be a philosophically dubious concept, but it can still be a potent practical reality.

In your essay on Jameson from 1982 you argue that it's sometimes difficult to tell the difference in his work between exegesis and critique. It seems to me that one of the strengths of Literary Theory *is that you deliberately exploit the indistinct boundary between the two. The book thus popularizes and polemicizes at the same time, speaking in both a neutral and a partisan voice.*

Raymond Tallis, who is one of my most implacable enemies, said that he was impressed by the way I was able to ventriloquize positions I didn't agree with – whereas one of the things I dislike about his work is that he can't resist polemical pokes even when he's supposed to be explicating. I suppose there is a lot of that going on, in that the critique is often implicit in the exegesis. It's significant, of course, that I don't talk about Marxism explicitly, except to hint at the end of the book that that's what it's really been about all along.

I like popularizing; I like trying to write for a larger audience. Indeed, some of the most interesting responses to *Literary Theory* came from people who had never seen the inside of a university. These were simply intelligent general readers who wanted to know what was going on in the field. Radical intellectuals have a duty to reach a wider constituency; or, at the least, to be intelligible within their own constituency. I am sometimes horrified by the implicit acquiescence in academicism maintained even by supposedly quite radical thinkers and writers. This is particularly objectionable in the case of literary theory, because I believe that – contrary to all appearances – it is a genuinely democratic activity. Genuinely democratic in the sense that what it sets out to replace is a kind of criticism that says: 'Look, in order to be intelligent, you have to have a certain kind of intuition, one bred into you by a certain sort of culture.' It's a matter of blood and breeding. Literary theory stands out against this and says, 'Anybody can join in this activity if they are prepared to learn certain languages.' It is then particularly scandalous that people engaged in what is basically a democratic enterprise should write in such an obscurantist way.

But to say that one shouldn't write in a deliberate and wilfully obscure way isn't of course to say that one should always be easy to read. In an age of consumerism, and one that includes and encourages the habits of intellectual consumerism, there's an attitude on the part of some students that can be summarized as, 'If I don't get it in the first two paragraphs then there must be something wrong with it, rather than me.' At a certain level that's a completely understandable response for literary students to make, since there is supposed to be something about literature itself that makes it generally available. So writing *on* literature is expected to be immediately accessible too. But it's as well to remember that those who do react in this consumerist way – 'If it doesn't go straight down then it's indigestible' – would never say that about reading, for example, an engineering textbook. And just as in engineering, there is a specific set of skills and languages to be learnt in literary theory in order to understand it. What I'm saying is that populism need not be the only opposite to élitism. When jargon means a wilfully obscure, in-group language, it is politically objectionable. But jargon can also quite properly refer to an inevitably specialized idiom. I think one has to distinguish between these different meanings of the term.

*In the afterword to the recent anniversary edition, you cover quite a
lot of ground that, for historical reasons, you couldn't cover in the
original edition. For example, you summarize the characteristics of the
new historicism and identify it as 'a historiography appropriate for a
postmodern age in which the very notions of historical truth, causality,
pattern, purpose and direction were increasingly under fire'. You also
discuss post-colonial theory. The current that you don't consider at all
is queer theory.*

That's true. I hadn't thought of that. I must admit there's a bit of a
blank with me about queer theory. That's partly a measure of the
distance between the moment of *The Rape of Clarissa* [1982] and the
present. I was intensively engaged with the idea of sexual politics
in *The Rape of Clarissa*, partly as a result of Toril Moi's influence,
partly because it was unavoidable, but I suppose my involvement
with ideas of sexuality since have been more psychoanalytic than
political. That's a limitation that I ought to put right.

You followed Literary Theory *with* The Function of Criticism
*[1984]. It's a polemical history of criticism as an institution, from 'the
Spectator to Post-Structuralism' — from the London coffee house to the
Parisian café. You argue that, though modern criticism emerged from
the struggle against the absolutist state, it has in the present climate
lost 'all substantive social function'. The book opens with an account
of the motivation behind it: 'Perhaps I could best describe the impulse
behind this book by imagining the moment in which a critic, sitting
down to begin a study of some theme or author, is suddenly arrested by
a set of disturbing questions. What is the* point *of such a study? Who is
it intended to reach, influence, impress? What functions are ascribed to
such a critical act by society as a whole?'*

I think that, having written two books that were largely concerned
with ideas, *The Rape of Clarissa* and *Literary Theory*, I wanted to
get back to the political and institutional aspects I'd discovered
in writing the Benjamin book. So there's an odd underground

connection there. Having dealt with texts and ideas and figures, I was more and more interested in raising meta-questions about the nature of criticism, the rationale for criticism, the status of criticism and how that had historically evolved. In the mid-eighties there was a point where it was less and less clear what that role was. People were certainly taking it for granted, and assuming that the thing had a point and that writing their works on this or that actually mattered. In a recent lecture called 'The Death of Criticism?' I come back to that question, so it has been with me for a long time. There is an *a priori* need to justify the whole enterprise of criticism – not in a guilty or grovelling way, but in order to make sense of it.

The Function of Criticism *located criticism historically in the space between civil society and the state that Jürgen Habermas identified as the bourgeois 'public sphere'.*

Like many others, I've argued that Habermas's theory is too rationalistic as it stands, but I was interested in those aspects of it that could be redeemed and could figure alongside a politics of the body. Aesthetic thought runs back to an anxiety about the absence of the body in certain rational discourses, though the various attempts to put the body back in have fallen foul of various modes of idealization and stylization. I felt I had to think that project through again, but this time from another, more corporeal standpoint. It was a project fraught with risk: partly because the body had now become such a fashionable theme, and partly because it's not easy to know how to avoid various forms of reductionism, naturalism, or the supposed self-evidence of body experience.

One of the other things you do in this book is deconstruct the ideology of 'disinterestedness' that you identified as structural to the bourgeois public sphere. Could you clarify that?

Notions of disinterestedness begin to crop up in the eighteenth century with the emergence of the bourgeois public sphere, and what is striking about that disinterestedness is its obvious interestedness. That is to say, only those who have an 'interest' can be disinterested, only those who have a stake in the culture, who are propertied, are entitled to enter into a certain 'disinterested' form of discourse, the whole discourse of Enlightenment reason for example. So what one is looking at in that whole history becomes visible as a highly élitist and exclusionist class formation – although certainly one which, like many class formations, needs to cast its language in universal terms. The idea of disinterestedness is most forcefully understood today in terms of that history. What happens with the growth of the commodification of literature, which was taking place throughout the eighteenth century, is that there is now a sense in which literature is in principle available to everybody – whatever the actual restrictions of social access to literature and power. Nonetheless, the commodification of literature actually liberates literary production from a very specific range of interested institutions – only to abandon it to the marketplace. Ironically, then, and by a striking contradiction, the very possibility of disinterestedness as a critical concept, as an intellectual posture, depends upon a sort of promiscuous availability of the literary commodity. Anybody is capable of judging this commodity, any 'gentleman', that is. This situation itself, in turn, is an effect of commodity production. If one looks at the history in that way then one sees where the so-called disinterested intellectual comes from.

What I tried to do in *The Function of Criticism* was to go on to trace the destiny of the concept into the nineteenth century and beyond. I think that the great crisis, the crisis around Matthew Arnold for example, is that it becomes implausible to believe either that you can transcend sectional and social interests, or that there is any longer a total body of social and intellectual knowledge on which intellectuals can get a fix, as it were, transcendentally. It seemed to me that one of the problems that dogged the institution of criticism is that either you try fruitlessly to reproduce that role of the disinterested intellectual, in all its various liberal-humanist guises, or you candidly recognize that the role is now historically devalued, it is past, and you try and do something else. The problem is that 'something else' tends either to be a kind of technocracy, a specialized, professionalized technocracy that has abandoned any hope of speaking more relevantly to a society beyond the academy; or, as with the left, you try and work out some other set of functions for criticism. I don't think criticism has solved that problem, and so long as it doesn't follow the path of the left I think it is actually structurally incapable of doing so.

Your institutional history of criticism effectively skips from Arnold, at the end of Chapter 3, to Leavis, at the start of Chapter 4, so the function of criticism at the fin de siècle, the criticism of Pater, Wilde and aestheticism, constitutes an aporia. *Pater and Wilde are surely important because, in seeing the object as it really isn't, as the latter once put it, they deconstruct the opposition between the cognitive and the creative, and so anticipate post-structuralist criticism in some respects.*

That should be there. I talked a little bit about the growth of the specialist journal, the increasing division of intellectual labour and so on; but there is a bit of a sea-change there, I agree, with the rise of notions of the critic as artist.

Patrick Parrinder, who'd been one of Raymond Williams's students, criticized your use of the concept of the counter-public sphere and in effect dismissed it as a politicized and de-professionalized version of Stanley Fish's concept of the 'interpretive community'. Do you have any thoughts on that?

I would have thought that it was almost the other way round – that Fish's 'interpretive community' is a depoliticized version of a politically conscious public sphere. Fish is thinking about different schools of criticism or interpretation, whereas the counter-public sphere means more than that. If it did come into being it could do so only on the back of a mass movement, a political movement. I suppose that was part of the point I was trying to make in the Benjamin book – that you can recycle the critic, or he or she can do it themselves, but it's only going to stick, it's only going to have force as opposed to meaning, if it's done in a certain political context. As far as that goes, we don't call the tune. I think that would still be my case today.

In the mid-1980s you edited a series of student introductions to canonical authors for Blackwell called Rereading Literature. *Steven Connor produced one on Dickens, for instance, Alan Sinfield one on Tennyson, and Rachel Bowlby one on Woolf. You've said that the book on Shakespeare that you contributed to this series has been underrated. Why is that the case?*

I've no idea. That series didn't do very well, both to my surprise and the publisher's, though the book on Shakespeare probably sold the best. I don't understand why not. It wasn't because of competition, since nobody else was doing it. My former student Philip Carpenter conceived it and I thought it was an excellent idea. But the sales were generally unimpressive and in some cases positively dismal. The books bombed in the States, so Blackwell did some market research and discovered that the Americans didn't regard them as real books. For an American, apparently, the definition of a book is something you can't put in your pocket. These were 'brochures'. So we tackled that problem by putting them in hardback, making the print bigger and so on – but it didn't work. It had seemed just the right moment, a high point in theory, but it didn't take off.

Why did you do the book on Shakespeare?

There was no one else to do it, and it had to be done since the series was supposed to deal with widely studied authors. But I did it with some alacrity because I'd maintained an interest in Shakespeare since the early Shakespeare book. In fact, as I said earlier, shortly after I'd published *Shakespeare and Society* [1967] I returned to Shakespeare and produced a terribly mangled and clotted manuscript, trying to develop some of the same ideas but in a much too fuzzy way. I was convinced I'd seen something about Shakespeare's plays that hadn't generally been seen – questions of exchange value, signification, identity and the like. When I came to put these claims in publishable form, alas, it was in a format that just didn't catch on. I still value this book, though.

How was it received?

There was a strangely dual response among the reviewers. Some of them disliked what they took to be its aloofly superior tone, as though Shakespeare were being given four and a half out of ten for not being modern. Others, strangely, thought it smacked of idolatory and was too uncritical of Shakespeare's assumed status. There was in this book a certain provocative appropriation of Shakespeare, a deliberate attempt at a demystifying approach for students who might otherwise find his status intimidating. In other words, there was some point and some pleasure in showing how he could be 'knocked off' for those critical purposes, and I think I probably did that with a certain provocative *élan*, though clearly with a serious point behind it. When I said in the introduction to the book that it was surprising to discover that somehow Shakespeare had managed to read Marx and Wittgenstein, this was to claim on the one hand that Shakespeare should be looked at in these modern terms, and on the other hand to acknowledge that, in certain senses, he seems to have pre-empted us. Both emphases – demystifying Shakespeare, and seeing what we can still learn from him – were coupled together.

It's an exhilarating book to read, I think, but it arguably has so much fun with the post-structuralist ideas it finds in Shakespeare that it neglects the important task of providing a historical and materialist reading of the plays.

I think that charge is pretty just, actually. It wouldn't have been hard to push the argument in that direction; it was open to being done. My interests were ideological and theoretical rather than historical. Historically speaking, I simply didn't have the necessary grounding. By contrast, I felt that, in its concentration on historical context, there was a certain skimping of ideas in the new historicism. I thought that the new historicists had failed to see some of the astonishing ways in which Shakespeare prefigured contemporary theoretical interests. That was the impulse behind the book. But I felt that, in its relatively brief compass, I couldn't cover both the theoretical and the historical, even if I had been competent enough in the latter area. That was a task that remained to be done.

In one of the reviews collected in Figures of Dissent *[2003] you memorably stated that 'the new historicism, for all its occasional brilliance, is theoretically speaking a set of footnotes to Foucault.' You haven't, however, discussed the new historicism especially extensively in your work. What did you make of Stephen Greenblatt?*

I was intrigued. I had met Greenblatt in California, and I was interested by the fact that he had started out as a pupil of Williams at Cambridge before moving into a very different position, one that he would himself identify as left-wing, but much more Foucauldian and much more pessimistic. From a distance, I saw that whole Californian new-historicist phenomenon as a sign of the political times. It was part of a general shift – not from left to right exactly but from optimism to pessimism. I don't think they were aware of this – the last thing you historicize is yourself – and I think it needed to be brought to their attention.

What about the British cultural materialists, like Jonathan Dollimore and Alan Sinfield, who were also products of Williams's influence? How did their work relate symptomatically to that political shift, do you think?

I suppose there was a sense in which after the hard-nosed literary Marxism of the seventies, epitomized by the Essex conferences, cultural materialism was a softer Marxist alternative. One of the unanswered questions I had about cultural materialism was how it differed from the traditional sociology of the arts. I don't think the theoretical distinctions were ever defined. It was effectively a British offshoot of new historicism, which was increasingly a fashionable movement. It put people on the map. So one answer to the question I raised before – 'What happened to the University of Essex conference groups?' – is that some of them became cultural materialists. It fitted better with the times.

In some respects, this seems rather harsh to me. In their emphasis on the politics of pedagogic practice, and above all in their treatment of sexuality, the cultural materialists were openly political, even if their politics were transparently post-Marxist.

Culture is always a deepening of the political as well as a potential displacement of it, and that was certainly true of a great deal of cultural-materialist work in sexuality, power and the like.

From the late 1980s you engaged in an intensive process of creative as opposed to strictly academic composition, and produced a novel and several plays. The novel, Saints and Scholars *[1987], is an intellectual fantasia in which after a series of set pieces in Dublin, Vienna, Cambridge and St. Petersburg, four characters (Nikolai Bakhtin, James Connolly, Ludwig Wittgenstein and Leopold Bloom) are holed up in a cottage on the west coast of Ireland. How did you come to write this novel?*

I don't remember, as I don't remember how I came to write anything, but it has always struck me that it was the first text I'd written about Ireland. I approached Ireland through creative writing first of all – there was the novel, and then three plays – and only subsequently through critical writing. So it was my first tentative engagement with the issue of Ireland. At that time I didn't have anything like the kind of historical knowledge that I later tried to acquire, and the novel form saved me from the need for it. Then the Bakhtin-Connolly-Wittgenstein triumvirate seemed to me to have both comic and intellectual potential. It drew together several of my interests. Finally, I think that, after the experience of writing the Benjamin book, with its more laid-back form, I was ready to chance my hand at fiction – I wouldn't have been earlier. So I passed it to Neil Belton, who was then the editor at Verso. He was Irish himself, though not of a Republican persuasion, and he took a personal interest in the novel, so that's how it ended up at Verso.

What I hadn't anticipated was people saying, 'Oh, how brave! You've written criticism about the novel and now you've put your money where your mouth is!' – partly because for me there was much more continuity between the critical and the creative than that implied. To my surprise, a number of people responded like that. Then a paperback firm picked the novel up. I remember the director, who was a bit of a thug, telling me very solemnly how interested in philosophy he was and that he was publishing it as a personal favour to himself. I had a bizarre interview with him in which he said, 'This is going to be a cult novel!' Indeed his parting words to me were: 'Bring them back! Bring them back!' – meaning the characters. I could just about see what he meant. He had glimpsed in it a kind of knock-about intellectual novel. So it did appear in paperback, but it didn't do all that well. The firm has long since gone bust. I hope I wasn't responsible for that.

If the novel staged an encounter between Bakhtin, Connolly and Wittgenstein, it also perhaps dramatized three different aspects of Terry Eagleton: there's Bakhtin the comic sensualist, Connolly the political activist, and Wittgenstein the intellectual ascetic.

I wasn't thinking about that consciously, but I was to some degree thinking consciously about places. Wittgenstein signified for me Cambridge, a certain dissident Cambridge, askew to the place as he was. I identified with him to some extent; in fact, I'd had supervisions in Whewell's Court in Trinity, where he'd lived. Then there was the growing interest in place in terms of Ireland. I was getting to know Ireland better. So I wasn't consciously pulling together fragmented aspects of my psyche, but I think I was conscious that there was an autobiographical thread in this representation of places. Wittgenstein did of course live for a while in the west of Ireland, which then neatly coupled together two dimensions of my own life.

What did Bakhtin represent in this spatial economy?

Perhaps he embodied the carnivalesque, as theorized by his brother Mikhail; and the ability of my work to explore humour and play more than it had. I think I was groping for that in the image of Bakhtin, a certain robust, earthy scepticism of the theoretical that I think is politically necessary. I was playing that sort of scepticism off against the high political seriousness of Connolly, which might reflect another aspect in myself.

Saints and Scholars *might be described as a Bakhtinian novel of ideas; and as such it pulls off a fairly delicate balancing act between the bodily and the cerebral. Its main characters clearly signal its philosophical influences, but were you also conscious of specific literary influences?*

Not really. In what I would now see as a typically Irish phenomenon, I didn't get much out of English realism. To a certain extent I saw it as a novel about language or languages. There are a lot of different idioms in the text. That caught up both my theoretical and political interests. But I have a strange sense of having written it, in literary terms, in a virginal kind of way, not feeling particularly influenced.

Perhaps it was an immaculate conception. Flann O'Brien probably hovers somewhere in the background, along with Joyce – the nightmare from whom Irish writers have been trying to awaken.

Do you think the novel represented in part a rejection of Williams's realist fiction?

I would think it did. Of course, there are those who would rightly point to Williams's interest in the experimental avant-garde, but his fiction is undoubtedly realist. When Joyce says he couldn't get anything out of English literary realism, I think that's extraordinarily important. In a much more minor way I felt I couldn't either. Realism usually serves up its ideas in domesticated form, which didn't interest me.

Were others from an Irish tradition at the back of your mind? It seems to me there are Beckettian qualities to Saints and Scholars, *albeit mixed up with Rabelaisian ones – as if a thin man and a fat man are fighting it out for dominance. And, rereading it, I was certainly reminded of O'Brien, who's not someone you've discussed in your criticism.*

Obliquely, O'Brien was an important influence. More broadly, I suppose, I was influenced by the black comedy characteristic of Beckett and O'Brien and others in the Irish tradition. I was later struck, when writing about the indigenous Irish novel, with how *Saints and Scholars* unconsciously reflected its ambiguous relationship with realism. Also, there's more of a tradition of the novel of ideas in Ireland, from Jonathan Swift to John Banville. Real life in Ireland was something mostly to get away from. Think of Wilde and Yeats. And medieval Irish writing is full of fantasy, hyperbole and word-play.

So there weren't any English models I was consciously following in *Saints and Scholars*. One point of comparison might be the kind of fiction that David Lodge, another Catholic literary critic, was writing at this stage: comic campus novels. But Lodge didn't really write novels of ideas. He's interested in the culture of Catholicism, not the theology. One might almost claim that the campus novel is a kind of English substitute for the novel of ideas. Its interest lies in the quirky ways of dons, rather than ideas. In contrast, I suppose I was looking for a fictional correlative for theory.

One that rejected the parochialism of the campus novel, and reflected instead the social and intellectual diaspora that had shaped theory . . .

Yes, that's right. I was also looking for a form that could accommodate a fairly broken-backed narrative, and allow me set pieces like the various cameos of place. It wasn't deliberately conceived as an experimental novel, but that's partly the way it came out. In writing it I realized that, for good and ill, I didn't have much patience with realism; and later I discovered that the easiest way to handle that problem was to write drama, which pares a lot of that away. Unlike English fiction, the Irish novel isn't all that enthralled by individual psychology, and I found myself spontaneously sharing this predilection.

I did however write an article for *New Left Review* in the late seventies, on *Aesthetics and Politics*, in which I tried to say that the whole argument about realism versus modernism suffers from a drastic shortage of history. The collective memory has repressed the moment of the revolutionary emergence and challenge of realism as a progressive force, as a rapidly secularizing, demystifying genre against the aristocratic forms of non-realism, the great feudalist and traditionalist genres. It is only by virtue of such a repression that we can now look back at realism in a universalizing way and say that it will always have a reactionary effect in its fixing of the sign or whatever. But whether representation will have a reactionary effect really depends on where you happen to be standing at the time. It may well be that the anti-realist moment is still right for this political moment – that it will be the forms we've received from the great revolutionary avant-garde currents, from the Futurists through to Brecht, that will be most viable. It may indeed be that intellectuals tend grossly to overestimate the extent to which the masses are in the grip of realism. Indeed, if one looks at many popular cultural forms, they don't use realism very much. They use techniques that are akin to the techniques of modernism.

Saints and Scholars might be said to use 'magic-realist' devices. I'm thinking for example of the end of the opening chapter, when you suddenly freeze-frame the bullets destined to execute Connolly in order, in Benjaminian fashion, to 'blast him out of the dreary continuum of history'. The book ostentatiously plays fast and loose with history. Is it then in some senses a 'postmodernist' novel?

Well, I suppose one might claim that modernism plays fast and loose with history too. But yes, another aspect of the Irish suspicion of realism is its indifference to the linear, evolutionary narrative. It's not easy to read Irish history as a stately progression towards a *telos*. So Ireland and Benjamin converged here.

As I indicated when we discussed The Rape of Clarissa, *one theme that frequently recurs in your work is martyrdom, which you characterize as a kind of dialectic of humiliation and redemption. In the novel it's the character of Connolly that incarnates this dialectic. Throughout the narrative, though, there's an interest in the religious and political forms that this dialectic assumes. It persistently probes the relationship between resurrection and insurrection, so to speak, the martyrdom of the monk and the militant.*

You describe the novel far better than I could myself. Yes, martyrdom was embedded deeply enough as a theme to re-emerge in my play about Connolly, *The White, the Gold and the Gangrene* [1993], so it must have been an abiding concern. I don't know at what point it was that, looking back, it struck me that I always wrote about martyrs – even in the Wittgenstein screenplay. The idea of abnegation was coming much more strongly into my work, and I felt somehow more comfortable handling it in a fictional rather than theoretical way, in terms of a character I could fictionalize, like Connolly or Wilde. Wilde was another Irish martyr, incidentally, as a man who at one time – I'm thinking of *De Profundis* – mistook himself for Jesus Christ.

Do you think this interest in martyrdom came purely from the religious formation you'd had, or was it also shaped by a secular spirit of romanticism?

I don't think it was purely religious. The idea was of course familiar to me from my religious background, but it also came out of a lot of brooding on the idea of death and self, failure and breakdown. So there was a lot in that early fictional work that anticipates the book on tragedy. Interestingly, I did it fictionally first and theoretically later.

Have you ever wanted to write another novel, if only in order to use it once again as a kind of laboratory for ideas?

No, I became bored with writing novels altogether – partly because of this impatience with realism. Writing novels is just more of the same thing as writing criticism. Theatre gets you out of the house. It's an entirely different world.

I'm struck again by how closely you seem to identify the novel form with realism. Given your sympathy with the anti- or post-realist novel, I wonder why that is.

Of course the novel is much wider than realism. But I thought that the particular sort of non-realist effect that I was after could somehow be achieved more easily in drama. There's a lot of dialogue in *Saints and Scholars*, which points forward to the plays.

It would be an easy novel to dramatize, though it would be hard to put St. Petersburg on stage.

Let's move on to the drama, then. Your most successful play, Saint Oscar, *was first staged in 1989. In addition to* The White, the Gold and the Gangrene, *which you've briefly mentioned, you've also written* Disappearances *[1987] and, for radio,* God's Locusts *[1995]. Perhaps you could begin by telling me about the genesis of* Saint Oscar.

I remember having a long wait in Palermo airport and beginning to scribble a ballad about Oscar Wilde. So the songs actually came first, or that one did at least. Then I began to write snatches of dialogue. The final version of the play was a surprisingly untransformed version of all that. In other words, it came very spontaneously. And it was easy and pleasurable to write. I wrote it with no idea of what to do with it, or even if it would be staged, but Field Day were looking for a play at that point. They wanted to do a new Irish play every year but didn't have one to hand, so they were rather glumly resigned to doing *Coriolanus* or something rather un-Celtic. Then I gave the manuscript of *Saint Oscar* to Tom Paulin, who was a member of the Field Day Group.

Perhaps you could explain what Field Day is . . .

Field Day had been started by Brian Friel and Stephen Rea in 1980; that's to say, by an Irish playwright and an Irish actor. They were then joined by Paulin, Seamus Heaney, Seamus Deane, a famous Irish folk musician called David Hammond and another dramatist called Tom Kilroy. It was an extraordinary mixture of intellectuals, actors and writers. All except one of them were from the north, and therefore, to put it slightly crudely, from the cultural wing of nationalism. They exemplified the old saying that in the north the Protestants have the power but the Catholics have the culture. They deliberately sited themselves in Derry rather than

Dublin, and had a grand opening there for the new play every autumn. Each play would open in the Guildhall, and there would be bunting around the town, so it was quite a big deal. Dublin was rather wary of them for that reason.

Tom Paulin instantly saw that *Saint Oscar* would make a Field Day production. Trevor Griffiths, an old friend of mine, who somehow got to read it, volunteered to direct it, although he'd only ever directed one of his own plays before. So it rapidly went into production for Field Day in 1989, and that was enormously exciting. Although I was teaching at Oxford at the time I tried to be as much part of the tour as I could. I kept chasing the play around Ireland, rewriting it as we went along and seeing it alter before my eyes. I knew enough about the situation not to interfere with the directing, and I'd sit at the back with the tea boy and the wardrobe mistress. Trevor Griffiths would have been a hard man to interfere with in any case. We played both in the legitimate theatres like the Abbey and in community centres and town halls – places where the parish priest insisted on taking a raffle after the performance and Stephen Rea had to dip his hand in the tin and read out the number. I learnt a lot about the mechanics of theatre. The play was greatly appreciated by Field Day, though they saw that it needed to be, in Trevor Griffiths's words, 'theatred'. There were too many instances of two people standing talking to each other. And I discovered I had difficulty moving people from the door to the French window. The plays I wrote after that were for a Belfast-based theatre group, some of which were also broadcast on radio.

Were you conscious of being part of a tradition of leftist, socialist theatre at the time, inherited from the seventies? Tariq Ali, Howard Brenton, Caryl Churchill, David Edgar and others were all writing plays at this time, weren't they? The dark days of Thatcherism threw up all sorts of interesting oppositional theatre. Were you conscious of that axis as well as the Irish one?

Yes, although the immediate engagement was with an Irish cultural, critical environment. Field Day was very much that. It had forged an identity for itself in that way. Trevor Griffiths provided an interesting link back to British political theatre of the seventies, though, and brought that experience to bear on it. But the British political theatre was past its heyday by that point, and there were cultural possibilities in Ireland that simply weren't available on what some Ulster Protestants like to call the mainland.

The stage production of Saint Oscar *was screened by LWT [London Weekend Television], wasn't it?*

Yes, about a year later. We could hire the studio for three days, so we transposed the stage set into the studio and filmed it. It was part of a series of plays that were filmed as if they were theatre pieces. Our hearts were in our mouths because it cost something like twenty thousand pounds a day to hire the studio. At the end of the process, whether we'd finished or not, they were just going to pull the plug. We took a whole day just to do the music.

Were you aware of literary influences on the play in a way that you weren't with the novel? Brecht is the obvious point of reference, I suppose, and Wilde himself perhaps.

Not really; again, as with the novel, I wrote it without any very conscious literary model in mind. Even the allusion to *Saint Genet* was only semi-conscious. *Saint Oscar* wasn't the original title. There was a more boring title: 'The Fall of Oscar Wilde'. However, Bobby Crowley, who comes from Cork and is a very fine designer on the West End stage, but who hadn't ever designed in Ireland before, couldn't get any inspiration out of that, so he homed in on the phrase 'Saint Oscar'. That suddenly liberated Crowley's visual imagination and he had a big statue of St Sebastian, pierced with arrows, hanging on the stage. I've argued in *Sweet Violence* [2003] that the saint and the sinner are to some extent in cahoots (it's a Graham Greene-ish notion) – as opposed to what I call the moral middle classes, who probably wouldn't even recognize evil if it fell into their laps.

Were you using Saint Oscar *to think about the defeats of the working class at that time? There's a character called Wallace, a socialist activist, who becomes increasingly pessimistic, increasingly defeatist, in the aftermath of the dock strike of 1889. Indeed in the final act he declares that 'the most we can hope for is a more humane form of capitalism'.*

To which Wilde replies that that's like hoping to contract VD in one ball only . . . Yes, he becomes pretty disenchanted. I was conscious of a number of different dimensions to this. On the one hand, as somebody once said, writing about Irish history is always double-coded, because to write about the past is also to write about the politics of the present. In places like Ireland, above all, whatever stance you take in relation to the past is going to reflect a stance toward the present, so there's that baggage. On the other hand, there's the anti-colonial theme. I saw that the socialist, anti-colonialist dimension of Wilde was very little known by the English. So the play was a way of highlighting that. In the English presentation of Wilde there were a number of key elements missing. And it was part of the purpose of the play to try and retrieve those. When I gave a lecture on Wilde in Lancaster recently, there was a very erudite member of the general public who came along and said that he hadn't known Wilde was Irish. But then for some of the time neither did he . . .

When we discussed the conclusion to Shakespeare and Society, *you said that you'd treasured 'The Soul of Man Under Socialism' long before you'd become interested in Wilde's drama. How did this essay, which is in many respects an anarchist statement, fit into your interest in Wilde in the 1980s?*

Wilde sees that socialism is about pleasure and leisure, and that, perversely, its precursor in the present is in some ways the aristocrat he himself aspired to be. What's wrong with Wilde is that he doesn't see the individual subject as relational. But the 'Soul of Man' essay rehearses certain vital themes in Marx about the self-development of the individual. I'd always argued that Wilde was closer to Marx than Morris was in terms of the abolition of labour. I suppose I was also dealing with notions of indolence, leisure, privilege, utopian prefiguration, anti-labour, play, art and so on.

Why is it that Wilde doesn't see the subject as relational? Is it a product of his aristocratic conception of socialism, so to speak, or of his social isolation as a homosexual in late nineteenth-century London?

It's because he inherits a libertarian tradition for which the individual self is absolute and inviolable. In a sense, the argument with Wilde's individualism in *Saint Oscar* was a critical dialogue with contemporary post-structuralism too. It was an argument about how far the non-normative, the aberrant, the dissident, is inherently radical; how far it might sometimes be a form of privilege, how far it might be politically premature, and how far it might be prefigurative. Wilde provided a highly economical means of exploring an extraordinary number of rich, suggestive issues, both theoretically and politically – though that's not why I wrote the play.

Wilde conjured his identity out of a lack of self-identity. But I think one must also see it as turning a certain rather dire necessity to advantage. There was something painful for him in this problematic identity, both sexually and ethnically. It wasn't just a matter of deconstructive exuberance. In a colonial situation the question of identity becomes a kind of daily burden. It's the rulers who have the luxury of not fretting about who they are. What Wilde does, magnificently I think, is turn all that into a kind of ecstatic comedy. To turn a lack of identity – which has potentially tragic implications both for him and for his society – into a more positive kind of ethic. The point is to get to the point where it doesn't matter to you who you are – not to get to the point of some solid, absolutely affirmed identity but to the point where the whole question of identity has somehow lapsed as part of an outmoded epoch. I think Wilde is trying to prefigure that utopian moment. But to do so in the present is to lay yourself wide open to travesty and hostility.

Is this the only place in your work where you've addressed homosexuality?

Well, the original screenplay for *Wittgenstein* [1993] had something of that, because there was a scene in which Ludwig picked up a young homosexual lover. Like a number of other scenes, it was written out by Derek Jarman and didn't appear in the final version of the screenplay. I think I wanted to see Wilde's gayness as part of a wider dissidence – political, intellectual, artistic. I thought this was enriching, by opening it out, but I think there was also a certain suspicion of that from some people in the gay community, who thought I was too quickly displacing the issue. There might have been something in that. One of the things I admired about Stephen Rea's performance was his refusal to camp it up. Anyway, there have been a lot of gay plays about Wilde. This was meant to be different. For one thing, it opened not in the West End but in Derry.

Tell me how you came to write a script for Jarman's film about Wittgenstein.

Tariq Ali conceived the idea of producing several TV films on philosophers. He himself scripted one on Spinoza, which was screened on Channel 4, and then commissioned me to do one on Wittgenstein, mainly because of *Saints and Scholars*. Derek Jarman had already been intending to do his own film of Wittgenstein, so Tariq brought him in on our project. Jarman then rewrote substantial portions of my screenplay without my permission. I suddenly found, for example, that a little green man had been excruciatingly added to the script. There was then a semi-public row about this. Jarman and I didn't hit it off, partly for temperamental reasons, partly because I wasn't a member of his coterie. The film was stuffed with people he knew, whereas I was an outsider. I don't think that Jarman took to outsiders much. The fact that I was an intellectual might not have helped much either. Jarman wasn't interested in Wittgenstein's ideas – it was the life and the ideas about colour that mattered to him.

But he deleted a scene in which Wittgenstein picks someone up?

Yes, he cut that out. I had set most of it in Cambridge, including that scene, and he said, 'We're not going to shoot in Cambridge.' I said, 'Why not?' and he said, 'Firstly, everybody does it; secondly, it's very expensive.' That was fair enough, and I didn't object at all to his putting it in a blacked-out studio. But I had an agent for theatrical purposes in those days and she was getting more and more restive about the way they were treating the screenplay. She told me not to attend the filming process, for example, because it might have signalled a certain complicity in what was going on. So although a fair bit of my script is still in the film, there is quite a lot of stuff I didn't agree with as well. Eventually a third writer was also credited. This was a man called Ken Butler, who was Derek Jarman's assistant. Jarman was very ill at the time – he died shortly after – so Butler was ghosting him as it were. He was a kind of assistant director, highly competent technically but very much Jarman's man. The first my agent and I knew of his contribution to the script was when we saw the credits and his name appeared on the screen. We had no idea that he had been brought in on it. He actually wrote very little, I think, but this was typical of the cavalier approach Jarman took. I suspect Jarman never really had any intention of letting me be an autonomous screenplay writer. He was an auteur, so no doubt it was one of his strengths that he controlled and put his stamp on everything. But although very brilliant visually and cinematically, I didn't think that Jarman was a particularly good writer. And I didn't think that he improved the script. The humour, for example, became broader and blander. So there was some bad feeling over it for a while. The BFI published a volume called *Wittgenstein: The Terry Eagleton Script and the Derek Jarman Film* [1993].

What did you think of the film when you finally saw it?

In the end I was too close to it to judge. There was enough of my stuff still there for me not to feel that I'd been completely taken for a ride, but I'd nonetheless been left on the outside. I thought there were some rather absurd things in it. I also thought that the actor who played Wittgenstein, Karl Johnson, apart from looking amazingly like him, was exceedingly good. A lot of people liked it; a lot of people enjoyed it. But whenever I watch that film with friends I tell them I'll raise my hand when I need to disown a scene.

Reading

Bloch, Ernst, et al., *Aesthetics and Politics*, trans. Ronald Taylor et al. (London: New Left Books, 1977).

Eagleton, Terry, 'Aesthetics and Politics', *New Left Review* 1:107 (January–February 1978), pp. 21–34.

Eagleton, Terry, *The Rape of Clarissa: Writing, Sexuality and Class Struggle in Samuel Richardson* (Oxford: Blackwell, 1982).

Eagleton, Terry, 'Interview: Terry Eagleton' (with James H. Kavanagh and Thomas E. Lewis), *Diacritics* 12:1 (Spring 1982), pp. 53–64.

Eagleton, Terry, 'Fredric Jameson: The Politics of Style', *Diacritics* 12:3 (1982), pp. 14–22 (repr. in *Against the Grain: Essays 1975–1985*, London: Verso, 1986, pp. 65–78).

Eagleton, Terry, *Literary Theory: An Introduction* (Oxford: Blackwell, 1983).

Eagleton, Terry, *The Function of Criticism: From the* Spectator *to Post-Structuralism* (London: Verso, 1984).

Eagleton, Terry, 'Politics, Theory and the Study of English: An Interview with Terry Eagleton' (with Richard Freadman), *English in Australia* 70 (December 1984), pp. 32–7.

Eagleton, Terry, *Against the Grain: Essays 1975–1985* (London: Verso, 1986).

Eagleton, Terry, *William Shakespeare* (Oxford: Blackwell, 1986).

Eagleton, Terry, 'Interview with Terry Eagleton' (with Andrew Martin and Patrice Petro), *Social Text* 13/14 (Winter/Spring 1986), pp. 83–99.

Eagleton, Terry, *Saints and Scholars* (London: Verso, 1987).

Eagleton, Terry, 'Action in the Present: An Interview with Terry Eagleton' (Richard Dienst and Gail Faurschou), *Polygraph* 2/3 (1989), pp. 30–36.

Eagleton, Terry, 'Criticism, Ideology and Fiction' (with Michael Payne), in *The Significance of Theory* (Oxford: Blackwell, 1990), pp. 71–89.

Eagleton, Terry, and Derek Jarman, *Wittgenstein: The Terry Eagleton Script and the Derek Jarman Film* (London: BFI, 1993).

Eagleton, Terry, *Saint Oscar and Other Plays* (Oxford: Blackwell, 1997).

Eagleton, Terry, 'A Grim Parody of the Humanities: An Interview with Terry Eagleton' (with John Higgins), *Pretexts: Literary and Cultural Studies* 9:2 (2000), pp. 215–23.

Eagleton, Terry, 'A Conversation with Terry Eagleton' (with José Manuel Barbeito Varela), *Atlantis: Revista de la Asociación Española de Estudios Anglo-Norteamericanos* 23:2 (December 2001), pp. 169–85.

Eagleton, Terry, 'Peter Brooks on Bodies', in *Figures of Dissent: Essays on Fish, Spivak, Žižek and Others* (London: Verso, 2005), pp. 129–35.

Eagleton, Terry, 'Ludwig Wittgenstein', in *Figures of Dissent: Essays on Fish, Spivak, Žižek and Others* (London: Verso, 2005), pp. 109–12.

Eagleton, Terry, *Literary Theory: An Introduction*, anniversary edition (Oxford: Blackwell, 2008).

Eagleton, Terry, 'On the Importance of Not-Being Earnest: A Dialogue with Terry Eagleton' (with Patrick O'Connor and Seán Daffy), *Irish Studies Review* 16:1 (February 2008), pp. 55–69.

Habermas, Jürgen, *The Structural Transformation of the Public Sphere: An Inquiry into a Category of Bourgeois Society*, trans. Thomas Burger (Cambridge: Polity, 1989).

Negt, Oskar, and Alexander Kluge, *Public Sphere and Experience: Towards an Analysis of the Bourgeois and Proletarian Public Sphere*, trans. Peter Labanyi et al. (Minneapolis: University of Minnesota Press, 1993).

Parrinder, Patrick, 'The Myth of Terry Eagleton', in *The Failure of Theory: Essays in Criticism and Contemporary Fiction* (Hemel Hempstead: Harvester Wheatsheaf, 1987), pp. 30–8.

CHAPTER EIGHT

Oxford/Dublin

The late 1980s and early 1990s were of course the period in which actually existing socialism disintegrated and the Soviet Union collapsed. What position did you take at the time?

I remember doing a lot of arguing and writing at the time. I tried for example to point out to people that a call for the overthrow of Soviet power went very far back in left thinking, and that there had been important left calls for something far beyond mere reform in the Soviet Union, so this was not something that started in Tiananmen Square. People seemed to be extraordinarily memory-less, or history-less, in this respect. I argued that if you wanted a historically and materially based analysis of the Soviet bloc that was also politically uncompromising, you had to go to the left and not to liberalism. I saw this as an episode that showed up the limits of the Western liberal critique, as well as of the Soviet system itself. Here were these people calling quite rightly for individual freedom and so on, but ignorant of the fact that for a very long time there have been whole currents of the left that have worked against this kind of narrow definition of freedom. And although that didn't of course mean that you then greeted the restoration of capitalism with glee, it did at least mean you were able to point out that there was another possibility. I suppose that, having gone through the IS and the WSL — a quasi-Trotskyist group and a straight-down-the-line Trotskyist group respectively — I was at least equipped with various arguments or ways of looking that didn't leave me disorientated. I would say for example to students or to colleagues that the last time that the Western left had illusions *en masse* about the Soviet Union was probably the 1930s. I would also point out that the Western left was in deep trouble long before the Berlin Wall came down. It wasn't just the collapse of the Soviet bloc that undermined it.

Raymond Williams died in 1988. The following year you edited a collection of essays on him: Raymond Williams: Critical Perspectives *[1989]. Did that book represent a deliberate attempt to re-evaluate his reputation?*

It did. It was started while he was alive, and indeed I had some contact or correspondence with him over the shape of it. He wasn't very satisfied with it in its early stages: he thought it was too conventional and contained too many of the usual suspects. He was right about that. He suggested a couple of alternative ways of doing it, which I largely took on board. The idea of a volume on him of some kind had been much in the air for some time. As I say in the introduction, it then turned into a posthumous volume because he died while it was being published. So the book became one element in the general activity that happened after his death. I remember speaking about him at a number of different venues. There were meetings about his work and memorial events of various kinds. The book was fairly recent and there was a fair bit of discussion of it largely for that reason.

In The Function of Criticism, *which contains a sustained discussion of Williams, there seems to be a deliberate attempt to undo some of the damage that was allegedly done by* Criticism and Ideology *[1976]. You point out that, in its consistent commitment to a 'semantic materialism', his work constituted a critique of semiotics from the outset: 'While other materialist thinkers, including myself, diverted into structuralist Marxism, Williams sustained his historicist humanism only to find such theoreticians returning under changed political conditions to examine the case less cavalierly, if not to endorse it uncritically.' Did you continue to re-evaluate your relationship to him?*

Yes, though in a sense it remains an oddly ambiguous relationship, because there's a lot of the original critique in *Criticism and Ideology* that I'd continue to defend, even though it's one-sided and mistaken in tone. I think you could say that throughout the eighties and nineties there was a growing rapprochement with his work. Perhaps I had needed to plant my own flag and establish my own base, and once I'd done that it was possible to look more positively at Raymond's achievement.

It's when you come back to the idea of culture — this is something we've touched on before — that your return to Williams becomes most apparent. The shift in your work from ideology to culture seems to signal this rapprochement.

It does. I went back and reread some key texts of Williams, and found myself greatly impressed by him again. I had of course been moulded by these works in the early period, but I was so close to him and to his work that I wasn't able to step back and evaluate it or take the measure of the importance of that influence. I rather took it for granted, and proceeded instead with the easier task of criticizing it. It's a familiar mistake.

After the collection on Williams, there's a slim volume called The Significance of Theory *[1989], which was published as part of a series of books based on lectures commissioned by Bucknell University in the States. It consisted of the lecture on Theory you'd given at Bucknell, an article on Adorno entitled 'Art after Auschwitz', and an interview.*

I deeply objected to that volume. It was no part of my plan to publish that book, and I had hardly any hand in it. I did indeed give a series of lectures at Bucknell University in the States, and they did have a habit of publishing the lectures, but I thought it was a terrible idea. It was Bucknell's attempt to put itself on the map, I think, so it was useful from their point of view but not from mine. I thought there was very little in the book that I hadn't said already. I included the chapter on Adorno, which came out of the work I was doing for *The Ideology of the Aesthetic*, because I desperately needed to pad the book out. I was asked to go over and speak in the States to a group of bookshop reps and salespeople from the US branch of Blackwell, and I said to them, 'I really sympathize with you guys, trying to peddle this book.' They were wised-up people with PhDs who knew exactly what they were selling, and they said, 'Yes! What are we going to do with this book?' So it was a non-event as far as I was concerned.

The introductions, by Michael Payne and M. A. R. Habib, sketched your significance – 'The Significance of Terry', if you like. Was it interesting to observe this institutionalization of your reputation?

I suppose it was. Taking that point more generally, though, I must say, at the risk of sounding arrogant, that I've actually learnt exceedingly little from a lot of commentary on my work. In general, either the critic is too sympathetic to be interestingly critical or they're coming from a position that's so unsympathetic that there's no common ground. This applies to Williams too. There were a lot of people who revered him and there were a lot of people who assailed him. I thought I was one of the very few that tried to do both. I tried to look at him critically – maybe too much so at one point – and I always felt that that was probably what he would have valued himself. He certainly had a very brisk way with uncritical veneration.

Let's move on to The Ideology of the Aesthetic *[1990]. In this book you excavated the history of the aesthetic as a philosophical category in European thought since the eighteenth century, and argued that aesthetics has in this epoch functioned as a displaced discourse on ethics and politics – one that, in spite of its apparent unimportance, has been absolutely central both to the ideological consolidation of capitalist society and its critique. It was widely regarded as your most ambitious and challenging book to date. Were you conscious at the time of making a 'philosophical turn'?*

No, I don't think I was. Unlike my earlier book, to be sure, it addressed professional philosophers. But I saw it much more as a theoretical continuum, as a new area of theory. I never quite was able to work out what I was doing with those philosophers. I remember talking to other people and asking for some kind of illumination about this. I was explicating these philosophers, discussing certain elements in their work relevant to aesthetics, but it was also to some extent – and this takes me back to *Saints and Scholars* – an imaginative recreation of philosophy. It was rather similar, I think, to the kind of thing that Jameson sometimes does. I was writing about Kant, for example, in ways that professional Kantians in the States found objectionable. I remember giving a couple of lectures from the book there and running into a lot of opposition. Somebody in Berkeley asked me, 'Are you at all disquieted by the fact that no professional analytical philosopher would accept your theory of Kant?' And I said, 'On the contrary, I would be horrified, or at least extremely surprised, if they did!' I still don't quite understand what's going on in that book methodologically.

It presents the history of aesthetics in the form of an intellectual, or, more accurately, ideological, drama.

Yes, I was dramatizing certain ideas. The book appeared more or less at the same time as another book about the aesthetic, by Andrew Bowie, and somebody, maybe Andrew himself, pointed out that whereas my book was rather critical of aesthetics but was written in an 'aesthetic' style, his book was the opposite. So there was something about the form of the book that was important. I attended closely to the writing, with the creative writing at my back, as it were. I don't remember feeling this at the time, but it was an extraordinarily ambitious kind of book. Somebody had said, in some review in the eighties, 'Eagleton's books are getting shorter and shorter', and I had done a number of books that for contingent reasons had indeed been short. Then suddenly I saw an unwritten history not of aesthetics but of the politics of aesthetics.

Were you conscious of the so-called new aestheticism, for all its differences from your approach? In addition to Bowie's book, Aesthetics and Subjectivity *[1990], Jay Bernstein's* The Fate of Art *[1992] appeared at roughly this time.*

I was to a minor degree. I was aware of Bowie's work and Bernstein's work, which has been useful to me over the years. But I thought what I'd seen was quite independent of that. I certainly didn't have any sense of the book as part of a current, when I wrote it. Isobel Armstrong took issue with the book – I actually wrote to her about it, though I don't normally reply to critical responses – and argued that it presented an implacably negative critique of the aesthetic. It wasn't true. This was a common misreading of my book and Andrew's. The whole point of my book was that there is this ambivalence or dialectical quality about the aesthetic, such that politically it could go either way. If you like, it's both ideology and utopia.

Another criticism of the book was that it seems unlikely that a discourse as marginal as the aesthetic could bear the kind of weight I ascribed to it historically and politically. It's an interesting criticism but it is mistaken, in the sense that what I meant by the aesthetic is not simply art or the production of art, but the way in which a particular ideology of the artefact took hold in the eighteenth century. So the aesthetic for me is not identical with just any discourse on art; it means a very particular historical discourse which begins in that period and which tries to reconstruct the work of art in a way that is relevant to the ideology of the early bourgeoisie. What is developing in that early bourgeois ideology is the need for the notion of a subjectivity or subject that is autonomous, that is a law unto itself. This in fact really defines what the work of art is, and it explains why I argue that the bourgeois subject is secretly an aesthetic subject. I didn't mean that the bourgeois subject is particularly concerned with art, but that the aesthetic provides a certain language of subjectivity, certain issues regarding form and content, law and freedom, individuality and universality and so on, that the bourgeoisie can then reuse.

The book excavates a materialist history of the category of the aesthetic and its ideological functions in bourgeois society. Could you briefly reconstruct that?

Historically, the concept of the aesthetic has become increasingly narrow and specialized. It has become a technical concept, so that journals of aesthetics today deal with highly technical problems of aesthetic perception and evaluation. That is not the way it started. The aesthetic began in the broadest possible way as a concept covering the whole of our bodily, sensual life. Indeed, it was not even about art at all when it first appeared, and it is one of the paradoxes of the aesthetic that it emerges as a discourse at the time when actual artistic production is being commodified. Art simply provides a peculiar paradigm of the sort of things that the aesthetic is interested in. There were other paradigms too, such as the life of the body or other models of autonomy.

The aesthetic in Kant, for instance, is a form of ideology, especially since the beautiful is defined as that which momentarily reconciles the human subject to the world. For Kant the aesthetic links the category of moral freedom to the category of nature or reality. The category of the beautiful is then important because, in a world which now seems to turn back on human subjectivity – a commodified, reified world – some provisional encounter between humanity and nature is ideologically essential if humanity is to feel at home in the world. The category of the sublime is also ideologically necessary as a kind of countervailing force that therapeutically disrupts this imaginary register every now and then in order to remind us of the kind of dynamism, enterprise and rivalry that were also necessary values in early bourgeois society.

As artistic production is gradually separated from other kinds of social production in the modern period, the discourse of the aesthetic becomes correspondingly narrow. In the twentieth century, after modernism, it ceased to be a concept of political relevance. In fact, modernism is the last moment when the aesthetic can still be political, albeit in a largely negative mode. After that, the discourse passes into the hands of the academics and the specialists and its history changes. But the aesthetic is an area that is at once a kind of specialization and a 'non-specialization', an ill-defined region where you hope you can raise certain problems jettisoned by the more official academic disciplines. The problem for politically radical movements is that art itself or the notion of culture has become so deeply bound up with the aesthetic in the bourgeois sense that either you say, as the avant-garde says, 'Away with art and the aesthetic altogether! Let's go right back to the beginning and start again!' or, as with Adorno, 'Let's accept some of these aesthetic categories, let's accept that the work of art is autonomous, but let's try to turn them to radical political use.' That is an astonishing enterprise – for Adorno and others the very ineffectuality of art in bourgeois society is somehow transformed into a radical statement. Art is supremely useless and that is its most politically important aspect.

So Adorno is paradigmatic of the agonized relations between politics and aesthetics for the intellectual in the twentieth century?

Adorno was of course devastated by the political history he lived through. Every word he writes is resonant with this sense of devastation and sometimes despair, and at the same time he

believes that the activity of critique in some form, although it may
be a critique beyond critique, must at all costs be perpetuated if
this form of politics is not to happen again. Adorno is therefore
caught in an intolerable and agonizing position between witnessing
the necessity of critique and yet seeing its ineffectuality and its
privilege compared to the sufferings that his people endured. On
the one hand, the work of art is intolerably privileged in a world
after Auschwitz. On the other hand, art has to go on. It must find
some way, as for Adorno and Beckett, of enclosing within itself
a kind of silence that speaks of all that is not privileged, of the
suffering. This must be the position of any radical intellectual, and
not necessarily one who has been scarred by the same experience
that Adorno lived through.

There is something profoundly contradictory about the act of
intellectual critique, in that at the very moment at which it aims
to be emancipatory it must find itself distanced from that which it
hopes to emancipate. I don't think this contradiction can be solved
within a class society; and all the individual critic can do is find
a way of living within that contradiction as best he or she can. It
is not our fault if this contradiction is there, produced by a class-
divided society, and will only be abolished with the abolition of
class society itself. Meanwhile, we find ourselves inevitably torn
between the offensive privilege of our being able to address these
problems only in relation to the aesthetic – offensive because the
aesthetic is hardly the most important political issue – and an
awareness that simply abandoning it, in a crisis of guilt, plays right
into the hands of a social order whose aim is actually to eliminate
radical ideas altogether. A radical intellectual dares not be complicit
in this system, even if the result of this refusal is the perpetuation
of a discourse that stands at a distance from the daily experience
with which he or she should be concerned.

As you've said, The Ideology of the Aesthetic *posits the aesthetic as
at once ideological and utopian. It's noticeable though that it doesn't
make extensive use of the concept of utopia. There is, however, an*

interesting passage in which you argue that art figures as the ideal
paradigm of material production for Marx because of its autotelic
quality. You cite that extraordinary passage from the Economic
and Philosophical Manuscripts *in which Marx writes that when*
communist workers gather together, even if their immediate aim is
propaganda, they act out the communist idea of fraternity in proleptic
form. The association is an end in itself as well as a means to an end:
'Smoking, eating and drinking, etc., are no longer means of creating
links between people.'

The aesthetic is simultaneously a generous utopian critique of
bourgeois individualism, and something utterly idealist and
ineffectual. One of the ways in which the aesthetic provides a frail
utopian impulse is that it seems to figure a form of community and
a way in which subjects are intersubjectively linked to one another
in the act of aesthetic judgment. But at the same time, how pathetic
that apparently only in aesthetic experience can such a community
be found! There must be something very wrong with society if the
aesthetic is the only area that seems to provide a sense of solidarity.

I suppose my conception of utopia assumes that you have to
have some kind of immanence, an immanent presence of the
possible, otherwise people will desire uselessly and fall ill with
desire. That was what gripped me about the passage from Marx –
apart from its moving and splendid nature. It was saying that it's
something you can see and handle now, and that it's prefigurative.
Actually, I've not done enough thinking about utopia, although it
obviously surfaces every now and then in my work. I don't discuss
Marcuse in this book, for instance, and if I had done I might have
highlighted that utopian dimension more.

One of the book's most original contributions to Marxist thought was
its argument that the body is absolutely central to Marx's materialism.

At the time I was increasingly impatient with the number of
books that deployed the word 'body' in their titles in order to sell

themselves. At the same time, I think that the body is a crucial category, and in the chapter on Marx in *The Ideology of the Aesthetic* I did indeed claim that the ambitiousness of Marx is that he is trying to work himself up from the body itself, from what he calls 'species being'. From what we are as material creatures, he tries to work his way up to a certain politics, to a certain ethics. That is what I think Marxism is trying to do. The body is absolutely essential to Marxism. It is of course the labouring rather than the sexual body – and to that extent it is at once crucial and limited. It suppresses the dimension of sexuality, but there is no doubt in my mind that the body is present from the earliest moment of Marx's work in his *Economic and Philosophical Manuscripts* of 1844.

My work is unequivocally concerned with socialist ethics, as *Trouble with Strangers* [2008] makes most explicit. The conclusion to *The Ideology of the Aesthetic* was my first attempt to write about this, about the question of whether one can derive an ethics from a certain view of how human beings as material animals are or could become. Even then I thought that this was a vital project. For one thing, I thought it was vital to oppose postmodernist trends that either skirted the question of ethics, or reduced it to the pragmatic subjective, or the intersubjective. I didn't think there was much future in that, and that is one reason why Marxism appeals to me.

Rereading The Ideology of the Aesthetic, *I was certainly struck by its emphasis on ethical matters – love and evil for example – which once again connect up your earliest and most recent publications. In the discussion of political love, in particular, the ethical strand in your work reappears: 'Radical politics addresses the question of what this love would mean at the level of a whole society, as sexual morality tries to clarify what counts as love in sexual relationships between individuals, and medical ethics tries to define what counts as love in our treatment of bodies which are suffering. It is because love is such a highly vexed, obscure and ambiguous topic that such ethical discourses are necessary in the first place.'*

One of the more unexpected aspects of the reception of *The Ideology of the Aesthetic* was that Frank Kermode gave it a very positive review in the *London Review of Books*. I think perhaps he mistook the generality of the final discussion for some sort of congenial liberal-humanist reflection on the nature of human life and so on.

The aesthetic, when it first sees the light of day in the Enlightenment, is concerned among other things with a form of rationality that would stay faithful to material, corporeal existence. It also finds in the work of art a kind of utopian community, in that each element of the work is brought fully into its own through its complex configuration with all the others. The 'law' or regulatory structure of the artwork isn't imposed coercively on its components, but simply *is* their intricate interrelations. This is a bit like Marx on communism – on the 'form' of an emancipated future.

Your next book was Ideology: An Introduction *in 1991, which is in some respects co-extensive with* The Ideology of the Aesthetic. *What prompted it?*

That was one of the few books of mine that came directly out of a lecture course. I'd been doing a lot of lecturing and seminar teaching on ideology in Oxford. Of course, it wasn't any part of the English course, so to some extent the lectures and seminars were a strategy or occasion for pulling in people who wanted some sort of political dialogue. I consciously had the idea of doing a student textbook, a book that did not primarily attempt to make an original theoretical contribution. Instead, I wanted to write a straight-down-the-line popular book on the concept of ideology in a period in which the concept was increasingly falling out of favour. That was the political impulse behind the book.

So it was an attempt to clarify the concept of ideology and to examine the reasons for it appearing superfluous or redundant. One of these is that the theory of ideology seemed to depend on a concept of representation. Certain models of representation had been called into question, and consequently so had the notion of ideology. Another reason is that it is often felt that in order to identify a form of thought as ideological one needs to have access to absolute truth. If the idea of absolute truth is called into question then the concept of ideology seems to fall to ground with it. There were two further reasons why ideology was no longer fashionable. One is what has been called 'enlightened false consciousness', meaning that in a postmodern epoch the idea that people labour under false consciousness is too simple-minded, since they are actually much more cynically or shrewdly aware of their interests than that would suggest. This again calls the concept of ideology into question. Finally, there is the argument that what keeps the system going is less rhetoric or discourse than its own systemic logic. This is the idea that advanced capitalism works all by itself, that it doesn't any longer need to pass through consciousness to be validated, that it somehow secures its own reproduction. I was dubious about whether all that was sufficient to ditch the concept of ideology. I was prepared to accept that there is some force to those various points, but one reason I wanted to retain the concept of ideology was that I do think there is something that corresponds to the notion of false consciousness. Indeed, not to think so seems to me absurd. How we explain this socially necessary illusion is another matter.

Interestingly, there's nothing on the Situationists in this book. At the beginning of The Society of the Spectacle *[1967]*, Debord effectively redefines ideology as 'an immense accumulation of* spectacles', *and announces that 'all that once was directly lived has become mere representation'. This is surely a significant attempt to theoriẓe ideology in advanced capitalist society.*

You're right. There was a different emphasis in my work at that time. The theory of the spectacle never particularly enthralled or enthused me. I was more interested in the Bolshevik and German avant-gardes, and I really ought to have followed that up with a critique of the later French work. I never did. I became more interested in the Situationists later, and even supervised the odd doctoral thesis on them, but somehow I've never yet worked it into my writing. Maybe that's to come.

It was of course the second edition of this book, in 2007, that contained the introduction that, because of its attack on Martin Amis, caused all the controversy. Scandalously, Amis had announced in the aftermath of the bombings in London in 2007 that 'the Muslim community will have to suffer until it gets its house in order.' You compared his comments to the ramblings of a British National Party member, and pointed out, among other things, that if he 'were to have his trousers forcefully removed on the streets of Dhamar or Damqawt, he might justly protest to the authorities that not all Westerners wish the Arab world harm; that only a small minority of them are raving Islamophobes; and that to characterize the lot of them as potential murderers is outright racism.' A number of Amis's liberal friends then leapt to his defence. At approximately the same time Amis was appointed as Professor of Creative Writing in the English department at Manchester, where you were teaching . . .

I never thought anybody would notice it! A journalist from the *Independent* spotted it, and saw its potential because of the Manchester connection. I'm not even sure that when I wrote it I knew he was coming to the department.

Amis's panic-stricken remarks about Muslims were outrageously authoritarian. He has since commented that he no longer believes what he said, but he has very notably failed to apologize to those he offended. He just said, 'I don't believe it any more', as though you might call a perfectly innocent neighbour a disgusting child-molester and then, once you've recovered your cool, say 'Oh, I don't think that any more.' So that's all right then . . . I suspect that Amis does indeed continue to harbour a good many illiberal sentiments on this score, even if he has graciously ceased calling for Muslims to be publicly hounded. What's now stalking abroad in these erstwhile liberal literary and intellectual circles, some of which centre upon that mythological region of the mind known as North Oxford, is a new species of what I call liberal supremacism, which finds in the benightedness of radical Islam fresh grounds to feel smug and self-satisfied about its own civilization at a time when that's not otherwise very easy. Dawkins falls squarely in this camp, and so does Hitchens, as I argue in *Reason, Faith, and Revolution* [2009]. But it was that Western smugness and hubristic self-belief which helped to breed an ugly Islamic fundamentalism in the first place.

Liberalism is supposed to treat arguments dispassionately, and all the best liberals do this magnificently. So what is one to make of those like Hitchens and Salman Rushdie who seem to believe that disinterestedness is fine except when it comes to defending your friends for saying the indefensible? Both of them tried to excuse Amis's redneck remarks on the most specious, spinelessly disingenuous of grounds. Rushdie even claimed, absurdly, that Amis wasn't talking about discriminating against Muslims, whereas this is a term he explicitly used in the offending interview.

Looking back, how would you characterize the career of ideology since you published that book?

The emergence of radical Islam and of fundamentalism in general has of course put it back on the agenda. I find myself now talking and teaching and lecturing quite a lot about it, which is one gain of the ebbing of post-structuralism. Real political history has pushed the concept into prominence again. But I actually think that in the minds of a lot of students, a lot of people, it never really went away. They simply didn't buy the case that the concept was now *passé*. I've had numerous discussions about the book on ideology – more than I'd expected, given that it was intended as a popularizing textbook. I think it struck a chord with a lot of readers.

How was the book received in its first edition?

Right-wing reviewers like Eric Griffiths at Cambridge – now why would you give a book on ideology by Terry Eagleton to Eric Griffiths? – found it too eclectic, too hospitable to different and divergent meanings. Some people on the left thought the same. Maybe I was reacting against an austere Althusserian focus, but it did seem to me justified by the topic. There are a number of different, sometimes incompatible but indubitably useful definitions of ideology, and I was loath to jettison them. But the other strength of the book – not deliberately intended – was that it appealed right across the spectrum of the humanities. I've talked to anthropologists, political scientists, all sorts of people, who found it helpful because they could take it straight into their own areas. There's nothing particularly literary about it. But the fact that it took a literary type to write it at that time may be significant.

In the introduction to the second edition you classified the outset of the twenty-first century as a 'post-post-ideological era'. Do you think there's a way of classifying the present conjuncture in terms of a positive rather than a double negative, so to speak?

So many different areas are now at stake politically, both literal, geographical areas and areas of work and living – and not least because of the economic crisis. A lot of the old concepts discarded by post-structuralism – totality, for instance – have been forced on our attention by history itself. It was an interesting case of the intelligentsia, in the shape of people like Francis Fukuyama, being caught napping by real developments. Far from being *en avance* of history, the intelligentsia was left behind by it.

The concept of totality is a good example. And so-called grand narratives are no longer quite as unacceptable as they were at the end of the last century. What about the concept of dialectics, though? Is that also on the agenda again?

Incidentally, I hope I've never in my work used the phrase 'the dialectic', whereas some Marxists seem quite insouciant about using this awful reification. No, in general it isn't on the agenda again. When I'm talking to a younger political generation, I have no trouble talking about the plausibility and the importance of grand narratives or totality, but 'dialectic' is a word they hardly know.

I've been somewhat quiet on the issue of dialectics because I am a little wary both of a certain sort of full-blooded dialectical philosophy – shades of Engels's 'dialectics of nature' – and of the way the concept has become rather sloppy. Having said that, I value dialectical thought in the sense of trying to salvage what is valuable and usable from an essentially negative phenomenon, trying for example to rescue from the great bourgeois tradition what is positive and productive about it. This has to be cherished in the face of a postmodernism that is drastically undialectical, that looks at complex, many-sided historical developments such as modernity or the Enlightenment and just takes a negative attitude to them. I neither back the case that present-day radicalism is simply an extension of the Enlightenment nor do I support the case that the Enlightenment was the moment of the Fall, some catastrophe from which we've never recovered. A dialectical assessment of the Enlightenment is, in principle, Marxism itself. Marxism understands itself, on the one hand, as the child of the Enlightenment. It would not have been possible without that marvellous bourgeois resistance to autocracy and absolutism. On the other hand, Marxism tries to revolutionize the Enlightenment, to revolutionize the social order that it created. That kind of dialectical approach is disastrously absent from most radical thought today.

Of course, the extraordinary one-sidedness of so much postmodern theory is ironic in this context, because it is itself so suspicious of binary oppositions. I do think dialectical thinking is a habit that's been lost, politically. To praise and to criticize in the same breath seems to me the most natural attitude. We do it every day – we do it about people, we do it about institutions, we do it about critical thought. The moment that it is deemed slippery or evasive to say, 'I think this is a major artist, but look how dreadful he is too!' I will sign off. A dialectical thought to me is one that gives the devil his due but at the same time insists that he is the devil. What distinguishes it from mere polite even-handedness is the way each position is inscribed within the other. Some Marxists have a compulsion to add the term 'dialectical' to any mention of contradiction or opposition. But not all of these things are always and everywhere dialectical.

You became the Thomas Warton Professor of English Literature at Oxford in 1992, which in light of your politics seems a surprising appointment. What were the circumstances in which you were elected to the post?

After I'd been elected to the Lectureship in Critical Theory at Oxford, I applied for promotion and was informed that I could only put in for a competitive readership. This was at a time when I was being offered various posh chairs in the States, so I accepted a chair at the University of Pennsylvania. I felt deeply ambivalent about the idea of going to the States, and doubtful whether it was the right decision, but I seemed to have come to something of a dead end at Oxford. This was partly because the Oxford English Limited campaign had shot its bolt. It was also because I'd been somewhat sidelined in the University lectureship. I had postgraduate teaching, but I was now cut off from my undergraduate teaching. But I became increasingly doubtful about going to the States. Then John Carey asked me to put in for the Warton professorship. He told me that if Christopher Ricks put in for it he would certainly get it, but as it happened Ricks didn't want to leave Boston. I thought there was nothing to be lost. I was told that there was blood on the floor at the meeting. There were certainly a couple of very strong internal candidates from Oxford apart from myself, and some fairly strong contenders from outside. I was astonished that they gave it to me, and very glad. For one thing, it rescued me from going to the States. On the other hand, it wasn't the English faculty that gave it to me, and I'm pretty convinced that they would not have done so had it been in their gift. It was a collection of odds and sods, heads of houses and people from outside and so on. But anyway they did. So that was how, in a rather surreal way, I followed in the footsteps of John Bayley. He was very charming, and courteous enough to conceal any dismay that he might have felt at the nature of his successor. He welcomed me to St Catherine's College in a letter and told me that the place looked like a modern-day office block, hastily adding, 'But I'm sure that's a very good thing!'

In your inaugural lecture, in a practical extension of the polemical argument with which you'd concluded Literary Theory, *you adumbrated a programme for English at Oxford which involved teaching 'writing in English' rather than English literature. 'The English language is now homeless and centreless,' you said, 'and our syllabus, which by and large stops short of Dover, has dismally failed to register the fact.' Did that fall on deaf ears?*

Not entirely, because not long after I'd left Wadham the post-colonial critic Robert Young moved there and became an increasingly important figure in the faculty. The thing about that inaugural lecture is that, although it had a utopian dimension to it, I no longer felt I was the person to make these changes. I'd been fighting too long, and had begun to lose interest at the very moment I was given the chair. So there was already a sense of disenchantment underlying that positive and programmatic statement, and this then bore fruit when I left Oxford, not that long afterwards.

At the end of the inaugural lecture, the pro-vice-chancellor turned to me as we processed out and said, 'I imagine now you expect to be arrested, don't you?' He was horrified. He regarded me as a silly adolescent who had made some indecent gesture of rebellion. Max Beloff went on record to say that it was the most disgraceful inaugural lecture he'd ever attended – but he can't have heard much of it, as I remember seeing him sleeping soundly most of the way through. Afterwards, I asked that it should be published. There had been no move to do so, but I specifically asked Oxford University Press to reproduce it as a pamphlet so it would get around the place, and they did.

When I first started teaching at Oxford, no postgraduate was allowed to work on a living writer. I think the syllabus went up to 1900, but there was some suspicion that Tennyson was a bit of a new-fangled modernist who might be a little too close to us to assess. Enormous gains have been made since then, and I don't think they should be underestimated. The cultural left has effected some major and substantial achievements, and it would now be very hard to roll these back. But, on the other hand, there is a danger of fetishization – a danger for example that the left should fetishize the issue of the canon. After all, you could have a canon consisting of nothing but black, working-class, female writing, and still treat it in an extremely conservative way.

You moved to Ireland shortly after you took up your chair . . .

I moved to Dublin in 1993, at almost precisely the time that the Celtic tiger began to roar, so I was coming into an Ireland strikingly different from the one that I'd known as a young man. On the one hand Ireland was an increasingly confident and sophisticated nation; and on the other, relatedly, it was a nation with a huge identity crisis. The conflict between tradition and modernity is of course a dire cliché, but Ireland at this time seemed to be a society trapped right in the middle of it. It was a society in which, unlike Britain, history was tangibly shifting beneath one's feet. The country was affluent for the first time in its history, and a new dispensation was emerging, but there were severe conflicts of value and vision. What happens when you become postmodern without ever having been fully modern in the first place? So intellectually the place was edgy but exciting. In terms of everyday life I found it relaxed and friendly – I've been accused of conforming to the cliché of the indolent Irishman in this respect, but then I'm a champion of stereotypes on materialist grounds. Even with the growing freneticism of an economy deeply mortgaged to the United States, there was still a more relaxed and friendly quality to Irish life than to English life.

Did the move reflect a frustration with Oxford?

I suppose I'd had enough of Oxford. It wasn't intended to be but it might have seemed like a slap in the face to Oxford – though Oxford was used to slaps in the face from me. No sooner had they invited me in from the cold than I removed myself physically across the water. I think one or two of them were rather sore about that. The chair at Oxford was seen by some people as a hopeful beginning, but for me it was to some extent the end. I felt that I'd struggled, that Oxford English Limited had struggled, for a long time, and that we hadn't really got very far. The physical move to Dublin probably reflected an increasing psychological distance from Oxford. I knew Dublin pretty well already and felt very much at home there. I also had at least as many friends in Ireland as I did in England, and certainly more than I had in Oxford, which I always found a deeply unfriendly place. I relished the small-town feel of Dublin, the network of writers and artists. I participated in the cultural life of the city quite intensively – lectures, book launches, writing for the Irish press and so on. I also appeared regularly on a TV programme about books.

Your next major publication – the first of three books in which you took a sustained look at Irish literature – was Heathcliff and the

Great Hunger *[1995]. In the introduction to* The Ideology of the
Aesthetic *you said that you'd originally conceived that book 'as a
kind of doubled text, in which an account of European aesthetic theory
would be coupled at every point to a consideration of the literary
culture of Ireland'. That material then formed the basis of* Heathcliff
and the Great Hunger; *but presumably the move to Ireland shaped
its composition significantly . . .*

Yes, my writing about Ireland very much emerged from that
context. I put myself through an intensive autodidactic course
in Irish history and culture – to the dismay of some of my Irish
political antagonists, who had up to that point consoled themselves
that at least I hadn't officially entered the field of Irish Studies but
had just sniped at them from a distance. The book caused a lot
of discussion, partly because there was so little being written in
Ireland from a Marxist or even far-left point of view. There was
post-colonial stuff, and feminist stuff, but very little Marxist stuff.
It was a kind of breakthrough for me because, after a couple of
tentative forays into the Irish arena in fictional form, I had finally
put my academic cards on the table. Obviously, all apparently
dispassionate historical or cultural writing about Ireland is
caught up in a fiercely controversial background. Indeed, it
would be interesting to see how the course of contemporary
Irish historiography was partly set by the IRA – that is to say, by
opposition to the IRA, and the consequent rewriting of nationalist
history. I was aware of intervening into that, but as a semi-outsider
and as an Englishman. I wasn't seen as an invading imperialist at
all, rather as a potential romantic and sentimentalist. I struggled
hard to avoid that stereotype, but it became a convenient way of
denigrating my work on the part of Irish critics. The outsider in
Ireland is caught in a classic double bind: if you sympathize with
them you are being romantic; if you don't you're being a colonialist.

*Were you trying to build an alternative genealogy for modernist Irish
literature?*

To some extent I was. I was conscious of constructing a different historical narrative, not simply a different literary one, as in the chapter in *Heathcliff* on the Anglo-Irish. I was writing in the teeth of what seemed to be a certain emollient revisionist discourse that took the catastrophe and the conflict out of Irish history. That discourse was written very much from the interests of the middle-class Irish present, so part of the task – and it wasn't by any means confined to me – was to show up that project as thoroughly ideological behind its dispassionate historiographical stance. The book roams around quite a lot, and I enjoyed the fact that I wasn't focusing on a particular topic, that I could move from Burke to the ascendancy to the famine.

The book employs certain strategies that are in a sense derived from your fiction, like the thought experiment you conduct in the eponymous opening chapter. There you argue that 'Heathcliff is a fragment of the Famine' in order to demonstrate that Emily Brontë's novel is profoundly – if codedly – imbricated in the Irish cultural politics that she inherited from her father Patrick. In a footnote, you offer a playful provocation to the historiographers: 'I have indicated already that Heathcliff may not of course be Irish, and that even if he is the chronology is awry as far as the Famine goes. But in this essay Heathcliff is Irish, and the chronology is not awry.'

One leading revisionist historian of Ireland described this as a disastrous chapter, precisely because the poor guy didn't know what was going on. I'm not sure I knew exactly what was going on myself, but there was certainly an interplay of history and fiction. I was able to exploit the fact that I wasn't an academic historian or even officially in Irish studies at all. So I didn't need to conform to the protocols.

There is a sustained discussion of Edmund Burke both in this book and in Crazy John and the Bishop *[1998].*

I am very interested in many aspects of Burke. I'm interested in Burke's whole theory of one's ambivalence towards the law and in the way he thinks about political authority. I'm also interested in the connection between Burke the political thinker and Burke the aesthetician. It seems to me that Burke is at this early point where the aesthetic means more than just art and has to do rather with sensation and perception, as I argued in *The Ideology of the Aesthetic*. As I've said, the aesthetic is born as a discourse of the body, and aesthetics is an attempt to make sense of the world in terms of one's physical and bodily location. It's an early species of phenomenology. Burke is fascinated by that project: for instance, what happens if you hear a certain sound or feel a certain texture? Indirectly, that is relevant to Burke the political theorist, because he has a highly developed sense of the dangers of the abstract, of political rationalism. You could trace a line from his interest in what happens when somebody taps you on the shoulder, in a very phenomenological way, to his insistence upon the lived and the tangible as against the terrors of the French Revolution. Some people have claimed that there is a certain Gaelic strain of concern with the concrete and particularized.

Burke's conservatism comes out *vis-à-vis* France; but his concern with the body operates as a radical critique in terms of the East India Company, where his great speeches to parliament are among other things all about the physical horrors of British rule. His own experience of colonialism in Ireland leads him to identify with colonial suffering. Of course, Burke is really arguing for a benign form of colonialism. His whole political thought concerns hegemony. He wants a hegemonic form of colonial rule, a form in which you actually love the law, so there are strict political limitations. But he is a searing critic of the ascendancy, and very bravely defends the American Independence movement at a certain cost to his own political reputation. All that, of course, was largely suppressed in the image of Burke the conservative, and I think there is value in putting back the other, bolder Burke. At the very end, he came about as near to supporting the United Irishmen as he decently could. Not bad for a member of the House of Commons – though Sheridan, another member, went even further.

Had you conceived the three books about Ireland as a trilogy? How do the second and third books on the history of Irish culture, Crazy John and the Bishop *and* Scholars and Rebels *[1999], relate to the first one?*

I don't think that 'trilogy' was a word I used. It certainly wasn't conceived as a whole project. But having put my cards on the table in *Heathcliff and the Great Hunger* I then wanted to explore a few neglected byways. I felt that Irish studies was being increasingly limited to a certain rather narrow canon. Everybody worked on Beckett, Joyce and Yeats, whereas there were all kinds of fascinating tributaries. *Crazy John and the Bishop* didn't sell very well partly for that reason. It's a book that deals with fairly tangential Irish figures that most people have never heard of, like William Dunkin and Frederick Ryan. The same probably happened with *Scholars and Rebels*.

Were you credited with the kind of scholarly discipline you demonstrated in Crazy John and the Bishop *in particular?*

Not really. I felt that the book missed its moment for some reason. I published it with Cork University Press because I wanted it to be part of the Field Day series – that was a political choice, I suppose – but Cork was struggling somewhat at the time, and that didn't help. So there were extraneous reasons. But I had also delved rather deeply into the arcane recesses of Irish history, so it was a very specialist study. Some people in Irish studies read it, but not many outside it I imagine.

Scholars and Rebels, *which is a slimmer, more readable volume, engages interestingly with Gramsci and the theory of the intellectual, so the book seems more closely tied to a specific theoretical framework.*

I'd seen a way of illuminating the general topic of the intelligentsia, the traditional and the organic one, and also the concept of the state intellectual, which is quite predominant, even paramount in nineteenth-century Ireland. There was a sense in which the Irish situation illuminated the Gramscian definition of the intelligentsia rather sharply, rather classically. It also allowed me to talk about some rather minor but neglected Irish figures I was interested in – scientists, economists, medics, antiquarians and so on, as well as the political figures. I also investigated the culture of Anglo-Irish ascendancy in more detail, an exploration I'd begun in the *Heathcliff* book.

In the year that Scholars and Rebels *appeared, you also published* The Truth About the Irish *[1999]. Slightly surprisingly, it's an A to Z of contemporary Irish culture, illustrated by cartoons, in which you playfully explode numerous racial and cultural clichés.*

Looking back, it seems an extraordinarily rash book to publish, because I hadn't been long in Ireland. I was in many ways accepted in Ireland, but I was nevertheless to some extent an outsider or semi-outsider still, so to write about the Irish so cavalierly was perhaps not the most diplomatic thing to do. I was naive enough about that to be rather taken aback by some inevitably hostile criticism in the Irish press and more generally in Ireland. I remember thinking at the time that just as the Irish were now priding themselves on having emerged as a fully-fledged, mature, Celtic-tiger nation, suitably cosmopolitan and liberal, they withered at the first hint of criticism from a Sassenach. Or at least a few of them did. A lot of people liked the book as well. So I think the book was an interesting litmus test of the nation's new-found liberalism. It was aimed at what might be called the intelligent tourist industry, and it still sells in a minor kind of way. A lot of Germans and other Europeans who come across to Ireland were pleased by it. So if the Irish were sometimes a little jaundiced about it, Continental tourists made up for that.

Reading

Armstrong, Isobel, 'The Aesthetic and the Polis: Marxist Deconstruction', in *The Radical Aesthetic* (Oxford: Blackwell, 2000), pp. 27–44.

Bernstein, J. M., *The Fate of Art: Aesthetic Alienation from Kant to Derrida and Adorno* (Cambridge: Polity, 1992).

Bourdieu, Pierre, and Terry Eagleton, 'Doxa and Common Life: An Interview', *New Left Review* 1:191 (1992), pp. 111–21.

Bowie, Andrew, *Aesthetics and Subjectivity: From Kant to Nietzsche* (Manchester: Manchester University Press, 1990).

Debord, Guy, *The Society of the Spectacle*, trans. Donald Nicholson-Smith (New York: Zone, 1994).

Eagleton, Terry, *Criticism and Ideology: A Study in Marxist Literary Theory* (London: New Left Books, 1976).

Eagleton, Terry, *The Function of Criticism: From the* Spectator *to Post-Structuralism* (London: Verso, 1984).

Eagleton, Terry, ed., *Raymond Williams: Critical Perspectives* (Oxford: Polity Press, 1989).

Eagleton, Terry, *The Ideology of the Aesthetic* (Oxford: Blackwell, 1990).

Eagleton, Terry, *The Significance of Theory*, eds. Michael Payne and M. A. R. Habib (Oxford: Blackwell, 1990).

Eagleton, Terry, 'Terry Eagleton on the Concept of the Aesthetic: An Interview by Maryse Souchard', *Recherches Sémiotiques/Semiotic Inquiry* 10:1–3 (1990), pp. 163–74.

Eagleton, Terry, *Ideology: An Introduction* (London: Verso, 1991).

Eagleton, Terry, 'Aesthetics and Politics in Edmund Burke,' in *Irish Literature and Culture*, ed. Michael Kenneally (Gerrards Cross: Smythe, 1992), pp. 25–34.

Eagleton, Terry, *The Crisis of Contemporary Culture: An Inaugural Lecture Delivered before the University of Oxford on 27 November 1992* (Oxford: Clarendon Press, 1993).

Eagleton, Terry, *Heathcliff and the Great Hunger: Studies in Irish Culture* (London: Verso, 1995).

Eagleton, Terry, *Crazy John and the Bishop and Other Essays on Irish Culture* (Cork: Cork University Press in association with Field Day, 1998).

Eagleton, Terry, *Scholars and Rebels in Nineteenth-Century Ireland* (Oxford: Blackwell, 1999).

Eagleton, Terry, *The Truth about the Irish* (Dublin: New Island, 1999).

Eagleton, Terry, 'Interview with Terry Eagleton', in *Lukács after Communism: Interviews with Contemporary Intellectuals*, ed. Eva L. Corredor (Durham: Duke University Press, 1997), pp. 127–50.

Eagleton, Terry, 'A Grim Parody of the Humanities: An Interview with Terry Eagleton' (with John Higgins), *Pretexts: Literary and Cultural Studies* 9:2 (2000), pp. 215–23.

Eagleton, Terry, 'Utopias', in *Figures of Dissent: Critical Essays on Fish, Spivak, Žižek and Others* (London: Verso, 2003), pp. 24–36.

Eagleton, 'Peter Brooks on Bodies', in *Figures of Dissent*, pp. 129–35.

Eagleton, Terry, 'Making a Break', *London Review of Books*, 9 March 2006, pp. 25–6.

Eagleton, Terry, *Ideology: An Introduction*, new edition (London: Verso, 2007).

Eagleton, Terry, *Reason, Faith, and Revolution: Reflections on the God Debate* (New Haven: Yale University Press, 2009).

Griffiths, Eric, 'Dialectic without Detail', *Times Literary Supplement* (June 28, 1991), pp. 6–7.

Kermode, Frank, 'Who Can Blame Him?' *London Review of Books*, 5 April 1990, pp. 13–14.

CHAPTER NINE

Culture/Civilization

I'd like to go back briefly to the year after Heathcliff and the Great Hunger *appeared, when you published* The Illusions of Postmodernism *[1996]. This was your first book-length engagement with postmodernism, though you'd critiqued the phenomenon in a number of places since the mid-eighties, when you published an important response to Jameson's 'Postmodernism, or the Cultural Logic of Late Capitalism' [1984]. Postmodernism exerted an almost magnetic influence on students and academics in the humanities throughout the eighties and nineties.*

It was so durable and pervasive that some sort of explanation like Fredric Jameson's, in terms of prevailing material and political conditions, must almost intuitively be right, whatever disagreements one might have with him here and there. Postmodernism wouldn't have had the tenacity it had unless it was somehow locked into that wider design. Postmodernism did seem to answer very immediately and spontaneously to a set of lived experiences in advanced capitalism. This bond is what secured its power, and – argue with it theoretically as you might – it was there, it was a whole cultural milieu, one that couldn't be dispersed in purely intellectual terms. One has to look, as David Harvey did in *The Condition of Postmodernity* [1990], at the material infrastructure, at the way that postmodernist theories themselves mime important changes in advanced capitalism and therefore important changes in subjectivity – in people's sense, or lack of sense, of themselves, and in the problems of orientating and coordinating oneself within that space. At the same time – and my book didn't highlight this enough – there are elements in postmodernism that can be used against the power of corporate capitalism. And if one then adds to that all the theoretical and practical reasons why it seems that Marxism is discredited, it's not hard to see why some people might want to scramble into those postmodernist positions, not least because they seem to keep a certain kind of radicalism warm, as post-structuralism had previously appeared to promise a radicalism that was often very difficult to identify in concrete political terms. Postmodernism and post-structuralism, however, aren't the same kind of thing: the latter is a set of theories, the former is a cultural formation.

The Illusions of Postmodernism *was nonetheless criticized for conflating the two. Is that a weakness of the book, do you think?*

Not entirely. It was written at a high level of generality and that was another source of criticism: I wasn't naming names. On the other hand it wasn't a book that was meant to name names. I didn't want to go through particular authors, like Baudrillard and Lyotard, in serial order. I wanted to capture a general intellectual ambience. And I think the book did that well enough. But it left itself vulnerable to certain criticisms in so doing. In discussing the book I've often found myself saying, 'Well, there are of course more radical currents of postmodernism that I don't really deal with . . .' It's very much a polemic, and I think I saw it as a political intervention rather than a theoretical text.

Has postmodernism, as both a political phenomenon and a theoretical one, been superseded? Can we refer confidently to its decline, even to its demise?

I think we may be in transition to a life after postmodernism with the new grand narrative of capitalism versus the Qur'an (or a particular reading thereof), but we have to remember that postmodernism was never wall-to-wall in the first place. It's not as though it's a whole condition we can either stay with or move beyond.

You edited a couple of extremely helpful anthologies that appeared in the early and mid-nineties. One is a collection of documents on ideology, which is in a sense a companion to the Verso book, though Longman published it. The other is an introductory selection of essays in Marxist literary and cultural theory, from Marx himself to contemporary Marxist critics of postmodernism, which you and Drew Milne edited for Blackwell. Were you conscious of constructing a kind of counter-canon of theoretical texts to challenge the dominance of postmodernism at this time?

Yes, to some extent. I saw the pedagogical value of having the major ideological texts made available. The editor of the series, Stan Smith, mooted the idea of the collection on ideology and I instantly leapt at it. It was worth doing; but it was a chore, it wasn't interesting to do. As far as the project with Drew was concerned, there was a hope that this might put Marxist criticism back on the map. It hadn't of course entirely gone away, so there was a sense that there was still something to build on. There was also a sense that the more fashionable discourses were not really delivering on the big questions that still concerned people; so there was an opening there.

You then produced an excellent little introductory book on Marx and Freedom *[1997]. Its emphasis on the 'anthropological' content of Marx's early thought, and the concept of species-being, was especially useful.*

That was certainly a discourse that had been buried for a long time, even by Marxists themselves. I'd been very influenced by Norman Geras's book on *Marx and Human Nature* [1983]. I'd always thought that Norman was onto something important there. And before I wrote the Marx book, for quite a long time in my teaching and discussion, I'd been trying to float those ideas, sometimes against the grain of other Marxist orthodoxies. It's one of the most forgotten of my books, so I'm glad it seemed useful.

You characterize Marx's ethics in this book in terms of the aesthetic, since the aesthetic 'is traditionally that form of human practice which requires no utilitarian justification, but which furnishes its own goals, grounds and rationales'. You've returned to this argument more recently . . .

As I've mentioned already, this interest in what one might technically call the autotelic runs like a thread throughout my work, taking in everything from God and Oscar Wilde to art and ethics; and now, of all un-Marxist topics, evil, which is similarly non-utilitarian, done simply for the hell of it. And on which I've just written a book.

The Idea of Culture inaugurated Blackwell's 'Manifestos' series in 2000. There you demonstrate among other things the dialectical relationship of nature and culture; and argue, in opposition to postmodernism, that 'the very word culture contains a tension between making and being made, rationality and spontaneity, which upbraids the disembodied intellect of the Enlightenment as much as it defies the cultural reductionism of so much contemporary thought.' What prompted this intervention on the question of 'culturalism'?

The book was a direct commission. Blackwell had dreamt up this series and commissioned me to do one on culture. It was, however, part of an ongoing attempt on my part to grasp the very slippery concept of culture, which one always either overestimates or underestimates. I wanted to get it into focus at a time when, because of identity politics, postmodernism and the media in general, it was obviously of vital importance. I was increasingly restive with the growing culturalist context of left thought. So part of the impulse behind the writing of *The Idea of Culture* was a feeling that the whole area of culture was being steadily drained of theoretical substance. I felt that cultural studies – not all cultural studies but a certain American mainstream – was largely responsible for that. It was as though each time I visited the States the theoretical environment had become more impoverished. Theory wasn't feeding into the actual study and analysis of culture, and important arguments were not only no longer current but not even known. I felt at the time that, after an intensive period of the laying-in of theoretical capital about the idea of culture and politics – and there of course Raymond Williams was my original point of reference – there was a danger of that being lost. And that was not simply because of an academic trend; it was because capitalism itself was shifting. With the increasing globalization of capitalism – the intensifying grip of that system and the apparent failure or collapse of various antagonists – it seemed that there was an enormous displacement of attention to the concept of culture. I felt the idea of culture needed to be rapped over the knuckles, as it were, and smartly put back in its place. That's how I end the book. Since then, I've come up with another slogan: 'Culture is what people will kill for'. So you see, the problem with culture is that it's immensely important in one sense and not at all primary in another. This is why it's so hard to get into focus or proportion. In that sense it's like sexuality.

The final chapter, 'Towards a Common Culture', makes the book's indebtedness to Williams even more explicit. What were you trying to do with his legacy in The Idea of Culture?

It wasn't only a matter of his legacy. When Williams read my early essay, 'The Idea of a Common Culture' [1968] – and I was very pleased about this – he told me that it had clarified something for him about the idea of a common culture. I think he meant the distinction between a culture commonly shared and a culture commonly made. That is in effect the distinction he had been arguing for between, say, Eliot and himself, but he hadn't formulated it to himself in those terms. I think all my essay did was to hit on that crucial discrimination. I'd emphasized that the phrase 'common culture' could be mystifying because it was open to different meanings – some of which were entirely acceptable to the cultural right, to the tradition of *Kulturkritik*, and some of which weren't. In the tradition of *Kulturkritik*, as for example Eliot or Leavis, the idea of a common culture could be quite compatible with stratification, hierarchy, subordination. Williams was trying to get beyond that in order to stress the process of common making, which incidentally involves much greater diversity. My essay helped him to formulate that, I think, and I was glad of the fact.

Do you think this notion of making or producing a common culture became especially useful again in the face of concepts of culture that were fixated on consumption?

I think so. There'd also been an attempt to radicalize the idea of consumption in the form of the New Times current of the nineties, which I'd always been somewhat sceptical about. The interesting point about Williams's stress upon production was that he was not of course in any sense a left fetishist of production. Instead, the concept of production, for him as for Marx, was extraordinarily wide. Again and again throughout his work, he uses phrases like 'active making' to shift the emphasis from the idea of a passive receiving of a culture primarily defined elsewhere. I think that's what he was insisting on too in *Culture and Society* [1958]. Culture isn't first decided and then disseminated; it doesn't pre-exist its active, collective making.

And he insisted on this in opposition to Eliot's notion of tradition, for example?

Yes, although I think Williams backs the case that tradition is a vital concept, albeit one that we've allowed to be appropriated. At one point in the conclusion to *Culture and Society* he talks about tradition as being a selection and re-selection of our ancestors, which on the one hand puts the emphasis upon active making but on the other hand is almost a translation of Eliot's idea of tradition.

What you advocate in The Idea of Culture *is effectively a politics of culture, as opposed to a cultural politics. Could you clarify that distinction?*

I was very gratified to see a convergence between my line of thought and the thinking of Francis Mulhern. Mulhern is one of the British cultural thinkers I respect most, because his level of rigour and reflectiveness is considerably higher than that of many people in the field. Partly because of his Marxist background, and partly because he didn't come to this simply through contemporary media. Mulhern has also been trying to whip a somewhat inflated notion of culture back into place – culture as a displacement of the political

I was going to remark on the coincidence of Mulhern's Culture/ Metaculture *and* The Idea of Culture, *both of which came out in 2000. Your book, like Mulhern's, examines and at the same time exemplifies or enacts what he calls a 'metacultural discourse', a discourse 'in which culture addresses its own generality and conditions of existence'.*

It was interesting that the two books should have coincided like that. It was time, as I said, to refocus this keyword, or buzzword, which for Williams's generation had been a terrain on which to fight politically but which was now in danger of coming to be a substitute for that. A shift had taken place from a politics of culture to a cultural politics, to revert to the distinction you mentioned. In a curious way, the concept itself had not only survived its previous history but become even more insistent, even more part of the buzz of intellectual discourse; but at the same time it had become increasingly depoliticized. It was the relationship between those two moments that interested both Mulhern and myself.

How does the CCCS [Centre for Contemporary Cultural Studies] in Birmingham, and the work of Stuart Hall more generally, fit into this narrative?

I wrote a piece in the *London Review of Books* in 1996 in which I reviewed a collection of essays about Stuart Hall. This was a brief and inadequate attempt at an overview of his work – much more would need to be said – but the more I think about the seminal role that Stuart played in that period, the more I see it as defined again and again, in different ways, by an ambiguous relationship to Marxism. I'm not saying that exhausts Stuart's contribution by any means, but if you look at the various moments of encounter or confrontation or theoretical mutation, I think they all involve some ambiguous relationship between Marxism and something else – whether it's culture, populism, ethnicity, feminism, democracy, post-structuralism or cultural studies. I would imagine that this can then be traced back to his experience as a post-colonial immigrant. That's to say that, from the start, Marxism was at once deeply relevant to Stuart Hall and never relevant enough. There were facets of his experience that Marxism simply couldn't capture. I think that if you're going to take your distance from Marxism, as Hall eventually did, then that's a much more reputable reason for doing so than because you think the bandwagon has stalled and it may be time to leap off it.

Do you think that even a book like Jameson's on the 'cultural logic' of postmodernism conceded too much to the depoliticization of culture?

From our European vantage point I think we can see how much the concerns of the Americans in this field – including Jameson, the most eminent and intelligent of them all – were shaped by depoliticization, by the lack of availability of socialist memory, let alone active contemporary socialist activity. That's not a criticism of them so much as of the system. It was the same with feminism back in the late seventies and eighties, in that if one came from Europe one assumed that feminism would have a roughly radical or socialist background, which one could certainly not take for granted in the States. That was a major problem of communication. Besides this, Jameson's theory of postmodernism is primarily economic rather than political. That's probably another reflection of his American milieu – of the insistence on the commodity, the media and so on, along with the problems of the political left. But at the same time these unpropitious conditions allow him to produce a powerfully totalizing, distancing, materially grounded vision of postmodern culture which – along with David Harvey's work on the subject – makes so much other discussion look shallow and two-dimensional. Jameson and Harvey both refuse to locate the phenomenon simply at the level of culture or ideas.

The Idea of Culture *is the first of your books to register the effects of reading Slavoj Žižek, whom you describe at one point as 'one of our leading technicians of otherness'. Can you recall first reading him?*

Žižek would of course quite rightly detest that particular phrase – did I really use it? – because it makes him sound like a disciple of Levinas, which is the last thing he is. Maybe my understanding at that point was rather limited. I remember reading *The Sublime Object of Ideology* [1989] with great excitement and I've followed his career closely since then. I was intrigued by the way that he seemed to move rather anachronistically from post-Marxism to Marxism. One of the keys to Žižek's thought is perversity – perversity in a more profound sense than simply being awkward, being part of the awkward squad. Like Wilde, Žižek loves ripping received ideas inside out, turning orthodoxies on their head. In *Trouble with Strangers* [2008] I discuss his small-nation relation to Europe, which I very much understand through Ireland. I've just come hotfoot from a conference organized by Žižek, at which I spoke amongst other things about Oscar Wilde, with his extraordinarily ambiguous relation to metropolitan culture. I think there's a lot of that in Žižek too. I once visited Slovenia, and one of the few words I didn't hear was 'Žižek'. Perhaps that's how small nations sometimes react to those of their number who become famous. In Ireland it can take the form of: 'Has that bastard really been taken up by Faber?'

The critical discourse of The Idea of Culture *occasionally seems stylistically comparable to that of Žižek's books too. For instance, there's a passage about the American middle class's fear of smoking in which you argue that it's a terror of extraterrestrials as much as of lung cancer. 'Like the loathsome creatures of* Alien, *smoke and cancer are those dreadful bits of otherness which manage somehow to insinuate themselves at the core of one's being.' There's a distinctly Žižekian flavour to that sentence.*

Yes, there is. One of the common elements in our work is humour, although the difference is that Žižek tells jokes and I don't. The other common element, I suppose, is a certain carnivalesque intermingling of the high and the low, or the theoretical and the everyday, though with him this is so pronounced as to win him the title of 'postmodern philosopher'. Interestingly, one of his responses to *Trouble with Strangers*, which he liked, was to see it as a very Anglo-Saxon critique of a certain French philosophical élitism. He sympathized with my critique of this philosophical current in the chapters on the Real, but didn't fully agree with them. I talk in that book about the bathos or earthiness of certain British and Irish theorists. One disreputable reason for this may be the pressure of empiricism, but it also has a therapeutic effect. Žižek in a curious sense does that in his work, but he doesn't really defend it in theory. His ethical theory is much more high-minded and élitist than his own style of writing.

In the past, Žižek has praised the way in which you combine theoretical sophistication and common sense. Common sense is in general denigrated in the Marxist tradition for being the deepest repository of the ideological, but there have been those – Gramsci is one that comes to mind – who have tried to reclaim common sense as a terrain in which a proletarian intelligence might use the experience of everyday life to undermine the ideological. Can common sense be reclaimed?

There are some Continental leftist philosophers who like common sense in moderation – like a couple of gin and tonics – and Žižek is one of those. But philosophy in Europe has accrued so much cultural capital that there are strict limits to its indulgence in common-sense debunkery. Even so, it's arguable that most of the really interesting Continental philosophers, from Kierkegaard, Marx and Nietzsche to Freud, Wittgenstein, Heidegger, Adorno and Derrida, are really anti-philosophers – thinkers who harbour profound suspicions about the whole philosophical enterprise as such, as they encounter it in their own times, and who in various ways are out to deconstruct it. This then involves a lot of satiric deflation, self-ironizing, bluntly materialist rereadings and the like, all of which gets transmitted in a different style reflecting the desire or compulsion to write otherwise. I also think of Derrida's curious attraction to Oxford philosophy. He liked its jokiness and laid-backness and everydayness, which were the last things one would associate with Derrida. As I've often said, French playfulness is a very solemn affair: you have to have several degrees before you can engage in French humour. So I think people like Žižek and Derrida have a certain ambivalent relationship to that current of English thought or English sensibility.

But, yes, Gramsci does go some way towards rehabilitating a concept that's been too easily dismissed. The concept of good sense in Gramsci seems to me to pick up – not necessarily consciously – a tradition of practical reason, of what Aristotle calls *phronesis*. It's a different way of reasoning, a way of reasoning which is closer to material technique than it is to abstraction. And this is to be found in thinkers as starkly divergent as Marx and Heidegger.

One of the concerns of The Idea of Culture *is the continuity of human history, its rootedness in species-being. You quote that wonderful passage from Sebastiano Timpanaro's* On Materialism *[1970 (1975)] about the transhistorical dimensions of human beings. Here you are refuting the characteristic postmodernist emphasis on discontinuity, on the dessication of human experience, which you identify as a form of left historicism.*

Or perhaps a conjuncturalism. This is not as extreme now as it was twenty years ago, when it seemed that the whole of the historical was pivoted on a single conjuncture or other. New historicism is one example of this: on certain meanings of the term historicism, new historicism might be better defined as a new anti-historicism, in the sense that it has a high degree of aversion to continuities, grand narratives and so on. The identification of history or historicization with local contextualization was part of the ideological thrust of that current, and indeed of postmodernism in general. Ellen Wood has criticized Quentin Skinner and others from the Cambridge School of History who have insisted on that kind of historicization. One of her points is that they locate political arguments in terms of discourse; the other is that they always mean a very local context, almost a pragmatic context, like arguments in parliament in 1689 or something. So the political arguments are not over historicization but over what that means, how far that stretches, how far down it goes.

When I look back at my work, one thing that strikes me is that I've never been a historicist. I don't just mean in the more disreputable senses but even in the more reputable ones, in the sense that I've consistently argued, against Jameson and others, that to historicize is not necessarily to politicize or to radicalize. Historicism has been as much a part of the right as of the left. It may well be that there's a Catholic universalism lurking somewhere at the root of this. But I also think the case is correct. I've never seen the idea of history with a capital 'H' as a foundation, or as that which conclusively resolves an issue. What history, what tradition, what historical context?

There is a sense in which, particularly in my work on Ireland, historical continuity has been important for me. It's been important in the sense that Irish historical revisionists have overwhelmingly stressed discontinuities, and although they've been right to dismantle the more egregious sort of vaunted continuities in Ireland, of the type that imagines there's been a single, heroic, unbroken struggle against perfidious Britain since 557 BCE, they've also tended to downplay some very important historical affiliations for their own political purposes. Besides, when the right-wingers say 'You can't change human nature', they use that among other things as an argument against socialism and many other kinds of change. But in a sense I would want to agree with them. I would want to say, 'Yes, and it's a good thing too,' because among those continuities are some positive ones such as resistance to oppression or the desire for justice. If you erase all continuities, you are erasing that as well.

In relation to Ireland, is your political point in part that there is in some even deeper sense a struggle for a united Ireland that underlies its divisive history?

There are definite continuities and historical affiliations in Ireland, from the United Irish movement to Daniel O'Connell to Young Ireland to Parnell's land movement and on up to Sinn Fein. Nobody is suggesting that there is some unchanging essence which threads those moments together – I think there's a cheap caricatural victory that the discontinuity camp sometimes scores in that respect, in the case of Ireland or elsewhere. But as long as Ireland was under the rule of Britain, that would remain an abiding question, whatever form it took historically. And of course the British complained that the Irish kept changing the question. That's a good instance of what I'm saying: they did indeed keep changing the question, in the sense that the question of colonial status was articulated in many different forms – it could be land, it could be repeal of the Union, it could be the Church, it could be universities or tithes, but it was the same question. In a colonial society like Ireland certain questions simply keep returning, stubbornly re-posing themselves and refusing to go away – it's not a matter of intellectual choice. This is perhaps one reason why Yeats, Joyce and Beckett see history more in cyclical than linear terms.

The Idea of Culture rehearses ideas about the relations between civilization and culture that you've recently extended and elaborated, and states at one point that the scandal of Marxism is that it has treated civilization as if it were culture. Can you say what you mean by that?

I had in mind to treat culture anthropologically, which is one of the resonances culture obviously had in the nineteenth century; to treat it as a specific, delimited form of life with its own internal laws and developments. I still believe, as I come to do the thinking for the book on Marxism that I'm writing, that that's an achievement of Marxism that's not been sufficiently stressed. Thinkers like Newton and Freud discovered something previously invisible, whether it was gravity or the unconscious. Marx in a sense does the same. Capitalism was so pervasive and unobtrusive as to be invisible as a determinable form of life. However, as far as the culture and civilization comparison goes, in *Reason, Faith, and Revolution* [2009] I argue that the opposition that is now increasingly opening up in the 'war on terror' is not between civilization and barbarism but civilization and culture. We have civilization; they have culture. Culture becomes a new name for barbarism.

Let's revert to the biographical narrative for a moment. In 2001 you left Oxford for Manchester University, where you became John Edward Taylor Professor of English Literature.

I'd intended to stick it out at Oxford and move to Manchester after retirement, but increasingly felt I'd served my time there. A particular index of this was that, while they expected me to administrate and be a senior manager on the one hand, on the other hand no sooner had I vacated the post that I'd had before the chair, namely the University Lectureship in Literary Theory, than they changed the definition of it from strict literary theory to something broader. I thought that was a sign of the times. So I was in talks with Manchester anyway and they said, 'Well, why not come now?' There seemed no reason not to. I left Oxford with no more twinge of nostalgia than I would have had if I'd left it the day after I arrived – whether that's a good or a bad thing I can't decide. Manchester offered me a very decent deal of simply teaching, with no administration and no examinations.

I'd also like to raise the question of autobiography at this point. The Gatekeeper, *the memoir you published in 2001, interweaves anecdotal accounts of your formative experiences with political and philosophical reflections. What sort of a reader did you have in mind for this book? In contrast to many contemporary memoirists, you weren't writing for the scum who want to have the cockles of their hearts warmed, as Brecht might have put it. And you deliberately problematize and complicate the conventions of autobiography. But isn't there something inherently heart-warming about the form?*

I've been notoriously critical in my work of the biographical or autobiographical form, and I'd stand by that position. I suppose my only defence is that my own effort attempts to be an anti- or non-autobiography, and it was certainly criticized as such. As far as the warm and genial genre goes, some critics, like Blake Morrison, felt that it wasn't anything like warm and genial enough. They felt deprived of what they conventionally expected from the genre. Some reviewers rather obtusely failed to realize that I was trying to do something different with the genre and interpreted that as a deficiency. Some of the slimier right-wing responses were to say, 'My goodness, these Marxists are human after all.' One's very humanity was used as a put-down! But that didn't last for very long. When I criticized Martin Amis for his anti-Islamic slurs a few years later, one newspaper had a sub-head reading, 'Where's Your Sense of Humour, Comrade?' Meaning, you understand, that because leftists are austere, thin-blooded, humourless types, they don't see what's riotously funny in rich white men urging people to harass poor Muslims.

The book doesn't have an epigraph, but one suspects that, if it did, your maternal grandmother's conviction that 'whatever you said you should say nothing' might be an apposite one. The book performs a kind of striptease, like all memoirs, but the reader finally realizes that you haven't in fact exposed yourself so much as assumed a series of different costumes. In that respect perhaps it's Wildean.

The equivalent image I used in *Saint Oscar* is that the mask is stripped off only to reveal another one. There was a practical reason for this when it was staged: Stephen Rea felt he wasn't fat enough to play Wilde, so we dressed him in layer after layer of costume and, as the play progressed, he gradually stripped off these gaudy, ludicrously extravagant garments to reveal his prison uniform underneath, in which he looked very thin and frail. 'Whatever you say, say nothing' is the title of a famous poem by Seamus Heaney, from *North* [1975], which my grandmother would have appreciated. In fact, as I say in *The Gatekeeper*, Heaney bears a surprising resemblance to my grandmother, so there's even a physical affinity between them. They probably came from much the same gene pool in Northern Ireland.

At times it's quite difficult to ascertain how ironic the tone of the book is. On the one hand, you're obviously satirizing the miserabilist confessional literature popularized by people like Frank McCourt in Angela's Ashes [1999]. On the other, you're emphatic about the grimness of your childhood in Salford, which you describe as a 'perpetual narrative of suffering'. Is there a tension here?

Yes, I think so. It's a book of mixed sensibility, or, in Eliot's phrase, of 'levity and seriousness'. I think that has been one of the hallmarks of my later work. There are dangers with that sensibility, and, as people pointed out in the case of *The Gatekeeper*, of seeming to strain for humorous effect. *Saint Oscar* is in that same tragicomic vein. Wilde himself was simultaneously hilarious and doomed, which may have been partly what attracted me to writing about him.

Why did you decide not to discuss your relationship with Williams in The Gatekeeper?

It hadn't even occurred to me that I hadn't done that. It would be interesting to know, and I still don't know, what principle of selection governed the book – apart from episodes that were interesting or funny or significant in some way. There's a lot of filtering out going on, of course, but I wasn't even aware that I don't talk about Williams.

By contrast there's a detailed portrait of Theodore Redpath, your tutor at Trinity. Interestingly, the book presents an almost archaic picture of society: there's a chapter entitled 'Aristos', and a pervasive interest in proletarian culture of course, but scarcely any bourgeois.

That's true. Certainly one wouldn't describe Redpath as bourgeois. What that does raise for me, however, isn't so much the class issue. What occurs to me now is that when I graduated from Cambridge – I don't say this in the book – Williams and Redpath were in a sense fighting for my soul. That's rather a dramatic way of putting it, but Redpath wanted me to stay on at Trinity, where there was some sort of Research Fellowship on offer, whereas Williams wanted me to go to Jesus. They met for the first time I think as a consequence of that. I'd love to have been a fly on the wall. I think it was perfectly amicable, and superficially at least they got on with each other, grotesquely disparate though they were as people; but some sort of genteel negotiation went on over this rather truculent twenty-one-year-old. Redpath knew I was a disciple of Williams, and for that reason it was settled in that direction; but I don't think he ever entirely accepted it. From then on Redpath became rather hostile to me, and at one point I was told to stop using him as a referee. He thought that I'd thrown up the possibility of a glittering literary career at Trinity. Perhaps he hoped I'd become his successor, inheriting his Spanish butler and Spanish housekeeper. Maybe I've missed my way.

One of the religious concepts that you invoke in The Gatekeeper *and other recent books is asceticism. You claim for example that the Carmelite nuns to whom you acted as gatekeeper embodied a crypto-political refusal of a capitalist society centred on consumption. In what sense can a gesture as remote or recessive as that be meaningfully regarded as political?*

I wouldn't want to overstate the political nature of what the nuns were doing, but I've sometimes rather mischievously claimed that all radical politics is other-worldly; it's just that when they hear the word 'other-worldly' people think 'up there' rather than 'beyond here'. These nuns were also quite literally communists. They didn't own the clothes on their backs. There is a sense in which the gesture of disengagement that you talk about is reminiscent of the negative politics of the modernist work of art according to Adorno. I don't think that's an entirely fanciful connection. There is a politics of refusal that relates to the ethics of the Real, as I try to spell out in *Trouble with Strangers*. Like Antigone or Clarissa, these women refused to enter the sexual market, rejected commodities and deepened and strengthened their existence by living perpetually in the shadow of death. They viewed their own radical self-dispossession as making up vicariously for our own inability to do so, yielding up their lives for others, as they saw it. I don't find any easy escapism in that. Indeed, a more apposite criticism might be that they were disengaging from a world they knew very little about. Is that a sacrifice? These were very young Irish girls . . .

Thereby hangs a tale, in fact. One of the readers of *The Gatekeeper* was one of those nuns, who is now seventy-eight and still a Carmelite nun, although only partly enclosed. She wrote a long letter to me and we're now in regular correspondence. She was an eighteen-year-old novice at the time I was gatekeeper, and because she didn't have much to experience, and didn't see anybody from the outside world apart from the priest and myself, she remembers much more than I do. I told her how spooky the whole experience had been for me. I think she understood that even at the time. She said she noticed that I used to recite the Latin very quickly, as if I wanted to run away from all these hidden eyes staring at me. She also annotated those bits of my account that are slightly awry in terms of memory. Among other things, she said, 'We had such fun!' They had an hour's so-called recreation, a bit like prison, but she wasn't talking about that. She insisted it was great fun. I think that's an extraordinary remark.

Perhaps the kind of Beckettian fun to be derived from waiting for God . . .

I'm sure that must have been the case with her. I thought of these people as plaster saints, but of course they weren't. They were women. And although she still knows very little about what's going on in the world, not least because they're not allowed television, she's very much alive, very shrewd and funny and down-to-earth, as in my experience most religious celibates are.

In 2003 you published no less than three books, Figures of Dissent, After Theory, *and* Sweet Violence. *They are generically rather different: respectively, a collection of reviews, a politico-philosophical polemic, and a theoretical study of tragedy. Perhaps I can begin by asking you about* Figures of Dissent, *which largely consisted of pieces that had appeared in the* London Review of Books *[LRB] in the course of the previous decade. Most of the articles reprinted in your earlier collection of this kind,* Against the Grain *[1986], had been culled either from the* New Left Review *or from more specialist academic journals. Could you say something about the role of a kind of higher journalism in your more recent work?*

I like to think that I can write in different styles, depending on the audience in question, and I immensely value writing intellectual journalism. I think I'm quite good at it, and I enjoy it a lot. The *LRB* has been wonderful in providing me with a platform of this kind. I suppose what we call a public intellectual is one who gets out of the house occasionally. A public intellectual has to discover arenas beyond academia, and there are of course precious few of them these days. So I'm always delighted when I'm invited to address an anti-war meeting, or a session of the Workers' Educational Association, or a group of worker-writers. I'm not an activist by temperament, and for a long time I felt guilty about this in a boring, middle-class-leftist way, before I realized that some people could no more *not* be activists than they could dispense with food (or more likely, in the case of left-wing activists, drink). So any chance I get to do something other than teach Flaubert or Max Weber I tend to seize gratefully. A lot of the early Catholic left work was of this non-academic kind.

I'm dismayed by radical intellectuals who *could* reach a wider audience, having already established their academic credentials – younger people often can't institutionally afford to write in this way – but who simply aren't interested in doing so, and don't see it as part of their political responsibility. Neither do some of them see it as a political responsibility not to write with such baroque obscurantism. Walter Benjamin once remarked that his prose style would have been improved by a German revolution. I suppose in our context this means that if one had a sharper sense of political urgency than is usual in Harvard or Columbia, one wouldn't write with such flagrant disregard for intelligibility since one simply wouldn't be able to afford it or get away with it. *Literary Theory* was read by a lot of people who had never seen the inside of a university. I don't think it's just some sentimental populism that makes me feel proud of this.

Perhaps the most controversial piece to reappear in Figures of Dissent *was your review of Gayatri Spivak's* A Critique of Postcolonial Reason *[1999], originally published in the* LRB, *in which you attacked her, among other things, for her eclecticism and her elliptical prose.*

There's one interesting aspect of my piece about Spivak – who, by the way, was typically gracious about it – that might be worth touching on. I doubt it could have been done in the USA – I mean, by a male academic like myself. The gender issues are simply too sensitive there, even though this wasn't at all what the review was about. It would be like a white American intellectual saying that a black American intellectual's book was utter garbage – which, needless to say, one must have the absolute right to do. Anyway, I stand by the case that there is something particularly scandalous in writing about men and women in the underdeveloped world, as it's amusingly called, in ways that they aren't even intended to understand. Innately difficult ideas are one thing; obscurantism is another. Nobody expects radical theory to be as luminously self-evident as a bus ticket, but that's no reason why it should read like Kabbalah. Theory is democratic, as I've already argued. It promises that all you have to do is learn a certain kind of language, as opposed to having high culture in your blood, as my own Cambridge tutors expected. So esoteric left theory is all the more outrageous. A writer like Žižek can produce some ferociously taxing ideas, but he does so in a lucid, companionable way. He isn't exactly witty, but he tells a lot of good jokes. If he can be clear about such complex matters, so that the difficulties belong to the content rather than the form, then so can others. It's just that they fear they will shed some intellectual kudos by doing so. I suspect that at the root of theoretical obscurantism lies insecurity as much as arrogance.

After Theory, *one of the other books to appear in 2003, proved to be among the most controversial of your career, and I'd like to ask you about it in slightly more detail. The book's initial premise is that we're living in the aftermath of high theory. By that you don't mean primarily that we're living in the era of what might by contrast be called low or mass theory – although there's a sense in which one could argue that high theory was mass-ified, to use a clumsy expression, in the form of cultural studies. The situation you sketch is more epochal than that. Could you say what you meant by it and what precisely the title was intended to designate?*

The title was slightly unfortunate, and some young academics who were struggling to introduce literary theory into courses were not pleased with it. I think I meant 'After "Theory"' – 'Theory' should be understood in quotation marks and with an upper-case 'T'. I did try and point that out in the book. I think the core of the book is the attempt to connect the acme of theory with the high point of the left. Of course, there's also a sense in which that theory was also a displacement of those leftist political beliefs – it kept certain radical ideas warm – but I think the historical coincidence was very marked. So I began thinking about theory more in terms of the *longue durée*. In a way, what happened was not that theory yielded ground to pragmatism in a purely philistine sense, although that also is a narrative to tell, but that non-pragmatic theory yielded ground to theoretical pragmatism. That was part of the postmodern intellectual cult. Theorists like Rorty and Fish were providing sophisticated theoretical defences of anti-theory. They weren't just anti-theorists in the sense that Brad Pitt probably is.

The book sets out a balance sheet of the losses and gains of cultural theory as part of an attempt to provoke cultural theory into thinking ambitiously again, so that it is once more capable of making sense of the grand narratives in which, inescapably, it is embroiled. Could you say something about this? The terrorist attacks on the Twin Towers aren't mentioned in the text, but the cover of the British edition was illustrated with a silhouette of a plane apparently nose-diving . . .

That wasn't my decision, but it was interesting that the publisher made that connection. The narrative I don't really relate in the book, though I perhaps should have done, is not the revival of theory as such but the revival of grand or grandiose thinking like US neo-conservatism in the wake of 9/11. I've often pointed out the irony that no sooner had the death of history been promulgated than history returned with a vengeance in the form of the so-called War on Terror. My point about that is not just that it's ironic, that the end-of-history theorists were caught on the hop; it's that it was logical, because the promulgation of the death of history itself reflected a certain political triumphalism that played its part in the imperial agenda, and then generated a backlash in the shape of a new grand narrative of terrorism. There was a sense in which, as has happened before historically, the act of announcing the death of history actually galvanized it again – just as Hegel's announcement of the death of history provoked ripostes from Kierkegaard, Marx and others. As with the artistic avant-garde, you find yourself opening up history in the act of trying to close it down.

The second half of After Theory *then rehabilitates some extremely unfashionable concepts: truth, virtue, objectivity, morality, revolution, foundations, death and love. If the first half revisits to some extent the terrain of* Literary Theory *[1983], the second half revisits the terrain of* The New Left Church *[1966]. It uses pre-modernist ideas, to put it schematically, as the premise of a post-postmodernist manifesto. Were you consciously returning to the early concerns?*

I don't know if I was actually returning to them. In a sense they had never entirely left me. I was increasingly concerned to highlight the ethical, and aware of the embarrassments it caused on the left. Almost in a campaigning, programmatic way, that book registered the fact that I was increasingly conscious of wanting to fight this ethico-political corner. What's happened on the left, though, is in fact a return to ethics, manifest in Derrida, Badiou, Agamben, Žižek and the interest in the Real. I see that in part as an attempt to come to terms with a foundational question that really refused to be staved off. In the case of people like Derrida and Levinas, that entails a certain displacement of the political. The ethical catches up with various motifs that are more properly political. So I think the question I was raising as early as that book, without really formulating it, was, 'What of the relation between the ethical and the political?' I then tackle that head-on at the end of *Trouble with Strangers*.

Let's come back to that in the context of Trouble with Strangers. *In the prefatory note to* After Theory, *to stick with that book for a moment, you state that 'the influence of the late Herbert McCabe is so pervasive on my argument that it's impossible to localize'.* Sweet Violence, *which came out in the same year, was dedicated to McCabe's memory. Could you clarify the ways in which he was important to the argument of the second half of* After Theory *in particular?*

It's interesting that I should have used that expression, because an influence that is so pervasive as to be non-localized is a metaphor for God. Not that Herbert was ever quite that. McCabe's work showed me from the beginning how Christianity was or could be political, without any concession to fashionableness. This is part of what I carried into the later work. He and Laurence Bright were the two figures who made theology make ethical, political and human sense to me – it certainly hadn't before. Herbert's work was so deeply influential on me not only because it showed me a way I could reconcile tradition with radicality – he was certainly a thorough traditionalist in the best sense of the word – but also in terms of sensibility. Laurence was the foppish Wildean figure who fascinated me but was very different from me; Herbert, who was from a lower-middle-class Irish, north-of-England background, and who was a radical from an early age, was much more of my kind. He had a positively Chestertonian sense of paradox, which I would relate to a certain intellectual perversity and a certain maverick quality odd in one so devoutly orthodox; and something of my attempt to introduce wit and humour into my own work came from him. The cast of his sensibility was spontaneously congenial to me.

In his comment for the back cover of After Theory, *Frank Kermode wrote, 'I should be surprised if this book didn't cause a considerable stir.' As I've already hinted, it did. Your old friend Eric Griffiths, for instance, published a screed against it in the* TLS, *attacking you for cynically pursuing what he called a 'cultural entrepreneurship', and concluding: '*After Theory *is stuffed to the brim with shoddy wares, and I advise you not to buy them.' Most of this attack can be dismissed as pathological, but what would be your response to his methodological criticisms, his claim that you present conclusions without arguing for them logically? Is he simply displaying an animus against polemic because it offends against the genteel codes of criticism? Or does he point more productively to the limits of the book's register?*

After Theory certainly has all kinds of flaws, some of which reflect its rather too buoyant, self-confident historical moment. The failure to argue fully for some of the positions is one symptom of that. So is a certain airy glibness of style. But the *Times Literary Supplement* has attacked every one of my books for the last forty years; in fact, it has sometimes reviewed subsequent editions of the same book, so as to boot it along its way. I suspect that certain *TLS* reviewers, Eric Griffiths among them, are paid a kind of anti-Eagletonian retainer, wheeled out of semi-retirement or at least semi-inertia whenever a book of mine appears but otherwise not very prominent in the publishing stakes. Because you have to remember, Matthew, that some of these poor souls haven't published a book of their own

since you were in diapers. This might have a little to do with their
ire, so one must feel a twinge of compassion here. Anyway, I'm
delighted to keep people like Griffiths in a job. I regard it as a form
of community service.

I'm sure that if I published a work announcing my conversion to
royalism and free market economics, conservative periodicals like
the *TLS* would find some way of savaging it. There are reviewers
in Ireland who pride themselves on their liberal pluralism, but who
are actually so virulently sectarian that they would be pathologically
incapable of passing a favourable comment on anything written by
an Irish Republican. Even if they agreed with it, they just wouldn't
be capable of bringing themselves to say so. I must say I find this
deeply depressing. It belongs to intellectual integrity to try to
meet one's antagonist's case at its most fruitful and persuasive –
Perry Anderson's work is an excellent example of this – and I fear
this is now a dying habit in an increasingly soundbite, partisan
culture. Dawkins and Hitchens on religion is one example of this
gradual death of disinterestedness – a virtue, incidentally, which
the postmodernists obtusely mistake for a God's-eye view of the
world, whereas what it really means is to attend for a moment to
someone else's interests rather than your own. Then, once you've
got what they believe right, you can put the boot in if you choose.
I've tried myself in my work to give as dispassionate an account as
possible of cases I disagree with.

I prize judiciousness very much, even though I'm a naturally
polemical, partisan thinker. But partisanship and fairness are not
necessarily antithetical. And yes, I do think that the conservative
distaste for my work has something to do with a dislike of the
polemical. But – come on! – the left is by no means in the ascendancy.
Are these people so fearful, malicious or insecure that they can't
stomach hearing even a few dissident voices? Haven't they ever
heard of intellectual democracy? It was probably the popularity
of *Literary Theory*, back in the early 1980s, which did for me in the
eyes of the political right, and *After Theory* revived memories of it.
Literary Theory had brainwashed and seduced people's students, and

I can appreciate how infuriating that must have been. It threatened to show up their own stuff as less fun. I know the feeling, because I remember trying to teach Mrs. Gaskell to Stephen Heath at Cambridge when all he wanted to do was to read Nietzsche and the Chinese novel. He was of course perfectly right in this.

After Theory was also attacked on the left, most sensationally in a review by William Deresiewicz for the Nation. *Much of this piece can also simply be ignored because it's blatantly* ad hominem *and based on feeble falsifications, like his claim that 'someone who owns three homes shouldn't be preaching self-sacrifice'. But, again, there are points that I'd be interested to hear you respond to, in spite of the embarrassingly crude nature of his attacks. He charges you with anti-Americanism, for example; and also with making 'virtually no reference to the present world in the second half of the book'. How would you refute these charges?*

I don't actually have three homes, unless you count the coal shed and the dog kennel. This is one of several myths I've heard about myself, though not quite as troubling as the report that I died of Aids in China some years ago. Nor am I anti-American. Some of my best friends are Americans. My wife, for example. And two of my five children, which is a reasonable percentage – as a Samuel Beckett character remarked of the fact that one of the two thieves on Calvary was saved. Not all of my US friends are even recovered Americans, though I do have a number of those as well, all loyal members of Americans Anonymous, who began by acknowledging that they were powerless in the face of US ideology and have now gradually progressed to becoming quite decent human beings. Relapses, however, are always a danger, not least around Thanksgiving.

It was in the year that After Theory *was published that the US and Britain invaded Iraq. What was your involvement in the anti-war movement?*

It was mainly confined to Ireland. I went on marches there and once had to prevent my young son from clambering over the rails of the US embassy in Dublin. There were some rather sinister-looking Marines lurking in the background who might not have been good for his health. I also spoke at a few public meetings, including one in a village in County Leitrim, very far from the metropolitan political centres. At a public meeting in Trinity College Dublin, some of the comrades were offended by my critique of Islamic fundamentalism, claiming that the word fundamentalism was simply a Western smear. Nobody mentioned that Saddam Hussein was a vile dictator. That's the kind of dishonest radicalism we have to resist.

Reading

Anderson, Perry, *The Origins of Postmodernity* (London: Verso, 1998).

Eagleton, Terry, 'The Idea of a Common Culture', in *From Culture to Revolution: The* Slant *Symposium 1967*, eds. Terry Eagleton and Brian Wicker (London: Sheed & Ward, 1968), pp. 35–57.

Eagleton, Terry, 'Capitalism, Modernism and Postmodernism', *New Left Review* 1:152 (1985), pp. 60–73 (reprinted in *Against the Grain: Essays 1975–1985* (London: Verso, 1986), pp. 131–47).

Eagleton Terry, ed., *Ideology* (Longong: Longman, 1994).

Eagleton, Terry, 'Terry Eagleton', in *Conversations with Critics*, ed. Nicolas Tredell (London: Carcanet, 1994), pp. 126–45.

Eagleton, Terry, and Drew Milne, eds, *Marxist Literary Theory* (Oxford: Blackwell, 1995)

Eagleton, Terry, *The Illusions of Postmodernism* (Oxford: Blackwell, 1996).

Eagleton, Terry, *Marx and Freedom* (London: Phoenix, 1997).

Eagleton, Terry, *The Idea of Culture* (Oxford: Blackwell, 2000).

Eagleton, Terry, *The Gatekeeper: A Memoir* (London: Allen Lane, 2001).

Eagleton, Terry, *After Theory* (London: Allen Lane, 2003).

Eagleton, Terry, 'Stuart Hall', in *Figures of Dissent: Essays on Fish, Spivak, Žižek and Others* (London: Verso, 2003), pp. 207–15.

Eagleton, Terry, *Trouble with Strangers: A Study of Ethics* (Oxford: Blackwell, 2008).

Geras, Norman, *Marx and Human Nature: Refutation of a Legend* (London: Verso, 1983).

Griffiths, Eric, 'The Pedlar's Wares', *Times Literary Supplement*, 17 October 2003, pp. 6–8.

Jameson, Fredric, 'Postmodernism, or the Cultural Logic of Late Capitalism', *New Left Review* 1:146 (1984), pp. 53–92.

Jameson, Fredric, *Postmodernism; or, The Cultural Logic of Late Capitalism* (London: Verso, 1991).

Mulhern, Francis, *Culture/Metaculture* (London: Routledge, 2000).

Timpanaro, Sebastiano, *On Materialism*, trans. Lawrence Garner (London: New Left Books, 1975).

Wood, Ellen Meiksins, 'Why It Matters', *London Review of Books*, 25 September 2008, pp. 3–6.

CHAPTER TEN

Death/Love

In purely literary terms, Sweet Violence *[2003], your recent book on 'the idea of the tragic', is perhaps the most ambitious book of your career, not least because it is as cosmopolitan in its references as it is historically wide-ranging. Is this a significant shift?*

I suppose with *Sweet Violence* I became for the first time what one might call a comparativist, investigating literary works from different cultures. Previously I'd been theoretically cosmopolitan but in literary terms rather parochial – though my excursus in the 1990s into Irish culture, which I had to teach myself almost from scratch, counts as an exception here. The idea of tragedy bestrides many – though, interestingly, by no means all – civilizations. I put a lot of myself – my middle-to-late self, as it were – into that book. It was one I was almost inevitably going to write ever since my student days at Cambridge, where to use Raymond Williams's terms from the first paragraph of *Modern Tragedy* [1966], tragedy as an idea, as a body of art, and as a personal reality, painfully converged in my life. Incidentally, despite my enormous admiration for *Modern Tragedy* – I was present at its making, so to speak, as Edward Thompson says of the English working class – I'd always felt that Raymond's book suffered from too provincial an artistic and philosophical range. There weren't really any ancient Greeks; there was no Racine, Corneille, Goethe or Schiller; there was a mere smattering of German theorists. Raymond always skated by on a surprisingly thin foundation of research. It was as though his

own personal thought was so deep and resourceful that he didn't
need it.

As early as The Body as Language *[1970] you'd asked, 'To what
extent is Marxism or socialist humanism capable of confronting, and
resolving, the problem of tragedy?' Why did you return to this question
at this point?*

Tragedy allowed me to get all sorts of things off my chest. Taken
together with works like *Holy Terror* [2005] – which I actually *like*
more than *Sweet Violence*, though I don't think it's as substantial –
I was able to articulate what I think was becoming an increasingly
coherent world-view. By this point I had overcome a certain
materialist coyness and was able to talk openly about certain
metaphysical or theological matters that concerned me; and in this
I was greatly inspired by the theological upfrontness of atheists like
Badiou, Agamben and Žižek. I mean, if they could do it, couldn't
a former altar boy do it too? Tragedy for me concerns the paradox
by which we can begin to move beyond our desperate plight in the
very act, and by the very power, by which we confess that this state
of permanent catastrophe is how things fundamentally are with us.

Sweet Violence was also an attempt to appropriate the idea of
tragedy – as critics like Jonathan Dollimore had done previously –
from the jealous clutches of the post-Nietzschean right, from those
for whom tragedy, in its sacred, heroic, hierarchical, mythological
way, was really an oblique onslaught on modernity as such. It
represented a trace of absolute value in a drably secularized
world, a hint of the gods, fate, religious ritual, blood sacrifice, the
chastening power of suffering and so on. Tragedy had become in
the hands of these commentators a code word for the rejection of
democracy, equality, materialism, reformism, humanitarianism
and the like. It was a form of *Kulturkritik* – an *ersatz* theology for
scholars who detested the modern world but couldn't quite drag
themselves to the synagogue or baptismal font and thus had rather
glumly to settle for this secular surrogate of transcendence. Of all

literary forms, it was perhaps the most ideologically charged. It was a deeply exclusivist terrain. So it seemed to me that we materialists had to get our grubby, plebeian hands on it, not just dismiss the whole mode in the manner of a Brecht. Rather, in Brecht's own style, the idea of tragedy had to be refunctioned, made available for another kind of politics and aesthetics altogether.

The book's political watchword is 'sober realism' as opposed to pessimism or fatalism. What does this entail in practice? Can it accommodate utopianism, an optimism of the will as well as a pessimism of the intellect?

I hope so. In common parlance, realism means something like 'Cool it', 'Back off', or 'Be moderate . . .' It would be interesting to trace the cultural history of this etymology, in which the real becomes synonymous with political compromise. For the young Hegelians, by contrast, to be realistic meant to be revolutionary. That's a case I would defend. When the Parisian sixty-eighters shouted 'Be realistic: demand the impossible!' they were being precise. How could anyone possibly take a soberly disenchanted look at the modern world and conclude that justice, freedom and happiness could come about without the most thoroughgoing of transformations, one that isn't currently proving possible? Who are these starry-eyed dreamers known as canny liberals and cynical right-wingers who find themselves able to believe otherwise? It's the hard-nosed pragmatists and sensible-minded reformists who are the anti-realists.

Tragedy, like psychoanalysis, reminds us that the real is in a certain sense impossible, but no less worthy of our desire for all that. Roland Barthes said something very similar about realist art: its hunger for the real is for something ultimately impossible, since we will never wrap the world up in words; but it's what keeps it in business. Without this it would lapse into silence. As for utopia, I suppose realism accommodates certain versions of it and rules out others. A genuinely free society would be in some ways more conflictive than the one we have now, because more men and women would be in on the arguments. And we would still be fragile, mortal animals, moving in the shadow of sickness, death and mutual injury. Only capitalists and the occasional A-list actor or actress want to live forever. Infinity is just a bourgeois plot, even more obviously than cosmetic surgery. Even so, a whole gamut of French radical thinkers, from Deleuze to Badiou, have fallen for this illusion in their own dissident, avant-garde way.

For the tragic outlook, redemption can only spring from bowing to our own mortality. That's what I've been calling tragic humanism, as opposed to liberal humanism, which doesn't see – in Yeats's words – that nothing can be whole or sole that has not been rent. For liberal humanism there's essentially a continuity between where we are and where we're heading. For tragic humanism there's a profound rupture between the two, a fissure in which something new and strange is born. In political life, this is known as revolution. The Christian term for this rupture is conversion. For some thinkers, tragedy and utopia are antithetical. For me, they implicate one another all the time. Without some fundamental sense of value there could be no tragedy. Why should we regard *Macbeth* or *Hedda Gabler* as tragic if things just couldn't have been otherwise?

So why does tragedy give pleasure? Might one answer to this perennial question be that in complex ways it is inseparable from the dream of redemption, that it is caught up in a dialectic of becoming as well as being?

Well, another answer to the question might be that it gives pleasure because we're all sadistic bastards. According to David Hume, we're sorry to witness the afflictions of others but glad about them as well, not least because it allows us to feel superior to them. Like the sublime, tragedy allows us to indulge the delights of the death drive vicariously, in the gratifying knowledge that we can't actually be harmed. And because it's art, we know that the characters aren't really being harmed either, which salves our sense of guilt. There's enjoyment in the knowledge that we survive even if Lear doesn't. There's also some guilt in it, which if Freud is to be credited is then an extra source of gratification.

Tragedy is a pleasure tinged with terror, as in that modern form of the sublime known as the horror movie. It also permits us to confront and rehearse our own death, and so in part to disarm it. And this, too, is a source of satisfaction to us. We also take pleasure in viewing a catastrophe that is bounded, limited by its aesthetic form and thus masterable – so that, as Yeats writes in his astoundingly crude poem 'Lapis Lazuli', it cannot grow by an inch or an ounce. We reap a malicious joy from seeing the mighty brought low; but we also revel in the protagonist's power to rise above his or her plight, which suggests a capacity for transcendence we find an echo of in ourselves. There are lots of other reasons – too many, in fact, rather than too few. Tragedy can satisfy our sense of justice as well as our rage for order. It caters to our sadism, masochism and moral conscience all at the same time. We want to see people suffer so we can indulge our masochism by suffering along with them, but to keep that masochism going means keeping them suffering, which is a kind of sadism. Above and beyond all this there's the gratification of art itself, whatever the obscure sources of that may be.

How would you characterize the relationship between Marxism and tragedy today? For Steiner, Marxism is anti-tragic, in effect because he regards it as utopian. In Trouble with Strangers *[2008] you describe socialism as a 'tragic project'.*

The most callow sort of Marxism simply apes bourgeois progressivism on this score – I mean bourgeois progressivism of the Hitchens or Dawkins kind. It's one long 'Hurrah for Humanity!' Simply get a number of oppressive obstacles out of the way – tradition, religion, the ruling class, superstition, the social relations of production and so on – and we can forge full steam ahead into socialism, Enlightenment, liberated humanity, the freedom of the middle-class individual. This ludicrous Just-So story, as astounding in its arrogant naivety as Graham Greene's quiet American, has rapidly become a sort of orthodox liberal wisdom after Islamism and 9/11. We possess freedom, but those bastards out there are trying to take it off us – A. C. Grayling-type nonsense, in short.

Williams's splendid chapter on tragedy and revolution in *Modern Tragedy* shows how socialist transformation is indeed a tragic project, in the most classical sense of the phrase. Only those who lack a sense of that legacy imagine that this means it won't work. Or that it simply comes down to saying that revolution has in the past involved a lot of bloodshed. That our condition must be broken in order to be remade is not an impossible process, but it is a tragic one. When Marx speaks of the total loss of humanity in the name of a total gain of humanity he speaks as a tragic humanist. He doesn't speak as a tragic anti-humanist, like George Steiner, or as a non-tragic humanist, like John Stuart Mill. That's not of course to say that Marx is thereby a pessimist; almost the reverse, in fact. Nobody could feel human wretchedness so profoundly without an equally deep sense of human possibility.

Would that this – this revolution or transformation – weren't necessary. Would that our condition wasn't such that only by dispossessing ourselves of ourselves could we flourish. The hardest form of emancipation is always self-emancipation, as feminists, psychoanalytic theorists and theologians know, but a lot of Marxists (even after Gramsci) don't appear to. Some of them find such 'spiritual' talk embarrassing. But then some materialists have a conception of spirituality as silly as Madonna's. It's just that they reject this conception of the spiritual, and she embraces it. Otherwise there's little difference. But as Wittgenstein once remarked, 'if you want an image of the soul, look at the body.'

You criticize Williams for the contradiction between his case that tragedy is an ordinary affair, which implicitly cannot ever be transcended, and his case that 'it has assumed in our time the shape of an epic struggle which can in principle be resolved.' Could you say something about the limits of his socialist humanism in this respect?

Williams is a tragic humanist – in my estimation an excellent thing to be, as I've been implying – but he retains rather too much for my taste of a different strain of liberal or socialist humanism. At times, this strain of humanism idealizes the common life – it's a generous error, unlike its opposite – and thus generates the contradiction I discuss, namely that tragedy for Williams is both commonplace and capable of being transcended. I don't see how this can be so. My own view is that tragedy is indeed commonplace, but that this means that it can't be transcended as such – as opposed to resolving this or that form of tragedy – without humanity transcending itself. And if that's not possible, then tragedy, alas, is here to stay. For the Christian gospel, tragedy is not epic or heroic but everyday; or rather, it's common and catastrophic together, a case with which socialists can sympathize. But its commonness in my view means that we can never move entirely beyond it as long as we're historical animals. You democratize tragedy, then, only at the price of confessing that in some sense it's here to stay. Freud would no doubt want to make parallel claims in a different idiom.

In his humanist generosity of spirit, Williams was reluctant to think the worst of human beings. I remember him once saying to Joy, his wife, 'You have to try to think well of people.' A lot of them sure didn't return the compliment. But sometimes you have to think the worst. No transformation of humanity in my view is worth having if you aren't at least prepared to entertain the view of Swift's king of Brobdingnag that the human species is a race of odious vermin. Only if you accept that human beings can behave in this way – I mean, acknowledge it in your bones, not just off the top of your head – is your desire to see them act otherwise more than sentimental wishful thinking. And only by confronting the worst can one release the power to glimpse something better, which might almost be a snap definition of the tragic spirit.

Let me put the point more sharply. In *Modern Tragedy*, Williams says of those like Steiner for whom the Holocaust signifies the absolute, unvarnished truth of humanity, 'Look, if there were people who did these things, there are also men and women who gave their lives to stop them; and to say the one thing but not the other is in its own way a blasphemy.' I utterly agree with this. Even so, I don't think Williams is prepared to say to himself, as the great tragic humanist John Milton was, 'If people could do these unspeakable things, can they ever redeem themselves?' By what well-nigh unthinkable paradox can human beings do such things yet there still be hope? Williams would baulk, I think, at that. Whereas my own point about tragic humanism is that unless you're prepared to stare that particular Medusa's head in the eyes you won't really get anywhere politically. Unless you start from Sophocles' or Schopenhauer's 'far better never to be born', you won't register the wretchedness that occasions this view. And if you don't register the wretchedness, you can't transform it. In this sense, only the tragic view is ultimately hopeful. Though there's a difference between hope and optimism . . .

Williams's book begins with an overtly personal gesture: 'In an ordinary life, spanning the middle years of the twentieth century, I have known what I believe to be tragedy, in several forms' – a form of tragedy 'at once more personal and more general' than the death of princes. Is this a necessary gesture?

As I've suggested before, I'm at one with him here. I knew a personal tragedy, the death of my father, on the very brink of entering an institution, Cambridge University, where I was invited to investigate the meaning of tragedy. I could no more dissociate this study from the broken, unfulfilled life of my father than Williams could from the life of his own father, Harold Williams, a Welsh signalman and socialist militant. Both Williams and I were struck by the discrepancy between the literary meaning of the word 'tragic' and its common meaning – the immense gap between them, as things then stood in academia. Both of us tried to do something to repair this situation. Every word I have written has been in the name of my father and people like him. Personally speaking, that's by no means an entirely healthy or desirable situation. To seek to compensate for the dead is to remain bound to them. To remain locked in a dialogue in which the other is eternally silent is not the most fruitful of conversations. It's just not a situation I can avoid.

Modern Tragedy *concludes with a play, a two-act tragedy called* Koba, *which Williams had been working on since the late 1950s. What did you make of this formal innovation?*

I thought Williams's inclusion of the play in the book was characteristically brave. I also thought it was uncharacteristically injudicious. The play is pretty poor; indeed virtually unperformable. Its language is painfully stilted, even if Williams's ponderous abstractions have a strange kind of music of their own. Williams was so massively self-identical a man, so deeply rooted in his own idiosyncratic style of being, that his capacity to project himself into the lives of other people was sometimes rather limited. There is thus something ironic as well as apposite about the fact that he occupied a chair of drama.

In Sweet Violence *you criticize the left's silence about religion and argue that, though contemporary religion 'represents one of the most odious forms of political reaction on the planet', this book is interested in exploring the 'theological ideas which can be politically illuminating'. How conscious were you of returning to the concerns of* The Body as Language *in this book?*

I was naturally aware that I was describing a sort of full circle in my work, though it's not entirely a circle. The theological preoccupations of the very early work differ a lot from those of the later, and this reflects a broader political and historical shift.

In the days of *Slant* and the Catholic left, the context from which both *The New Left Church* [1966] and *The Body as Language* emerged, the emphasis was very much on an affirmative theology, on community, brotherhood, liberation and so on – all very sixties. It didn't take much account of the darker dimensions of Christian faith: fallenness, death, suffering, mortality, sacrifice, finitude and the like. I was also too young to know much of these unpalatable realities at first hand. You can't be a tragic philosopher at the age of twenty-one. In the early work, for example, the Mass is about community, while in the later work it's about sacrifice and self-abandonment, a turbulent transition from death to life. Maybe any philosophy that doesn't encompass both these moments, that doesn't make sense of the one in relation to the other, isn't worth all that much.

So this early, rather euphoric work reflected a political left which felt it had the world at its feet – more specifically in this case the liberation theology of Latin America, though that in fact really only reached me after *Slant* had folded. I can see in much the same way how the concerns of my later work reflect a more sober, crepuscular political world. One might claim, for example, that for all its insights Lacanian theory, with its contempt for the common world, would probably have looked very different had it sprung from a more affirmative political history. So indeed might Freud's own writing. Even so, downturns of this kind bring to light ideas which might otherwise be unavailable. One can sometimes pluck a certain intellectual victory from the jaws of political defeat.

Can you say what you mean here by the term 'demonic' in this book, which you use in contradistinction to the satanic or evil?

I mean by the demonic a condition in which one's trapped between life and death, unable to die for real and drawing some kind of ghastly pseudo-existence from the deathly pleasure involved in destroying others, or sometimes oneself. Only by virtue of this destruction can the evil persuade themselves that they're still alive. The demonic is thus the opposite of that other life-in-death condition in which you can achieve an authentic sort of life by the 'death' of a self-giving to others. This is one reason why saints and sinners sometimes look much alike to the untutored eye. The saints or martyrs are those who have the courage to abandon their current condition in the faith – but by no means in the smug assurance – that this will result in an enhanced, transfigured existence. This is what the revolutionary subject is called upon to do – to turn its own dissolution and unmaking into an active remaking of society, with absolutely no guarantees beyond the fact that the future is unlikely to be much more intolerable than the present. It has to make something creative out of its 'death'. The demonic, by contrast, are those who are in the grip of the death drive – those who cling morbidly to the *jouissance* it yields them so as to con themselves into a vicarious sort of life. The demonic are in agony, but they can't renounce it because it's all they have left. In D. H. Lawrence's *Women in Love*, Rupert Birkin and Gerald Crich respectively illustrate these positive and negative forms of life-in-death, though they have more in common than the novel imagines, and the opposition between them is eminently deconstructible.

You self-consciously identified your next book, Holy Terror *[2005], with 'the metaphysical or theological turn' you referred to a moment ago, and remarked that this shift has been 'welcomed by some but looked upon with alarm and resignation by others'.*

As I said in *After Theory* [2003], there are certain ideas that the left – especially the male left – has been typically coy about discussing. They include love, death, evil, faith, ethics, tragedy, non-being, mortality, sacrifice and suffering. I see my most recent work as deliberately, provocatively trying to challenge, or open up a dialogue with, those leftists – I imagine the name of Fredric Jameson, a critic I greatly admire as you know, might stand in for many of them – who in my view shy away from such 'spiritual', 'ethical' or 'metaphysical' matters largely because they misconceive their character in what's really a rather conventional, not terribly intelligent way. For one thing, I don't think our political situation is such that the left is particularly well placed to look an intellectual gift horse in the mouth. For another thing, these and other such subjects strike me as offering us a chance to deepen and enrich our thought, and indirectly our practice, at a time when we face the most formidable of political challenges. None of the ideas I've just listed are as fashionable with today's cultural left as power, gender, the body and ethnicity. This is exactly why the cultural left should take them seriously, if it isn't to continue being stuck in these well-worn, increasingly repetitive political grooves.

So I hope I'm being sufficiently heterodox here, in a long tradition of Western Marxist thought. And I'm genuinely sorry about those comrades who feel that in raising these issues I'm making perilous overtures to some dubious bodies of thought. Some on the left think it's an excellent idea, others are perfectly neutral and indifferent about it, and others are really worried. I just want to say that I'm very sorry indeed for alarming colleagues and comrades for whom I have a lot of respect. And also that I have no intention whatsoever of ceasing to alarm them.

You use this book to further develop your notion of the pharmakos. *Could you say what you mean when you conclude that 'the terrorist is not the* pharmakos; *but he is created by it, and can only be defeated when justice is done to it'?*

Terrorists aren't scapegoats or *pharmakoi*, because they're guilty of horrendous crimes; whereas the *pharmakos* is, in Paul Ricœur's phrase, the 'guilty innocent'. The scapegoat takes on the burden of communal guilt, and thus becomes like Oedipus a frightful, hideously disfigured piece of humanity. It is the focal point of the violence and hatred of the community at large, as the proletariat for Marx embodies this total loss and deformation of humanity. But like the proletariat it is innocent in itself. If it's caught up in violence, then this is a violence done to it, not one perpetrated by it. And the more deliberately the scapegoat, like Christ, turns himself into a livid signifier of universal dispossession, the more repulsive, but by the same token the more selfless and blessed, he becomes. 'Sacred' in ancient times means both blessed and cursed. In this sense, the *pharmakos* blurs distinctions and undermines conventional social logics. It represents the way in which dissolution is power, as the scum of the earth become powerful through their very dispossession. Those who can fall no further are dangerous because they have nothing to lose. The ancient scapegoat, I'm arguing, is thus a harbinger of the modern revolutionary subject.

Although there is of course a danger, in identifying the 'shit of the earth' with the proletariat, of implicitly overstating the revolutionary importance of the lumpenproletariat, *or of simply idealizing it. One might make this case, inflected a little differently, against Hardt and Negri's influential concept of the multitude.*

I think that's probably true.

Holy Terror is another of your recent books to provoke the right. In an extraordinary attack on you written for the Social Affairs Unit, David Womersley accused you of a kind of intellectual incendiarism: 'It is a dangerous thing to trifle with a serious subject; and Holy Terror *is a dangerous, mischievous book.'*

I'm delighted to see that the Warton Chair, after my own brief, aberrant occupancy of it, has reverted to its proper function of promulgating old-school, backwoods Oxfordian values. If Womersley thinks the book is dangerous because it glamourizes terrorism then he can't have read it, since it explicitly rejects any such moral obscenity. The book's title refers not to this but to a whole series of phenomena – the Jewish biblical Yahweh, the pagan god Dionysus, the aesthetic concept of the sublime, the unconscious, the Real, the *pharmakos* or scapegoat and so on –

which are radically double-edged in their power both to create and destroy. (Shakespeare would have added: alcohol.) This kind of terror both enhances and annihilates, and so is by no means to be unequivocally affirmed. One of the original meanings of the sacred is that it's radically dangerous. The sacred has a perilous power to renew and negate, akin to that of the scapegoat or the wretched of the earth. But I wouldn't expect Professor Womersley to know anything of these arcane matters. He just pronounces on them. He probably thinks *pharmakos* is a posh word for the local chemist.

How did you come to write your next book, The English Novel *[2005], an introductory book on the history of prose fiction designed for students? At present, the libidinal energies of your writing, if I can put it like that, seem to be directed at the ideas elaborated in* After Theory, Holy Terror, Trouble with Strangers . . .

I wrote the book because it seemed time to produce another popularizing book that aimed radical ideas at literary students. So far, however, it hasn't been exactly a roaring success. The publishers were hoping it might end up as a textbook on US courses, like *Literary Theory* and, to a lesser extent, *How To Read A Poem*, but so far that hasn't happened very much. My publisher, who was also a student of mine at Oxford, said the book reads like one long Wadham tutorial. I suppose he was being complimentary . . .

You apologize in the preface for sticking to the literary canon, and excuse this on the grounds that these are the authors that students are most likely to encounter. But is this right, given the entrenchment of cultural studies? In After Theory *you evoke an image of 'quietly spoken middle-class students [who] huddle diligently in libraries, at work on sensationalist subjects like vampirism and eye-gouging, cyborgs and porno movies'. Why did you feel the need to apologize for rather than defend the canon, canonicity?*

The book was written for students of literature, and therefore had to intervene on the terrain they occupy, which in academic terms is mostly canonical. But too much fuss can be made about the canon. In English writing, this supposedly élitist, hierarchical, conservative way of framing things encompasses the revolutionary regicide John Milton as well as the political radicals Blake, Shelley, Wollstonecraft, Morris, Orwell and a great many more. Non-canonical writing, for its part, includes a lot of racist ballads and sexist fantasies, as well as more valuable material. Most of the values promoted by the major canonical works are to the left of the present-day political establishment. In any case, you can treat canonical writing in a radical way and non-canonical writing conservatively. Having said that, it's true that my work on English literature has tended to stick to canonical names, which is how I was academically reared. It's much less true of my work on Irish writing, as I've said to you before; though as one Irish critic wryly remarked: 'It's all very well for you English to deconstruct your canon. We don't even have one yet.'

A further criticism might be that the canon only goes up to Joyce and Woolf. Your short postscript, 'After the Wake', reads like some fiendish literary game in which you have to summarize subsequent developments in the English novel in the space of a few sentences or paragraphs (which, as at least one reviewer pointed out, you do extremely skilfully).

The postscript was the publisher's idea, not mine, and if I had my own way I'd cut it. If one reviewer described it as skilful, another dubbed it 'absurd'. My own view, as befits a middle-of-the-road moderate, is that the truth lies somewhere between the two; but undoubtedly tilted towards the absurd.

Your first chapter is entitled 'What is a Novel?' Isn't another opening chapter needed, entitled 'What is Englishness?'. . .? To an extent the book takes the notion of Englishness for granted. And, albeit in a semi-satirical tone, you not infrequently refer to alleged English traits — the English 'love a "character"', you state at one point, and on the same page refer to the 'very English reticence' of Woolf's novels. Would you indulge in this if you were writing about the Irish? Another way of putting this question might be to ask whether this is a book on the English novel written from an Irish perspective.

I'm a doughty defender of stereotypes, not all of which, of course, are negative: think of 'Arabs are a hospitable people'. For a materialist, it would be astonishing if groups of individuals who have shared roughly the same material and historical conditions down the centuries didn't manifest certain psychological traits and patterns of behaviour in common — whatever the liberal or postmodern cant that 'we're all individuals'. What sort of starry-eyed anti-materialism is that? Are people mysteriously unaffected by their common conditions? A belief in the (partial) reality of (some) stereotypes isn't necessarily racist or essentialist. Anyway, I'm also a champion of a mild form of essentialism, which is another story, and which puts me equally at odds with some current mealy-mouthed leftist pieties. It's true that Ulster Protestants aren't on the whole remarkable for their foppish, extravagant, surreal, fantastic wit and wordplay. I live among them a lot of the time and can vouch for the fact. This has nothing to do with ethnic essences, and everything to do with cultural and historical conditions. Nor does it mean that some Ulster Protestants aren't exactly like this.

Why don't you discuss Beckett's fiction in this book? It seems odd to me that, though there's an essay on his drama in Crazy John and the Bishop, *you've never written in detail about his novels.*

It's true I've never written on Beckett's fiction. I have, however, done the next best thing, which is to write a Beckettian-type fiction, an unpublished novel about nuclear war I produced years ago called 'The Last Days'. Even if I knew where the manuscript was at present, a point on which I'm a little hazy, I wouldn't dream of inflicting it on the world. It is, however, very like early Beckett, and not at all consciously. Someone had to point this out to me. It's just that I somehow found myself spontaneously writing in that poker-faced, mock-pedantic, surreal, blackly humorous style. Perhaps it's something to do with ethnic essentialism. Wasn't Beckett Irish or something?

In his recent monograph on your work, James Smith suggests that the subject matter of The English Novel *does not 'push criticism into new engagements, and instead presents a certain sense of uneasiness as to where [your] literary-critical project feels it should next move'. Is this a relevant criticism? Has your literary-critical project as such reached an end or impasse?*

I don't think so. I'm now writing a book trying to refute, one by one, the chief standard objections to Marxism, but after that I intend to write a book on 'pure' literary theory, a project that, interestingly, has almost dropped out of sight. Nobody writes any more on narratology or reader reception or semiosis, but this is what I intend to do. I think – don't for heaven's sake let this go beyond these four walls – that I may have stumbled on the literary equivalent of the physicist's Theory of Everything. Either that or I've finally lapsed into psychosis. But it won't be unveiled for another couple of years, since there are one or two more urgent political projects such as the defence of Marxism.

How to Read a Poem [2006], which you've briefly referred to, is in some respects a companion volume to The English Novel, *especially in its pedagogical commitment and its comparatively unfashionable subject matter. What prompted this book?*

Largely my sense when teaching at Manchester that students had mostly lost the habit of the close analysis of language – not because they aren't bright but because they aren't really taught it any more.

As I observe in the book, they simply can't say things like 'The poem's exuberant tone is curiously at odds with its shambling syntax'. In one sense, that's a silly kind of thing to say, and in another sense a vitally important one. You've got to be able to hear tone and feel texture and spot a shift of pace or mood in order to read well. As far as I can see, students of literature these days are almost entirely taught what's traditionally known as content analysis. They think an attention to form simply means knowing whether it rhymes or what metre the stuff is written in. Content analysis is fine as far as it goes, but in my view it isn't literary criticism. Criticism investigates the thickness and intricacy of the medium in which we come into our own as subjects: language. Although this project isn't everything, it's not to be sniffed at either.

Since poetry is the real test of this responsiveness to language as discourse or rhetoric, rather than as *langue*, I took it as the subject matter of the book. Anyway, it was fun to work on line-endings and synecdoche for a change, instead of ideology and class. As I said in a previous discussion, rhetoric in classical antiquity meant broadly two things, each in terms of the other: the art or science of figurative speech; and the practice of effective public oratory. In other words, the oldest form of criticism on record – rhetoric – was textual and political together. Most twentieth-century criticism then tilted the balance towards the textual, which in turn, from the 1970s, inspired a counter-alignment that tipped it towards the political. Both in different ways lose the interweaving of the textual and political typical not only of ancient rhetoric, but of most of the major moments of criticism ever since. An attention to the legendary words on the page should be at the same time an attention to the historical forces that constitute them.

Literary theory tried in its own way to reinvent this conjunction, since it raises hugely general, broadly political issues but also engages very closely with textual detail. The received idea that theorists don't read closely – is this true of Bakhtin, Adorno, Benjamin, Jameson, Kristeva, Hartman, Derrida, De Man? – hardly survives a close reading of a single one of the major theorists, though it's certainly true of many of their epigones. It's a shop-soiled cliché, rather like the claim that terrorists are surprisingly normal-looking people who always have a polite word for their neighbours but keep themselves to themselves. Beware of anyone who behaves like this.

The book's most specific or self-conscious contribution to the tradition of practical criticism is its concept of the 'incarnational fallacy'. Could you explain this?

Poetry can be a source of mystification because it looks as though there's a seamless identity within it between language and reality – language not just as denoting reality but somehow 'enacting' or 'incarnating' it, being iconic of it. On this theory, poetic language gives you the experience directly, in all its sensuous particularity, which then conveniently overlooks the way all such experience is socially mediated. So this identity is also a form of ideology – as Paul de Man, a critic who had excellent reasons for feeling shamefaced about ideology, recognized so well. My own hypothesis in the book is that it comes about through a slippage from the associational to the incarnational. Poetry does indeed pay peculiar attention to the materiality of the signifier, which then encourages us to imagine that the words somehow 'embody' things. But this is only because semantic materialism brings to mind, associatively, a more ontological materialism. In plainer English I mean that, while it seems to F. R. Leavis that a Keatsian phrase like 'mossed cottage trees' yields us a sense of the gnarled, thickly layered trees themselves, this is only because of what we might call semantic materialism. The prominence of the vowel-sounds in the phrase, the physical labour involved in pronouncing this mouth-filling phrase, puts us in mind of materiality as such – in this case the trees – and thus breeds the illusion that the words somehow incarnate the things. It's what you might call a sacramental, iconic or symbolic aesthetics, rather than a semiotic one.

Is there a sense in which your attention to the sensuous details of poems in this book, like Leavis's in his epoch, is a response to a society governed by abstraction and utility, and specifically to a culture of higher education that's increasingly governed by market values? Poetry, then, as non-pragmatic discourse, and hence as a potential repository of use value . . .?

Absolutely. I'm attracted by the high-modernist paradox that the work of art is political in its very autonomy, socially useful and instructive in its very refusal of utility and didacticism – though I wouldn't want to inflate this highly specific historical way of seeing to a general theory of art and politics. For one thing – *pace* the liberal critics – there's nothing wrong, aesthetically speaking, with didacticism as such. Think of Donne's sermons . . . As Adorno sees so superbly, aesthetic autonomy is both a kind of fetishism, a refusal of history and politics, and a negative politics of its own. The glorious uselessness of the work, its mute resistance to utility and the commodity form, is precisely its political point. The self-determining work of art prefigures the self-determining free man or woman of the future. Where art was, there shall humanity be. It's absolutely no accident that Oscar Wilde was an aesthete and a socialist at the same time. There's no contradiction at all here, whatever the more utilitarian species of Marxist might consider.

You conclude this book by asserting that 'to write the history of poetic forms is a way of writing the history of political cultures', since the poem mediates politics by materializing a prevalent structure of feeling. What would such a history look like? How would the present period figure in it?

It was Roland Barthes who remarked that to push form all the way though is to emerge into the domain of the historical. Formalists are simply people who don't push form far enough. Form always comes saturated in historical and ideological content, and historical or political content is always already formed, shaped, significantly organized, before either the artist or the critic comes to lay their hands on it. People who believe that art gives shape to the chaos of reality, or some such modernist banality, don't see this. Whoever saw an unshaped reality? Except perhaps Gilles Deleuze in what he calls transcendental empiricism, an interesting condition for which one may require a little aid from certain easily obtainable stimulants.

The Meaning of Life [2007], which followed How to Read a Poem, *was another deliberately populist book, albeit in a philosophical register rather than a literary-critical one. Was this book your idea or did Oxford University Press approach you with it?*

OUP asked me to contribute a volume to their Very Short Introductions series, and since I couldn't think of anything else to write on, I proposed this subject. I think they thought at first that I was joking, and of course to write a book on the meaning of life *is* a joke, however serious you intend it to be. The subject is so profound as to be both momentous and ridiculous, so deep as to be potentially meaningless – more Monty Python than Merleau-Ponty, one might claim. But this very fact appealed to a certain wayward, surreal streak in me.

You argue in this book that 'it is sport, not religion, which is now the opium of the people'. What roles does sport play in capitalist society? Is it both ideological and utopian, so to speak?

Sport combines the finest kinds of skill with the most extraordinarily popular appeal. It's thus the most obvious solution to the conflict between high and popular culture, rather as cinema can be, or genres like science fiction. At the same time, as I suggest in the book, it provides a surrogate version of certain political values: solidarity, tradition, festivity, competition, loyalty, a pantheon of heroes and so on. To this extent, it confiscates an enormous amount of energy that could be politically productive. Without sport, contemporary capitalist societies would be in deep political trouble. The bread-and-circuses argument really does apply here, at least to football. Where else in an alienated society would ordinary people derive these sorts of precious experiences? If sport is a unique safety-valve for mass political energies – and I don't of course mean this conspiratorially – then perhaps the best way to ensure millions of people coming out on the streets would be to abolish it. The only problem is that they would probably surge onto the streets simply to protest at its abolition. I speak, I should add, as one who was forced to play rugby at school when he would rather have been reading Albert Camus. But even a nerd's viewpoint has some validity.

You end up in this book by taking an idea from Gerry Cohen and arguing that jazz offers a metaphor for the good life, if not a solution to the intractable problem of the meaning of life, because of its dialectic of the individual and the collective. Perhaps you could elaborate this point.

John Gray was critical of this metaphor in a review in the *Independent*. He said that he could only take my word for it that jazz groups achieve this happy state, and pointed out that its distance from any political embodiment is striking. I suspect that the happy state of some jazz groups springs from something a bit more tangible than being a model for the good life. The image is really a way of concretizing Marx's dictum in the *Communist Manifesto* about communism as the development of each becoming the condition for the development of all. I've written that I can't think of any ethic deeper than this. In Christian terms, one might call it eucharistic. Jazz musicians do their own thing, but find what they do enhanced rather than inhibited by others in the group doing just the same. So what we have here is neither individualism nor uniformity, but some third condition which currently lacks a name and can be encompassed by neither of those two logics. John

Gray is right to imply that this is a utopian image. I just don't see why he should imagine that this is a criticism of it. Or perhaps that's disingenuous – given Gray's trek from ebullient young Thatcherite to grumpy middle-aged misanthropist, I can see exactly why he thinks this.

Simon Jenkins, another right-wing liberal, was rather more positive than Gray in his review for the Guardian. *'Since I regarded Eagleton as the Dave Spart of critical gobbledegook, I approached the book with trepidation,' he wrote. 'All I can say is that wonders never cease. This is popular philosophy by an amateur in the best sense of the word, a man who clearly loves the stuff and writes plain English.'*

I'm not sure that to be complimented by the former editor of *The Times* on writing plain English is quite the plaudit I was looking for. I hope my prose style is clear but not plain. But Jenkins is right that there's a distressing amount of critical gobbledegook around: 'symbol', 'allegory', 'eternal truths of human nature', 'metaphorical richness', and so on. Why can't people who talk about 'narrative viewpoint' or 'fully rounded characters' speak plain English? I never heard this kind of talk back in Salford. Come to that, why don't doctors write things in their notes like 'spot of trouble in the old tummy' rather than indulging in all this barbarous medical jargon?

You've recently consolidated and extended your commitment to constructing a materialist ethics in the form of Trouble with Strangers *[2008]. It's probably your most substantial publication since* The Ideology of the Aesthetic *[1990], a book that in important respects it complements. Why are ethics so important to you?*

I suppose my Catholic background peeps out there. Perhaps because of it, I've always been impatient with leftists who think that politics can take the place of ethics. This is merely an inversion of the liberal credo that ethics can take the place of politics. For both viewpoints, ethics is really about the bedroom rather than the boardroom. Instead, the book tries to explore the relations between the two domains, which isn't at all a matter of the relation of personal to public, inner to outer, individual to institutional and so on. That's just a middle-class mistake a lot of left-wingers make. To see why, however, you have to put in brackets that whole, disastrously misguided ideology of the ethical which descends to us from Kant, which is really quite anti-political, and which sees ethics primarily in terms of duty, obligation, responsibility and the like. I don't claim any originality on this score: Bernard Williams spent a lifetime on this task, as has Alasdair MacIntyre. I suppose the originality of my own book lies rather in its application to ethics of the Lacanian trinity of Imaginary, Symbolic and Real. I just mean that because of this lethal lineage it's now hard to recuperate that alternative inheritance, from Aristotle and Aquinas to Hegel, Marx and Nietzsche, for which ethics is about abundance of life, rich and diverse self-realization, power, enjoyment, wealth of capacity and so on. Marx is absolutely an ethical thinker in this sense, even if he quite often doesn't know he is.

There's still a Protestant Puritanism around today which wants to deny all this, but its names are now not Calvin and Luther but Badiou, Derrida, Lacan, Žižek and others. These avant-gardist philosophers resist the Judaeo-Christian scandal that ethics is ordinary, prosaic and everyday, fend off its claim that the only law that matters is the law of love, and recast classical notions of obligation in the rather more fashionable terms of some absolute Law or Real or Imperative, thus seeking to revive a largely discredited lineage. *Trouble with Strangers* does however also try to weigh what's positive and precious in this so-called ethics of the Real, and this connects with what we've been saying about tragedy. To my mind, the realms of ethics and politics can be neither divided nor conflated. Ethics deals with such questions as human values, purposes, relationships, qualities of behaviour, motives for action, while politics raises the question of what material conditions, power-relations and social institutions we need in order to foster certain of these values and qualities and not others. This is nothing to do with the relation between spiritual and material or personal and public.

Occasionally, for all your interest in the body as the basis of ethics as of aesthetics, the arguments in this book seem oddly disembodied; and for all your sense of history, it also seems oddly dehistoriciƷed. For example, there is comparatively little about capitalist modernity. At one point you accuse Hume of dealing with questions of law and property 'as concepts rather than social realities'. Mightn't the same be said of your concerns here?

That's fair enough, I think. The historical dimension needs more shading in. There's a kind of concealed narrative in the book, from early to middle to late capitalism, of which the trek from Imaginary to Symbolic to Real is in some sense allegorical. In a broad sense, you could maybe correlate each of these historical phases with each of these cultural and psychological registers. I make the merest gesture towards this grand narrative but don't develop it – I'm not sure why. Perhaps simply because I had enough on my plate already. One can't, after all, say everything at once – a phrase that might seem less trite if one thinks of those Marxists who stand up after an excellent feminist paper on metaphor in Adrienne Rich to ask why nothing was said about class struggle in nineteenth-century France, or those feminists who rise to their feet after a gripping paper on the feudal mode of production to ask why nothing was said about abortion rights.

Ethical discourse seems to be overwhelmingly a male discourse in this book . . .

I'm not so sure of that. The Imaginary, with its stress on the corporeal and empathetic, is very relevant to certain notions of femininity.

So, less predictably, is the Real, whose heroines are such figures as Antigone, Samuel Richardson's Clarissa (the English Antigone, as I argue in the book), and Emily Brontë's characters. I discuss these and other 'fictions of the Real' – *The Merchant of Venice*, for example – in the book, and see now that these are works which have always exerted a fascination upon me without my being quite aware of it. I wrote an early book on Richardson, when it was neither popular nor profitable to do so, an early work on the Brontës, and so on. I also return in this more recent book to a 'fiction of the Real', as I call it, that I found compelling as early as *The New Left Church*: Arthur Miller's *Death of a Salesman*. A lot of my work has moved in circles in this sense, haunted by certain spectres that refuse to lie down and die. In some ways it has been extraordinarily consistent, though I don't especially mean that as a self-compliment. Consistency isn't always a virtue, as Brecht and Barthes both appreciated.

The idea of a fiction of the Real is an elusive one, which I spell out in the book, but it involves among other things certain figures caught *in extremis* between life and death, trapped in a certain obdurate, uncompromising posture, driven on by a sort of deathly yet life-yielding *jouissance*, by a compulsion or commitment which is more their real self than they are themselves. It's an inability to back away from what Lacan would call the law of one's being. This connects in my thought to the tragic protagonist, and more particularly the martyr – another ghost that, as you pointed out on a previous occasion, has never ceased to haunt my writing, and especially my fictional work about Ireland, from Oscar Wilde to James Connolly. This is not something I particularly understand. This Real is both intimate with and strange to oneself, closer to us than breathing yet implacably impersonal and even anonymous, something terrible and traumatic yet also something one has to acknowledge rather than disavow. It has had many names in cultural history, as I argue in *Holy Terror*: God, the sublime, the Will, the unconscious, *jouissance* . . . But it's always at once life-giving and potentially annihilating. It's in love with death in what can be either a morbid or a transformative spirit.

This thing, which is terrible yet necessary to look on, and which is neither quite living nor quite dead, and therefore deeply uncanny, has also figured in my work since *Sweet Violence* as the scapegoat or *pharmakos*. On the one hand, this Janus-faced creature is the shit of the earth – utter failure, breakdown and mortal weakness – because it bears the burden of the crimes of the community as a whole. On the other hand, precisely because of this mortal weakness, the scapegoat – from Oedipus and Christ to Lear and later figures – presents a holy, violent, potentially transformative power. So in my recent work ideas of sacrifice, scapegoating, political revolution, the death drive, the sublime, and a sort of simultaneous holiness and disfigurement begin to merge together. Most people on the left understand the idea of sacrifice in its diminished everyday sense; I try rather to trace a line from ancient sacrifice to modern revolution. It's not the orthodox language of the political left – you won't find much reference to the *pharmakos* in the Trotskyist press – but I hope it can provide an enrichment of that language. It sure needs it.

Can you explain more precisely what you mean in this book when you advocate 'political love', an idea you'd previously invoked in the conclusion to The Ideology of the Aesthetic *[1990]?*

Love, once we've rescued this vital idea from its narrowing and impoverishment by those who see it primarily as an erotic, romantic, sexual or interpersonal affair, means the kind of reciprocity in which each represents the ground for the other's self-fulfilment. The political correlative of this is the phrase I quoted earlier from the *Communist Manifesto*, about the free development of each as the condition for the free development of all. Communism is just whatever set of institutional arrangements would enable us to approximate most closely to this utterly impossible condition. This is one reason why I find it hard to understand why anyone wouldn't be a communist. What more rewarding form of life than this might there possibly be? Christians believe this too, of course, but they also hold that it's finally beyond our power without that fleshly revolution they know as the resurrection of the body. In their view, what is most historically necessary is also what is least historically possible. Cynics and sceptics agree with this view from a quite different perspective, while some leftists regard such a condition as historically attainable. Liberals and conservatives tend to regard love as a private affair that doesn't impinge on politics – this is one of the catastrophic losses of modernity – so they aren't part of this particular quarrel. Love for them is no more a political concept than paring your fingernails is. This is true of the overwhelming mass of left-wingers as well, though it shouldn't be. For them, too, love is something you get up to after a hard day's leafleting. It's only a political matter in so far as sexuality is a political matter. One of the great blind spots of our era has been to imagine that it's only by virtue of sexuality that anything connected with love has any political relevance.

Reading

Cohen, G. A., *Self-Ownership, Freedom, and Equality* (Cambridge: Cambridge University Press, 1995).

Deleuze, Gilles, *Difference and Repetition*, new edition, trans. Paul Patton (Columbia: Columbia University Press, 1995).

Dollimore, Jonathan, *Death, Desire and Loss in Western Culture* (London: Routledge, 2001).

Eagleton, Terry, *The Body as Language: Outline of a 'New Left' Theology* (London: Sheed & Ward, 1970).

Eagleton, Terry, *Sweet Violence: The Idea of the Tragic* (Oxford: Blackwell, 2003).

Eagleton, Terry, 'Jonathan Dollimore', in *Figures of Dissent: Critical Essays on Fish, Spivak, Žižek and Others* (London: Verso, 2003), pp. 121–8.

Eagleton, Terry, 'Foreword', in Jonathan Dollimore, *Radical Tragedy: Religion, Ideology and Power in the Drama of Shakespeare and his Contemporaries* (Durham: Duke University Press, 2004), pp. x–xiii.

Eagleton, Terry, 'Political Beckett?' *New Left Review* 2:40 (2006), pp. 67–74.

Eagleton, Terry, *Holy Terror* (Oxford: Oxford University Press, 2005).

Eagleton, Terry, *The English Novel: An Introduction* (Oxford: Blackwell, 2005).

Eagleton, Terry, *The Meaning of Life* (Oxford: Oxford University Press, 2007).

Eagleton, Terry, *How to Read a Poem* (Oxford: Blackwell, 2007).

Eagleton, Terry, *Trouble with Strangers: A Study of Ethics* (Oxford: Blackwell, 2008).

Eagleton, Terry, *Reason, Faith, and Revolution: Reflections on the God Debate* (New Haven: Yale University Press, 2009).

Smith, James, *Terry Eagleton: A Critical Introduction* (Cambridge: Polity, 2008).

Steiner, George, *The Death of Tragedy*, with a new foreword (Oxford: Oxford University Press, 1980).

Williams, Raymond, *Modern Tragedy* (London: Chatto & Windus, 1966).

Conclusion

Since being forced in 2008 into premature retirement at Manchester University, a shameful episode that led to protests by students and impassioned letters in the national papers, you've taken up several other academic posts, including one at Galway and another at Lancaster . . .

Whereas Madonna collects African babies, I seem to have collected a number of academic jobs since I was forced to leave Manchester for being too long in the tooth. I think the tally is three or four at present, in Britain, Ireland and the United States. None of them, however, involves an excessive amount of that disagreeable phenomenon known as physical presence. I can just come in from time to time and teach postgraduates and be free of administrative or examining duties, which is an enviably privileged position to be in. But I did spend thirty years conducting Oxford tutorials, which is bloody hard work, and eight years before that in Cambridge doing the same thing, and I think I deserve parole.

Can I return in conclusion to the question of your so-called theological turn? In his recent book From Marxism to Post-Marxism *[2008], Göran Therborn sketches a 'broad cultural mood' characterized by a 'widespread fascination with religion and religious examples'. 'As an alternative future disappears or dims, what become important are roots, experience and background,' he writes. 'A classical European education, a maturation in a non-secular milieu, and a middle age at a safe distance from any demands of faith make Christianity a natural*

*historical experience to look at.' He cites you as a prime example of
this phenomenon, portraying you as 'a tough and unrepentant Marxist
literary and cultural theorist' who has returned to the left Catholicism
of your youth.*

Quite why everyone seems suddenly to be talking about God, after
his long enforced absence from the historical stage, is a question
I take up in *Reason, Faith, and Revolution* [2009]. I doubt there
would be such intense God-talk if the Twin Towers were still
standing, but fear of Islamic fundamentalism is by no means the
only reason for the Almighty's remarkable come-back so late in
his failing career. I think Therborn isn't quite right to see such a
dramatic reversal in my intellectual trajectory, since theology and
its emancipatory potential has long been an interest of mine. If I've
become more explicit about it, it's partly because of an intellectual
climate in which that seems easier than it did in the 1970s – though
Althusser was of course a former Catholic, as is evident in so much
of his work and sensibility (it takes one to know one . . .). A hostile
way of putting the point would be to say that when there's a major
political downturn, of the kind the left has suffered for quite some
time, people tend to look rather wistfully to alternative resources,
to false or surrogate solutions of various kinds. I think there's quite
a lot in that; but I've also argued that one of the few benefits of
such a downturn is a more sober sense of the limits of the political,
which is much harder when the left is in the ascendant.

As a materialist like Sebastiano Timpanaro was well aware,
there are vital aspects of human existence which politics doesn't
particularly engage, and which nobody should expect it to.
Marxism isn't some Theory of Everything, except for those who
need to get out more. It's also a strictly provisional, self-abolishing
project, not an eternal truth. An inflated view of politics has been a
traditional defect of the left, just as a playing-down of politics has
been a characteristic error of the right and centre. I suppose my
own recent work has argued that, far from providing some kind
of comforting retreat from the real political world, Christian faith

makes the most harsh, uncompromising political demands. This doesn't of course make it true. But it certainly makes it something more than the opium of the people. I began my memoir *The Gatekeeper* with an account of the enclosed order of Carmelite nuns I used to serve Mass for – we talked about this earlier – and I implied that it functioned as a kind of women's commune. It seems to me that nothing could be more banal than to claim in some cosy liberal or leftist wisdom that these young women were 'escaping from the real world'. On the contrary, there's a sense in which they deliberately threw away their lives out of love, in one strenuous, continuously staged encounter with the Real. This isn't the kind of thing a good, *bien-pensant* liberal would approve of. You don't find a lot of it in literary London, for example. But the good, sensible liberal wouldn't approve of throwing away your life as a guerrilla fighter either.

In Trouble with Strangers, *you cite Eric Santner: 'We don't [. . .] need God for the sake of divine things but for the sake of proper attentiveness to secular things.' The phrase 'proper attentiveness to' seems a slightly mealy-mouthed concession to me, but is this approximately your position too?*

Absolutely so. If you do believe in God, then the only God worth believing in is surely one who's hopelessly in love with finite, created things, as the God of the New Testament is portrayed as being. I understand the notion of infinity not as that which soars beyond such creatureliness, but as a quality of one's potentially inexhaustible attention to it – and in the first place to that form of creatureliness known to Judaism as one's neighbour. Infinity here just means that our concern with our neighbour – a term which for Luke's gospel means above all the needy, dispossessed members of the community – must be in principle unlimited. Any other sort of infinity is just science-fiction stuff or wrong-headed Parisian philosophy.

What, then, does 'God' signify to you?

The idea of God is utterly impossible. I mean, the very idea of someone or something who loves and embraces you simply and entirely for what you are, in all your shabbiness, viciousness and self-delusion! As Groucho Marx might have said, 'Would you really want to spend eternity with a sucker like that?'

According to Roland Boer, who has explored your recent theological thinking in some detail, you have been noticeably silent on sin. Why is that?

I'm not at all silent on sin, apart from my own. I write again and again in my recent work about selfishness, greed, violence, dominion, exploitation, aggression, even evil. My *An Essay on Evil* [forthcoming in 2010] has a lot to say about the idea of the Fall, which I try to demythologize. Or doesn't it qualify as talk about sin if you don't mention sex? Part of what I have against Dawkins and Hitchens is exactly that they don't talk about sin – or whatever suitably secular translation of the term one prefers. They don't seem to recognize that there's anything basically awry with our situation that cries out for fundamental change, as I argued in *Reason, Faith, and Revolution*. The really dangerous people are those who think it's basically okay. As Adorno observed, pessimists like Freud serve the cause of humanity in their bleak-eyed realism more than the doctrinaire cheerleaders.

In your introduction to the recent edition of the Gospels published in Verso's 'Revolutions' series you ask, 'Was Jesus a revolutionary?' How do you answer this?

Jesus didn't have much conception of politics because he wouldn't have had much conception of history – I mean secular history, history in our modern sense as the project of collective self-determination, as opposed to a sense of so-called salvation history, which he would have had in plenty. So it's anachronistic to see Jesus as a prototype for Trotsky. If you believe, as Jesus probably did, that the world is imminently about to end, then there's no time to bother about revolutionizing the place. You just have to stand surrendered in faith to the Yahweh who will make Creation whole – as some Kabbalists add, by making certain minor adjustments. On the other hand, Jesus led something of a revolutionary lifestyle – like Che he couldn't be hampered by a mortgage and a settled existence. And on Calvary he's very deliberately presented as the tortured, mangled victim of imperial political power who threatens the powers of this world by speaking up fearlessly for love and justice. The message of the gospel is that anyone idiotic enough to do this is going to get topped by the state. Indeed, that's Jesus's own explicit warning to his comrades, several of whom ended up in exactly this disagreeable situation. The reign of the powers-that-be has in principle come to an end in this executed body, overthrown by what Lacan calls a limitless love. This, for the gospels, isn't a reformist matter of pouring new wine into old bottles. Rather, it demands an unimaginable dissolution of all we know for something inconceivably different, and all this demands a terrifying passage through death, nothingness and self-dispossession. So I suppose in a sense that's revolutionary enough. It might be language unfamiliar to Lenin or Mao, but it seems to be well to the left of the World Bank.

For Herbert McCabe, in Law, Love and Language *[1968], Marxism and Christianity diverge over the issue of death and resurrection: 'If the Marxist is right and there is no God who raised Jesus from the dead, then the Christian preoccupation with death as the ultimate revolutionary act is a diversion from the real demands of history; if the Christian is right then the Marxist is dealing with revolution only at a relatively superficial level, he has not touched the ultimate revolution involved in death itself, and for this reason his revolution will betray itself; the liberation will erect a new idol.' Does your conception of death commit you, if only in some symbolic sense, to the resurrection of the body as well as the abolition of capitalism?*

First of all, I think McCabe is right to see that the traditional Christian belief is in the resurrection of the body rather than the deeply non-Judaic notion of the immortality of the soul. As Thomas Aquinas might have said, if a renewed form of existence doesn't involve my body it doesn't involve me. He identified people with their bodies – as Wittgenstein did in that remark that if you want an image of the soul you should look at the human body. Soul-language is just a way of accounting for what makes creative, historical, self-transformative bodies like human ones ontologically distinct from material bodies like CD players and paperclips. Once one has a sufficiently phenomenological account of the body, such language can drop out of the picture. It's no longer useful in one's battle with the mechanical materialists.

McCabe is also right – and entirely in line with Judaeo-Christian tradition – to see that there isn't something called an 'afterlife' (perhaps as a reward for the hellishness of this one). That's a pagan conception, not a Judaeo-Christian one. As Wittgenstein claimed, to cite him again, if there's something called eternal life – and he didn't imagine there was – it has to be here and now. He considers the logical impossibility of claims like 'eternal life will begin when I die at 3:33 pm.' Eternal life can't *begin*. Eternal life has to be an account of *this* life, in its full, visionary depth. Think of William Blake – that's orthodox Christian doctrine. It's a vision of how our life really is or could be were it to be liberated from certain illusions, oppressions and constraints. And one thing we know it would have to be is life for the sake of its own perpetual delight. This is why it's traditionally seen as the life of God, who is pure self-delight, and who unlike slaves and bedroom slippers exists just for the hell of it. For Christian faith, it isn't the body that gets in the way of this kind of life, since the body is good. It's sin – which is to say, the kinds of mutual injury and destructiveness that having, or being, bodies in the first place allows us to get up to. The opposite of sin is love. But sin can only be fully overcome if the creatureliness that allows us to harm one another is transformed out of recognition. And this is the doctrine of the resurrection of the body.

Do I believe, as McCabe maybe implies, that political revolution would finally have to penetrate that deep in order not to be in vain? No, I don't. That would be to belittle the political and historical. In what sense is people achieving justice and not going hungry superficial? We can abolish the major injustices that plague us without having to rise from our graves. Yet at the same time we need to be realistic about what political revolution can't do. It can't do away with human suffering, tragedy, mortality, or indeed with all forms of cruelty and exploitation. As long as we have, or are, bodies, these things will be part of us, bound up with our fleshliness. This, I think, is what the doctrine of the resurrection is trying to articulate. There is no utopia, no heaven on earth; but this should not deter us from stretching every nerve and bending every sinew to bring this strictly impossible state of affairs about.

I want finally to ask you about the function of criticism and the task of the leftist critic. Perhaps I can open this up by raising the issue of the Marxist critic's audience. There's an article by Edward Said, 'Opponents, Audiences, Constituencies, and Community' [1982], in which he criticized you for implicitly accepting that you too are limited to the rarefied sphere of academia that you had yourself criticized Fredric Jameson and Frank Lentricchia for inhabiting. Said writes: 'Eagleton, Jameson and Lentricchia are literary Marxists who write for literary Marxists in cloistral seclusion from the inhospitable world of real politics. Both "literature" and "Marxism" are thereby confirmed in their apolitical content and metholodology.' What do you make of this criticism?

I suppose it depends what Said means by 'literary Marxist'. I think that being a literary Marxist is all right so long as that isn't all one is. Said's implication is that that is all one can be . . . I did actually respond to his critique, albeit not directly, in an article I wrote for *Critical Quarterly*. In the course of that piece I commented that I wished Said had been present when I was turned down for a second time in applying for membership of the local Labour Party, on the grounds that I was too closely identified with a Trotskyist organization. I suppose that, in one precise sense, Said was fortunate in being able to bring his culture and his politics together. The kind of politics in which he was involved led to certain kinds of cultural or literary activity. In my own case, it was slightly more problematic; but then I had no great conviction that things that are disparate should always be brought together.

I'd add that, like a lot of intellectuals, I'm not temperamentally an activist – perhaps Said was an exception. I get no particular kick out of political activism; and in the various groups I was involved in I quickly came to realize that I shouldn't feel bad about that, because a lot of other people couldn't not have been activists. These people lived and breathed and slept politics. At the same time, I have always kept in mind an image of the narrowly academic Marxist as a warning of the dangers that 'cloistral seclusion' entails.

So what is the task of the critic?

I wrote in my study of Benjamin in 1981 that the primary task of the socialist critic was to participate in what I called the cultural emancipation of the masses; and I listed such activities as the organization of writers' workshops and popular theatre, the business of public design and architecture and so on. All this, needless to add, describes the task of the socialist critic in far more politically hopeful times than we're living through at present. I'm recalling the enormous cultural upheaval and excitement of the Bolshevik and Weimar eras. But I think we need to keep this goal in mind in order to prevent us from imagining that the task of the socialist critic is simply to write Marxist accounts of Henry James. In this sense, the true tasks of the critic are still to come. It isn't literally true, as Benjamin wrote, that any moment is the strait gate through which the Messiah might enter. But the future does have a habit of taking us by surprise; and to think of the critic's task in these terms is one way of not being disarmed by its arrival.

Reading

Benjamin, Walter, 'Theses on the Philosophy of History', *Illuminations*, ed. Hannah Arendt, trans. Harry Zohn (London: Fontana, 1973), pp. 245–55.

Boer, Roland, 'Terry Eagleton and the Vicissitudes of Christology', *Cultural Logic* 8 (2005) (http://clogic.eserver.org/2005/boer.html).

Eagleton, Terry, *Walter Benjamin; or, Towards a Revolutionary Criticism* (London: Verso, 1981).

Eagleton, Terry, 'The Idealism of American Criticism', *New Left Review* 1:127 (1981), pp. 53–65 (repr. in *Against the Grain: Essays 1975–1985* (London: Verso, 1986), pp. 49–64).

Eagleton, Terry, 'Literature and History', *Critical Quarterly* 27:4 (1985), pp. 23–6.

Eagleton, Terry, *The Gatekeeper: A Memoir* (London: Allen Lane, 2001).

Eagleton, Terry, 'Tragedy and Revolution', in *Theology and the Political: The New Debate*, eds. Creston Davis, John Milbank and Slavoj Žižek (Durham: Duke University Press, 2005), pp. 7–21.

Eagleton, Terry, 'Lunging, Flailing, Mispunching', *London Review of Books*, 19 October 2006, pp. 32–4.

Eagleton, Terry, 'Introduction', in *Jesus Christ, The Gospels*, ed. Giles Fraser (London: Verso, 2007), pp. vii–xxx.

Eagleton, Terry, *Trouble with Strangers: A Study of Ethics* (Oxford: Blackwell, 2008).

Eagleton, Terry, *Reason, Faith, and Revolution: Reflections on the God Debate* (New Haven: Yale University Press, 2009).

Eagleton, Terry, *An Essay on Evil* (Yale: Yale University Press, forthcoming 2010).

McCabe, Herbert, *Love, Law and Language* (London: Sheed & Ward, 1968).

Said, Edward W., 'Opponents, Audiences, Constituencies, and Community,' in *Reflections on Exile and Other Essays* (London: Granta, 2000), pp. 118-47.

Santner, Eric L., 'Miracles Happen: Benjamin, Rosenzweig, Freud, and the Matter of the Neighbor,' in Slavoj Zizek, Eric L. Santner and Kenneth Reinhard, *The Neighbor: Three Inquiries in Political Theology* (Chicago: Chicago University Press, 2005), pp. 76-133.

Therborn, Göran, *From Marxism to Post-Marxism* (London: Verso, 2008).

BIBLIOGRAPHY

Works by Terry Eagleton

Books

The New Left Church (London: Sheed & Ward, 1966).

Shakespeare and Society (London: Chatto & Windus, 1967).

The Body as Language: Outline of a 'New Left' Theology (London: Sheed & Ward, 1970).

Exiles and Émigrés: Studies in Modern Literature (London: Chatto & Windus, 1970).

Myths of Power: A Marxist Study of the Brontës (London: Macmillan, 1975).

Criticism and Ideology: A Study in Marxist Literary Theory (London: New Left Books, 1976).

Marxism and Literary Criticism (London: Methuen, 1976).

Walter Benjamin; or, Towards a Revolutionary Criticism (London: Verso, 1981).

The Rape of Clarissa: Writing, Sexuality, and Class Struggle in Samuel Richardson (Oxford: Blackwell, 1982).

Literary Theory: An Introduction (Oxford: Blackwell, 1983).

The Function of Criticism: From The Spectator *to Post-Structuralism* (London: Verso, 1984).

Against the Grain: Essays 1975-1985 (London: Verso, 1986).

William Shakespeare (Oxford: Blackwell, 1986).

Saints and Scholars (London: Verso, 1987).

Saint Oscar (Derry: Field Day, 1989).

The Ideology of the Aesthetic (Oxford: Blackwell, 1990).

The Significance of Theory, eds. Michael Payne and M. A. R. Habib (Oxford: Blackwell, 1990).

Ideology: An Introduction (London: Verso, 1991).

The Crisis of Contemporary Culture: An Inaugural Lecture Delivered before the University of Oxford on 27 November 1992 (Oxford: Clarendon Press, 1993).

Heathcliff and the Great Hunger: Studies in Irish Culture (London: Verso, 1995).

The Illusions of Postmodernism (Oxford: Blackwell, 1996).

Marx and Freedom (London: Phoenix, 1997).

Saint Oscar and Other Plays (Oxford: Blackwell, 1997).

Crazy John and the Bishop and Other Essays on Irish Culture (Cork: Cork University Press in association with Field Day, 1998).

The Eagleton Reader, ed. Stephen Regan (Oxford: Blackwell, 1998).

Scholars and Rebels in Nineteenth-Century Ireland (Oxford: Blackwell, 1999).

The Truth about the Irish (Dublin: New Island, 1999).

The Idea of Culture (Oxford: Blackwell, 2000).

The Gatekeeper: A Memoir (London: Allen Lane, 2001).

After Theory (London: Allen Lane, 2003).

Sweet Violence: The Idea of the Tragic (Oxford: Blackwell, 2003).

Figures of Dissent: Critical Essays on Fish, Spivak, Žižek and Others (London: Verso, 2003).

Holy Terror (Oxford: Oxford University Press, 2005).

The English Novel: An Introduction (Oxford: Blackwell, 2005).

The Meaning of Life (Oxford: Oxford University Press, 2007).

How to Read a Poem (Oxford: Blackwell, 2007).

Trouble with Strangers: A Study of Ethics (Oxford: Blackwell, 2008).

Reason, Faith, and Revolution: Reflections on the God Debate (New Haven: Yale University Press, 2009).

An Essay on Evil (Yale: Yale University Press, forthcoming 2010).

Edited Essay Collections

The Slant *Manifesto: Catholics and the Left*, eds. Adrian Cunningham, Terry Eagleton et al. (London: Sheed & Ward, 1966).

Directions: Pointers for a Post-Conciliar Church, ed. Terry Eagleton (London: Sheed & Ward, 1968).

From Culture to Revolution: The Slant *Symposium 1967*, eds. Terry Eagleton and Brian Wicker (London: Sheed & Ward, 1968).

Raymond Williams: Critical Perspectives, ed. Terry Eagleton (Oxford: Polity Press, 1989).

Edited Anthologies

Ideology (Longman Critical Reader), ed. Terry Eagleton (London: Longman, 1994).

Marxist Literary Theory, eds. Terry Eagleton and Drew Milne (Oxford: Blackwell, 1995).

Editions

Thomas Hardy, *Jude the Obscure*, ed. Terry Eagleton (London: Macmillan, 1974).

Charles Dickens, *Hard Times*, ed. Terry Eagleton (London: Methuen, 1987).

Oscar Wilde, *Plays, Prose Writings and Poems*, ed. Terry Eagleton (London: Everyman, 1991).

Selected Articles

'Language and Reality in *Twelfth Night*', *Critical Quarterly* 9 (1967), pp. 217–28.

'History and Myth in Yeats's "Easter 1916"', *Essays in Criticism* 21 (1971), pp. 248–60.

'Thomas Hardy: Nature as Language', *Critical Quarterly* 13 (1971), pp. 155–62.

'Class, Power and Charlotte Brontë', *Critical Quarterly* 14 (1971), pp. 225–35.

'Nature and the Fall in Hopkins: A Reading of "God's Grandeur"', *Essays in Criticism* 23 (1973), pp. 68–75.

'William Hazlitt: An Empiricist Radical', *New Blackfriars* 54 (1973), pp. 108–17.

'Thomas Hardy: The Form of his Fiction', *New Blackfriars* 55 (1974), pp. 477–81.

'Ideology and Literary Form', *New Left Review* 1:90 (1975), pp. 81–109.

'Pierre Macherey and the Theory of Literary Production', *Minnesota Review* 5 (1975), pp. 134–44.

'The Poetry of Peter Dale', *Agenda* 13:3 (1975), pp. 85–91.

'Criticism and Politics: The Work of Raymond Williams', *New Left Review* 1:95 (1976), pp. 3–23.

'First-Class Fellow Travelling: The Poetry of W. H. Auden', *New Blackfriars* 57 (1976), pp. 562–6.

'*Sylvia's Lovers* and Legality', *Essays in Criticism* 28:1 (1976), pp. 17–27.

'Marxist Literary Criticism', *Sociological Review Monograph* 25 (1977), pp. 85–91.

'Marx, Freud and Morality', *New Blackfriars* 58 (1977), pp. 21–9.

'*Aesthetics and Politics*', *New Left Review* 1:107 (1978), pp. 21–34.

'Translation and Transformation', *Stand Magazine* 19:3 (1978), pp. 72–7.

'Form, Ideology, and *The Secret Agent*', *Sociological Review*, Monograph 26 (1978), pp. 55–63.

'Liberality and Order: The Criticism of John Bayley', *New Left Review* 1:110 (1978), pp. 29–40.

'Literature and Politics Now', *Critical Quarterly* 20:3 (1978), pp. 65–9.

'Irony and Commitment', *Stand Magazine* 20:3 (1979), pp. 24–7.

'The Poetry of E. P. Thompson', *Literature and History* 5:2 (1979), pp. 139–45.

'Radical Orthodoxies', *Oxford Literary Review* 3:3 (1979), pp. 99–103.

'Marxism and Deconstruction', *Contemporary Literature* 22:4 (1981), pp. 477–88.

'The End of Criticism', *Southern Review* 14:2 (1981), pp. 99–106.

'The Idealism of American Criticism', *New Left Review* 1:127 (1981), pp. 53–65.

'Fredric Jameson: The Politics of Style', *Diacritics* 12:3 (1982), pp. 14–22.

'Pierre Macherey and Marxist Literary Theory', *Philosophy* 14 (1982), pp. 145–55.

'The Revolt of the Reader', *New Literary History* 13:3 (1982), pp. 449–52.

'Wittgenstein's Friends', *New Left Review* 1:135 (1982), pp. 64–90.

'Power and Knowledge in "The Lifted Veil"', *Literature and History* 9:1 (1983), pp. 52–61.

'The Task of the Cultural Critic', *Meanjin* 42:4 (1983), pp. 445–8.

'Nature and Violence: The Prefaces of Edward Bond', *Critical Quarterly* 26:1/2 (1984), pp. 127–35.

'Brecht and Rhetoric', *New Literary History* 16:3 (1985), pp. 633–8.

'Capitalism, Modernism and Postmodernism', *New Left Review* 1:152 (1985), pp. 60–73.

'Literature and History', *Critical Quarterly* 27:4 (1985), pp. 23–6.

'Politics and Sexuality in W. B. Yeats', *Crane Bag* 19:2 (1985), pp. 138–42.

'Marxism and the Past', *Salmagundi* 66–8 (1985), pp. 271–90.

'Marxism, Structuralism, and Post-Structuralism', *Diacritics* 15:4 (1985), pp. 2–12.

'Politics and Sexuality in W. B. Yeats', *Crane Bag* 9:2 (1985), pp. 138–42.

'New Poetry', *Stand Magazine* 26:1 (1985), pp. 68–72.

'The Subject of Literature', *Cultural Critique* 2 (1985–1986), pp. 95–104.

'The Poetry of Radical Republicanism', *New Left Review* 1:158 (1986), pp. 123–8.

'Frère Jacques: The Politics of Deconstruction', *Semiotica* 63:3/4 (1987), pp. 351–8.

'The End of English', *Textual Practice* 1:1 (1987), pp. 1–9.

'Estrangement and Irony in the Fiction of Milan Kundera', *Salmagundi* 73 (1987), pp. 25–32.

'Two Approaches in the Sociology of Literature', *Critical Inquiry* 14:3 (1988), pp. 469–76.

'Resources for a Journey of Hope: The Significance of Raymond Williams', *New Left Review* 1:168 (1988), pp. 3–11.

'Rereading Literature: or, Inside Leviathan', *Antithesis* 1:1 (1988), pp. 11–14.

'The Silences of David Lodge', *New Left Review* 1:172 (1988), pp. 93–102.

'J. L. Austin and Jonah', *New Blackfriars* 69:815 (1988), pp. 164–8.

'The Ideology of the Aesthetic', *Poetics Today* 9:2 (1988), pp. 327–38.

'Aesthetics and Politics in Edmund Burke', *History Workshop Journal* 28 (1989), pp. 53–62.

'Modernism, Myth and Monopoly Capitalism', *News from Nowhere* 7 (1989), pp. 19–24.

'Schopenhauer and the Aesthetic', *Signature* 1 (1989), pp. 3–22.

'Saint Oscar: A Foreword', *New Left Review* 1:177 (1989), pp. 125–8.

'Defending the Free World', *Socialist Register* 26 (1990), pp. 85–94.

'Shakespeare and the Class Struggle', *International Socialism* 49 (1990), pp. 115–21.

'Unionism and Utopia: *The Cure at Troy* by Seamus Heaney', *News from Nowhere* 9 (1991), pp. 93–5.

'The Crisis of Contemporary Culture', *New Left Review* 1:196 (1992), pp. 29–41.

'Emily Brontë and the Great Hunger', *Irish Review* 12 (1992), pp. 107–19.

'The Right and the Good: Postmodernism and the Liberal State', *Textual Practice* 8:1 (1993), pp. 1–10.

'Memorial to the Great Famine', *Actes de la Recherche en Sciences Sociales* 104 (1994), pp. 18–23.

'Oscar and George', *Nineteenth-Century Contexts* 18:3 (1994), pp. 205–23.

'My Wittgenstein', *Common Knowledge* 3:1 (1994), pp. 152–7.

'Ireland's Obdurate Nationalisms', *New Left Review* 1:213 (1995), pp. 130–6.

'Where do Postmodernists Come From?', *Monthly Review* 47:3 (1995), pp. 59–70.

'Marxism without Marxism', *Radical Philosophy* 73 (1995), pp. 35–7.

'Cork and the Carnivalesque: Francis Sylvester Mahony (Fr. Prout)', *Irish Studies Review* 16 (1996), pp. 2–7.

'The Irish Sublime', *Religion and Literature* 28:2/3 (1996), pp. 25–32.

'Priesthood and Paradox', *New Blackfriars* 77 (1996), pp. 316–19.

'The Contradictions of Postmodernism', *New Literary History* 28:1 (1997), pp. 1–6.

'Nationalism and the Case of Ireland', *New Left Review* 1:234 (1999), pp. 44–61.

'Things I'd Gladly Leave Behind', *Neue Rundschau* 110:4 (1999), pp. 17–19.

'A Note on Brecht', *Pretexts: Studies in Writing and Culture* 1 (1999), pp. 89–92.

'Self-Realization, Ethics and Socialism', *New Left Review* 1:237 (1999), pp. 150–61.

'Defending Utopia', *New Left Review* 2:4 (2000), pp. 173–6.

'Base and Superstructure Revisited', *New Literary History* 31:2 (2000), pp. 231–40.

'Subjects and Truths', *New Left Review* 2:9 (2001), pp. 155–60.

'God, the Universe, Art, and Communism', *New Literary History* 32:1 (2001), pp. 23–32.

'Capitalism and Form', *New Left Review* 2:14 (2002), pp. 119–31.

'Irony and the Eucharist', *New Blackfriars* 83 (2002), pp. 513–16.

'Norman Feltes', *English Studies in Canada* 28:3 (2002), pp. 473–7.

'Commentary ["Rethinking Tragedy"]', *New Literary History* 35:1 (2004), pp. 151–9.

'Evil, Terror and Anarchy', *Salmagundi* 148/149 (2005), pp. 148–9.

'On Telling the Truth', *Socialist Register* 42 (2006), pp. 307–26.

'Political Beckett?', *New Left Review* 2:40 (2006), pp. 67–74.

'Comrades and Colons', *Antipode* 40:3 (2008), pp. 351–6.

'The Art of Medicine: Literary Healing', *The Lancet* 371:9621 (2008), pp. 1,330–31.

'Must We Always Historicize?', *Foreign Literature Studies* 30:6 (2008), pp. 9–14.

'Introduction: The View from Judgment Day ["Devalued Currency"]', *Common Knowledge* 14:1 (2008), pp. 29–33.

'Culture and Socialism', *International Socialism* 122 (2009), pp. 91–9.

'Jameson and Form', *New Left Review* (forthcoming 2009).

Selected Chapters

'The Idea of a Common Culture', in *From Culture to Revolution: The* Slant *Symposium 1967* (London: Sheed & Ward, 1968), pp. 35–57.

'Eliot and a Common Culture', in *Eliot in Perspective: A Symposium*, ed. Graham Martin (London: Macmillan, 1970), pp. 279–95.

'Myth and History in Recent Poetry', in *British Poetry since 1960: A Critical Survey*, eds. Michael Schmidt and Grevel Lindop (Oxford: Carcanet, 1972), pp. 233–9.

'Lawrence', in *The Prose for God: Religious and Anti-Religious Aspects of Imaginative Literature*, eds. Ian Gregor and Walter Stein (London: Sheed & Ward, 1973), pp. 86–100.

'Marxist Literary Criticism,' in *Contemporary Approaches to Literary Studies*, ed. Hilda Schiff (London: Heinemann, 1977), pp. 94–103.

'Écriture and Eighteenth-Century Fiction', in *Literature, Society and the Sociology of Literature*, ed. Francis Barker (Colchester: Essex University Press, 1977), pp. 55–8.

'Tennyson: Politics and Sexuality in *The Princess* and *In Memoriam*', in *1848: The Sociology of Literature*, ed. Francis Barker et al. (Colchester: Essex University Press, 1978), pp. 97–106.

'Text, Ideology, Realism', in *Literature and Society*, ed. Edward W. Said (Baltimore: Johns Hopkins University Press, 1980), pp. 149–73.

'Psychoanalysis, the Kabbala and the Seventeenth Century', in *1642: Literature and Power in the Seventeenth Century*, ed. Francis Barker et al. (Colchester: University of Essex, 1981), pp. 201–6.

'Macherey and Marxist Literary Theory', in *Marx and Marxisms*, ed. G. H. R. Parkinson (Cambridge: Cambridge University Press, 1982), pp. 145–55.

'Ineluctable Options', in *The Politics of Interpretation*, ed. W. J. T. Mitchell (Chicago: Chicago University Press, 1983), pp. 373–80.

'Ideology and Scholarship', in *Historical Studies and Literary Criticism*, ed. Jerome J. McGann (Madison: University of Wisconsin Press, 1985), pp. 114–25.

'Political Criticism', in *Textual Analysis: Some Readers Reading*, ed. Mary Ann Caws (New York: Modern Languages Association, 1986), pp. 257–71.

'The God that Failed', in *Remembering Milton: Essays on the Texts and Traditions*, eds. Mary Nyquist and Margaret Ferguson (New York: Methuen, 1987), pp. 342–9.

'Reception Theory', in *Issues in Contemporary Literary Theory*, ed. Peter Barry (Basingstoke: Macmillan, 1987), pp. 119–30.

'The Critic as Clown', in *Marxism and the Interpretation of Culture*, ed. Lawrence Grossberg and Cary Nelson (Urbana: University of Illinois Press, 1988), pp. 619–32.

'History, Narrative and Marxism', in *Reading Narrative: Form, Ethics, Ideology*, ed. James Phelan (Columbus: Ohio State University Press, 1989), pp. 272–81.

'Joyce and Mythology', in *Omnium Gatherum: Essays for Richard Ellmann*, ed. Susan Dick (Gerrards Cross: Smythe, 1989), pp. 310–19.

'Nationalism: Irony and Commitment', in *Nationalism, Colonialism and Literature*, ed. Seamus Deane, with Fredric Jameson and Edward W. Said (Minneapolis: University of Minnesota Press, 1990), pp. 23–39.

'Marxism and the Future of Criticism', in *Writing the Future*, ed. David Wood (London: Routledge, 1990), pp. 177–80.

'The Politics of Postmodernism', in *Criticism in the Twilight Zone: Postmodern Perspectives on Literature*, eds. Danuta Zadworna-Fjellestad and Lennart Bjork (Stockholm: Almqvist & Wiksell, 1990), pp. 21–33.

'Aesthetics and Politics in Edmund Burke', in *Irish Literature and Culture*, ed. Michael Kenneally (Gerrards Cross: Smythe, 1992), pp. 25–34.

'Value: *King Lear, Timon of Athens, Antony and Cleopatra*', in *Shakespearean Tragedy*, ed. John Drakakis (London: Longman, 1992), pp. 388–98.

'Bakhtin, Kundera, Schopenhauer', in *Bakhtin and Cultural Theory*, eds. Ken Hirschkop and David Shepherd (Manchester: Manchester University Press, 1989), pp. 178–88.

'Free Particulars: The Rise of the Aesthetic', in *Contemporary Marxist Literary Criticism*, ed. Francis Mulhern (London: Longman, 1992), pp. 55–70.

'The Ideology of the Aesthetic', in *The Politics of Pleasure: Aesthetics and Cultural Theory*, ed. Stephen Regan (Buckingham: Open University Press, 1992), pp. 17–32.

'Deconstruction and Human Rights', in *Freedom and Interpretation*, ed. Barbara Johnson (New York: Basic Books, 1993), pp. 122–45.

'Introduction to Wittgenstein', in *'Wittgenstein': The Terry Eagleton Script/The Derek Jarman Film* (London: BFI, 1993), pp. 5–13.

'Self-Authoring Subjects', in *What is an Author?* eds. Maurice Bitiotti and Nicola Miller (Manchester: Manchester University Press, 1993), pp. 42–50.

'The Flight to the Real', in *Cultural Politics at the Fin de Siècle*, eds. Sally Ledger and Scott McCracken (Cambridge: Cambridge University Press, 1995), pp. 11–21.

'Ideology and its Vicissitudes in Western Marxism', in *Mapping Ideology*, ed. Slavoj Žižek (London: Verso, 1995), pp. 179–226.

'Self-Undoing Subjects', in *Rewriting the Self*, ed. Roy Porter (London: Routledge, 1996), pp. 262–9.

'Where do Postmodernists Come From?', in *In Defense of History: Marxism and the Postmodern Agenda*, eds. Ellen Meiksins Wood and John Bellamy Foster (New York: Monthly Review Press, 1997), pp. 17–25.

'Edible Écriture', in *Consuming Passions: Food in an Age of Anxiety*, eds. Sian Griffiths and Jennifer Wallace (Manchester: Manchester University Press, 1998), pp. 203–8.

'Prout and Plagiarism', in *Ideology and Ireland in the Nineteenth Century*, eds. Tadhg Foley and Sean Ryder (Dublin: Four Courts, 1998), pp. 13–22.

'Five Types of Identity and Difference' and 'Postcolonialism: The Case of Ireland', in *Multicultural States: Rethinking Difference and Identity*, ed. David Bennett (London: Routledge, 1998), pp. 48–52, 125–34.

'Marxism without Marxism', in *Ghostly Demarcations: A Symposium on Jacques Derrida's* Specters of Marx, ed. Michael Sprinker (London: Verso, 1999), pp. 83–7.

'Ideology, Discourse and the Problem of Post-Marxism', in *Postmodern Debates*, ed. Simon Malpas (Basingstoke: Palgrave Macmillan, 2001), pp. 79–92.

'Changing the Question', in *Theorising Ireland*, ed. Claire Connolly (Basingstoke: Palgrave Macmillan, 2003), pp. 76–90.

'Aesthetics and Politics', in *Between Ethics and Aesthetics: Crossing the Boundaries*, eds. Dorota Glowacka and Stephen Boos (New York: State University of New York Press, 2002), pp. 187–94.

'Tragedy and Revolution', in *Theology and the Political: The New Debate*, eds. Creston Davis, John Milbank and Slavoj Žižek (Durham: Duke University Press, 2005), pp. 7–21.

'The Decline of the Critic', in *Authorship in Context: From the Theoretical to the Material*, eds. Kyriaki Hadjiafxendi and Polina Mackay (Basingstoke: Palgrave Macmillan, 2007), pp. 185–93.

'Lenin in the Postmodern Age', in *Lenin Reloaded: Towards a Politics of Truth*, eds. Sebastian Budgen, Stathis Kouvelakis and Slavoj Žižek (Durham: Duke University Press, 2007), pp. 42–58.

'Heretic Adventures', in *Traversing the Imaginary: Richard Kearney and the Postmodern Challenge*, eds. Peter Gratton and John Manoussakis (Evanston, Illinois: Northwestern University Press, 2007), pp. 138–41.

'Commentary', in *Rethinking Tragedy*, ed. Rita Felski (Baltimore: Johns Hopkins University Press, 2008), pp. 337–46.

'"All Truth with Malice in it": Fictions of the Real', in *A Concise Companion to Realism*, ed. Matthew Beaumont (Oxford: Blackwell, forthcoming 2010).

Interviews

'Interview: Terry Eagleton' (with James H. Kavanagh and Thomas E. Lewis), *Diacritics* 12:1 (1982), pp. 53–64.

'The Question of Value: A Discussion' (with Peter Fuller), *New Left Review* 1:142 (1983), pp. 76–90.

'Politics, Theory and the Study of English: An Interview with Terry Eagleton' (with Richard Freadman), *English in Australia* 70 (1984), pp. 32–7.

'Criticism and Ideology: Andrew Milner interviews Terry Eagleton', *Thesis Eleven* 12 (1985), pp. 130–44.

'Interview with Terry Eagleton' (with Andrew Martin and Patrice Petro), *Social Text* 13/14 (1986), pp. 83–99.

'Action in the Present: An Interview with Terry Eagleton' (with Richard Dienst and Gail Faurschou), *Polygraph* 2/3 (1989), pp. 30–36.

'The Politics of Hope: An Interview' (with Raymond Williams), in *Raymond Williams: Critical Perspectives*, ed. Terry Eagleton (Cambridge: Polity, 1989), pp. 176–83.

'Criticism, Ideology and Fiction' (with Michael Payne), in Terry Eagleton, *The Significance of Theory* (Oxford: Blackwell, 1990), pp. 71–89.

'Terry Eagleton on the Concept of the Aesthetic: An Interview by Maryse Souchard', *Recherches Sémiotiques/Semiotic Inquiry* 10:1–3 (1990), pp. 163–74.

'Terry Eagleton: In Conversation with James Wood', *Poetry Review* 82: 1 (1992), pp. 4–7.

'Doxa and Common Life: Pierre Bourdieu and Terry Eagleton in Conversation', *New Left Review* 1:191 (1992), pp. 111–21.

'Terry Eagleton', in *Conversations with Critics*, ed. Nicolas Tredell (London: Carcanet, 1994), pp. 126–45.

'Interview with Terry Eagleton', in *Lukács after Communism: Interviews with Contemporary Intellectuals*, ed. Eva L. Corredor (Durham: Duke University Press, 1997), pp. 127–50.

'A Grim Parody of the Humanities: An Interview with Terry Eagleton' (with John Higgins), *Pretexts: Literary and Cultural Studies* 9:2 (2000), pp. 215–23.

'A Conversation with Terry Eagleton' (with José Manuel Barbeito Varela), *Atlantis: Revista de la Asociación Española de Estudios Anglo-Norteamericanos* 23:2 (2001), pp. 169–85.

'Talking after Theory: An Interview with Terry Eagleton' (with Matthew Jarvis and Liz Oakley-Brown), *English* 53:207 (2004), pp. 177–90.

'Edward Said, Cultural Politics and Critical Theory (An Interview)' (with Ibrahim Fathy, Ferial Ghazoul, Barbara Harlow, Rana El Harouny, Dalia Mostafa and Andrew Rubin), *Alif: Journal of Comparative Poetics* (2005) (http://www.thefreelibrary. com/_/print/PrintArticle.aspx?id=135888177).

'On the Importance of Not-Being Earnest: A Dialogue with Terry Eagleton' (with Patrick O'Connor and Seán Daffy), *Irish Studies Review* 16:1 (2008), pp. 55–69.

Works About Terry Eagleton

Books

Aczel, Richard, 'Eagleton and English', *New Left Review* 1:154 (1985), pp. 113–23.

Alderson, David, *Terry Eagleton* (Basingstoke: Palgrave Macmillan, 2004).

Anderson, Perry, 'A Culture in Contraflow', in *English Questions* (London: Verso, 1992), pp. 192–301.

Anderson, Perry, *The Origins of Postmodernity* (London: Verso, 1998).

Barnett, Anthony, 'Raymond Williams and Marxism: A Rejoinder to Terry Eagleton', *New Left Review* 1:99 (1976), pp. 47–64.

Bennett, Tony, *Formalism and Marxism* (London: Routledge, 1979).

Bennett, Tony, *Outside Literature* (London: Routledge, 1990)

Bennington, Geoff, 'Demanding History', in *Post-Structuralism and the Question of History*, eds. Derek Attridge, Geoff Bennington and Robert Young (Cambridge: Cambridge University Press, 1987), pp. 15–29.

Bergonzi, Bernard, 'The Terry Eagleton Story', *PN Review* 2:2 (1984), pp. 15–21.

Birchall, Ian, 'Terry Eagleton and Marxist Literary Criticism', *International Socialism* 2:16 (1982), pp. 114–24.

Boer, Roland, 'Terry Eagleton and the Vicissitudes of Christology', *Cultural Logic* 8 (2005) (http://clogic.eserver.org/2005/boer.html).

Burns, Wayne, 'Marxism, Criticism and the Disappearing

Individual', *Recovering Literature: A Journal of Contextualist Criticism* 12 (1984), pp. 7–28.

Clifford, John, and John Schilb, 'A Perspective on Eagleton's Revival of Rhetoric', *Rhetoric Review* 6:1 (1987), pp. 22–31.

Craib, Ian, '*Criticism and Ideology*: Theory and Experience', *Contemporary Literature* 22:4 (1981), pp. 489–509.

Connor, Steven, 'Poetry of the Meantime: Terry Eagleton and the Politics of Style', *Year's Work in Critical and Cultural Theory* 1:1 (1991), pp. 243–64.

Connor, Steven, 'Art, Criticism and Laughter: Terry Eagleton on Aesthetics', unpublished paper (1988), pp. 1–13 (http://www.bbk.ac.uk/english/skc/artlaugh.htm).

Cronin, Richard, 'Politicizing Literature', *Modern Age* 32:4 (1988), pp. 311–17.

Cunningham, Adrian, 'The December Group: Terry Eagleton and the New Left Church', *Year's Work in Critical and Cultural Theory* 1:1 (1991), pp. 210–15.

Donoghue, Denis, 'I Am Not Heathcliff', *New Republic*, 21–28 August, 1995, pp. 42–5.

Dupré, John, 'Comments on Terry Eagleton's "Base and Superstructure Revisited"', *New Literary History* 31 (2000), pp. 241–5.

Easthope, Anthony, 'On an Aside by Eagleton', *New Left Review* 1:110 (1978), pp. 95–6.

Easthope, Anthony, 'Iron on the Shoulder: For Young Terry at 50', *Year's Work in Critical and Cultural Theory* 1:1 (1991), pp. 288–93.

Elliott, J. H., 'Schlegel, Brecht and the Jokes of Theory', *MLN* 113 (1998), pp. 1056–88.

Freadman, Richard, and S.R. Miller, 'Three Views of Literary Theory', *Poetics* 17:1/2 (1988), pp. 9–24.

Frow, John, 'Marxism and Structuralism', in *Marxism and Literary History* (Oxford: Blackwell, 1986), pp. 18–50.

Gallagher, Catherine, 'The New Materialism in Marxist Aesthetics', *Theory and Society* 9:4 (1980), pp. 633–46.

Goldstein, Philip, *The Politics of Literary Theory: An Introduction to Marxist Criticism* (Tallahassee: Florida State University Press, 1990).

Goode, John, 'For a Pilgrim of Hope', *Year's Work in Critical and Cultural Theory* 1:1 (1991), pp. 294–301.

Habib, M. A. R., 'Marxism', in *A History of Literary Criticism: From Plato to the Present* (Oxford: Blackwell, 2005), pp. 527–54.

Harvey, J. R., 'Criticism, Ideology, Raymond Williams and Terry Eagleton', *Cambridge Quarterly* 8:1 (1978), pp. 56–65.

Haslett, Moyra, *Marxist Literary and Cultural Theories* (New York: St. Martin's Press, 2000).

Haslett, Moyra, 'Terry Eagleton', in *Modern British and Irish Criticism: A Critical Guide*, ed. Julian Wolfreys (Edinburgh: Edinburgh University Press, 2006), pp. 89–94.

Helmling, Steven, 'Marxist Pleasure: Jameson and Eagleton', *Postmodern Culture* 3:3 (1993) (http://muse.uq.edu.au/journals/postmodern_culture/v003/3.3helmling.html).

Henderson, Greig, 'Eagleton on Ideology: Six Types of Ambiguity', *University of Toronto Quarterly* 61:2 (1991–1992), pp. 280–88.

Higgins, John, *Raymond Williams: Literature, Marxism and Cultural Materialism* (London: Routledge, 1999).

Hogan, Patrick Colm, 'The Persistence of Idealism', *Social Scientists* 24:1 (1994), pp. 84–92.

Johnson, Pauline, *Marxist Aesthetics: The Foundations Within Everyday Life for an Enlightened Consciousness* (Balmain: Law Book Co of Australasia, 1984).

Kavanagh, James, 'Marxism's Althusser: Towards a Politics of Literary Theory', *Diacritics* 12:1 (1982), pp. 25–45.

Kimball, Roger, 'The Contradictions of Terry Eagleton', *New Criterion* 9:1 (1990), pp. 17–23.

Larissy, Edward, 'The Sign of Value: Reflections on Eagleton and Aesthetic Value', *Year's Work in Critical and Cultural Theory* 1:1 (1991), pp. 230–42.

McNeill, Dougal, 'Sounding the Future: Marxism and the Plays of Terry Eagleton', *Cultural Logic* 8 (2005) (http://clogic.eserver.org/2005/mcneill.html).

McQuillan, Martin, 'Irish Eagleton: Of Ontological Imperialism and Colonial Mimicry', *Irish Studies Review* 10:1 (2002), pp. 29–38.

Maley, Willy, 'Brother Tel: The Politics of Eagletonism', *Year's Work in Critical and Cultural Theory* 1:1 (1991), pp. 270–87.

Mulhern, Francis, '"Ideology and Literary Form": A Comment', *New Left Review* 1:91 (1975), pp. 80–7.

Mulhern, Francis, 'Marxism in Literary Criticism', *New Left Review* 1:108 (1978), pp. 77–87.

Mulhern, Francis, ed., *Contemporary Marxist Literary Criticism* (London: Longman, 1992).

Mulhern, Francis, *The Present Lasts a Long Time: Essays in Cultural Politics* (Cork: Cork University Press in association with Field Day, 1998).

Nakano, Yukito, 'Terry Eagleton as Critic', *Studies in English Language and Literature* 37 (1987), pp. 27–51.

Paananen, Victor N., 'Terry Eagleton: Sifting and Winnowing', *British Marxist Criticism*, ed. Victor N. Paananen (London: Routledge, 2000), pp. 291–363.

Palmer, R. Barton, 'Philology and the Material, Dialogical Word: Bakhtin, Eagleton, and Medieval Historicism', *Envoi* 1:1 (1988), pp. 41–57.

Parrinder, Patrick, 'The Myth of Terry Eagleton', in *The Failure of Theory: Essays in Criticism and Contemporary Fiction* (Hemel Hempstead: Harvester Wheatsheaf, 1987), pp. 30–8.

Pfeil, Fred, 'Portable Marxist Criticism: A Critique and a Suggestion', *College English* 41:7 (1980), pp. 753–68.

Poole, Roger, 'Generating Believable Entities: Post-Marxism as a Theological Enterprise', *Comparative Criticism: A Yearbook* 7 (1985), pp. 49–77.

Rooney, Ellen, and Brian Caraher, 'Going Farther: Literary Theory and the Passage to Cultural Criticism', *Works and Days* 3:1 (1985), pp. 51–77.

Regan, Stephen, ed., 'Barbarian at the Gate: Essays for Terry Eagleton', *Year's Work in Critical and Cultural Theory* 1 (1991), pp. 207–301.

Regan, Stephen, ed., *The Eagleton Reader* (Oxford: Blackwell, 1998).

Rolleston, James, 'The Uses of the Frankfurt School: New Stories on the Left', *Diacritics* 21:4 (1991), pp. 87–100.

Ryan, Michael, 'The Marxism–Deconstruction Debate in Literary Theory', *New Orleans Review* 11:1 (1984), pp. 29–35.

Said, Edward W., 'Opponents, Audiences, Constituencies and Community', in *Reflections on Exile and Other Essays* (London: Granta, 2000), pp. 118–47.

Segal, Alex, 'Language Games and Justice', *Textual Practice* 6 (1992), pp. 210–24.

Shumway, David R., 'Transforming Literary Studies into Cultural Criticism: The Role of Interpretation and Theory', *Works and Days* 3:1 (1985), pp. 79–89.

Slaughter, Cliff, *Marxism, Ideology and Literature* (London: Macmillan, 1980).

Smallwood, Philip, 'Terry Eagleton', in *Modern Critics in Practice: Critical Portraits of British Literary Critics* (Hemel Hempstead: Harvester Wheatsheaf, 1990), pp. 7–40.

Smith, James, *Terry Eagleton: A Critical Introduction* (Cambridge: Polity Press, 2008).

Soper, Kate, 'The Ideology of the Aesthetic', *New Left Review* 1:192 (1992), pp. 120–32.

Speirs, Logan, 'Terry Eagleton and "The Function of Criticism"', *Cambridge Review* 15:1 (1986), pp. 67–63.

Sprinker, Michael, *Imaginary Relations: Aesthetics and Ideology in the Theory of Historical Materialism* (London: Verso, 1987).

Sprinker, Michael, 'After the Revolution: Eagleton on Aesthetics', *Contemporary Literature* 32:4 (1991), pp. 573–9.

Wade, Geoff, 'Changes: A Critical Survey of Terry Eagleton's Work', *Year's Work in Critical and Cultural Theory* 1:1 (1991), pp. 219–29.

Wade, Jean-Philippe, '"The Humanity of the Senses": Terry Eagleton's Political Journey to *The Ideology of the Aesthetic*', *Theoria* 77 (1991), pp. 39–57.

Index